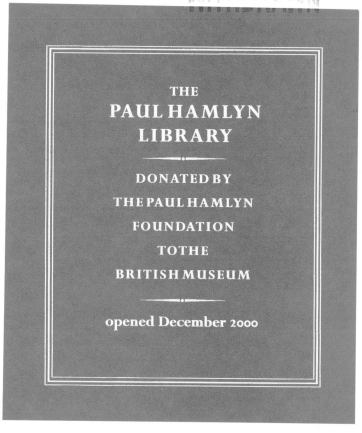

SCIENCE AND SPECTACLE IN THE EUROPEAN ENLIGHTENMENT

Science, Technology and Culture, 1700–1945

Series Editors

David M. Knight
University of Durham

and

Trevor Levere
University of Toronto

Science, Technology and Culture, 1700–1945 focuses on the social, cultural, industrial and economic contexts of science and technology from the 'scientific revolution' up to the Second World War. it explores the agricultural and industrial revolutions of the eighteenth century, the coffee-house culture of the Enlightenment, the spread of museums, botanic gardens and expositions in the nineteenth century, to the Franco-Prussian War of 1870, seen as a victory for German science. it also addresses the dependence of society on science and technology in the twentieth century.

Science, Technology and Culture, 1700–1945 addresses issues of the interaction of science, technology and culture in the period from 1700 to 1945, at the same time as including new research within the field of the history of science.

Also in the series

Entropic Creation
Religious Contexts of Thermodynamics and Cosmology
Helge S. Kragh

William Crookes (1832–1919) and the Commercialization of Science
William H. Brock

Jesse Ramsden (1735–1800)
London's Leading Scientific Instrument Maker
Anita McConnell

Science and Spectacle in the European Enlightenment

Edited by

BERNADETTE BENSAUDE-VINCENT
Université Paris X, France

and

CHRISTINE BLONDEL
CNRS, Paris, France

ASHGATE

Published by
Ashgate Publishing Limited
Gower House
Croft Road
Aldershot
Hampshire GU11 3HR
England

Ashgate Publishing Company
Suite 420
101 Cherry Street
Burlington, VT 05401-4405
USA

Ashgate website: http://www.ashgate.com

British Library Cataloguing in Publication Data
Science and Spectacle in the European Enlightenment. – (Science, Technology and Culture, 1700–1945)
    1. Science – Social aspects – Europe – History – 18th century – Congresses. 2. Science – Social aspects – Europe – History – 19th century – Congresses. 3. Science – Social aspects – Europe – History – 20th century – Congresses. 4. Technology – Social aspects – Europe – History – 18th century – Congresses. 5. Technology – Social aspects - Europe – History – 19th century – Congresses. 6. Technology – Social aspects – Europe – History - 20th century – Congresses. I. Bensaude-Vincent, Bernadette
    II. Blondel, Christine
    306.4'5'094

Library of Congress Cataloging-in-Publication Data
Science and Spectacle in the European Enlightenment / edited by Bernadette Bensaude-Vincent and Christine Blondel.
    p.   cm. – (Science, Technology and Culture, 1700–1945)
    Includes bibliographical references and index.
    1. Science – Social aspects – Europe – History – 18th century. 2.Science – Social aspects – Europe – History – 19th century. 3. Science – Social aspects – Europe – History – 20th century. 4. Technology – Social aspects – Europe – History – 18th century. 5. Technology – Social aspects – Europe – History – 19th century. 6. Technology – Social aspects – Europe – History – 20th century.
    I. Bensaude-Vincent, Bernadette. II. Blondel, Christine.
    Q175.52.E85S354 2007
    509.4'0903–dc22
                                                                2007038995

ISBN 978-0-7546-6370-6

This volume is printed on acid-free paper

Printed and bound in Great Britain by MPG Books Ltd, Bodmin, Cornwall.

Contents

List of Figures

Notes on Contributors

Bernadette Bensaude-Vincent is Professor of History and Philosophy of Science at the Université Paris X. She has authored a number of books about the history and philosophy of chemistry. She also devotes part of her research to issues related to science and the public.

Paola Bertucci is Research Fellow at the University of Bologna and works with the Institute and Museum of the History of Science in Florence (IMSS). She has published various articles on the history of eighteenth-century electricity and is now writing a book on the Italian journey of the leading French physicist, the Abbé Nollet (1749). She has been curator of two exhibitions: one at the History of Science Museum in Oxford, in 1998, one at the IMSS, which is currently open. She also coordinates the group of scholars at the IMSS who are planning a new exhibition format for the eighteenth-century collections; within this project, she is designing the rooms 'The spectacle of science' and 'Domestic Science'.

Christine Blondel is a researcher at the Centre national de la recherche scientifique (CNRS) and works at the Centre de recherche en histoire des sciences et des techniques (Cité des sciences et de l'industrie, Paris). She is working on the history of electricity in 18th and 19th century science, industry, medicine and culture. She has published books on the history of electricity, on the history of scientific instruments and on the relations between scientists and the occult.

Jan Golinski is Professor of History and Humanities at the University of New Hampshire. He is the author of *Science as Public Culture: Chemistry and Enlightenment in Britain, 1760–1820* (Cambridge University Press, 1992), and of *Making Natural Knowledge: Constructivism and the History of Science* (Cambridge University Press, 1998); and co-editor (with William Clark and Simon Schaffer) of *The Sciences in Enlightened Europe* (University of Chicago Press, 1999).

Oliver Hochadel is a historian of science based in Vienna, currently working on the history of zoos in the nineteenth century. He is the editor (with Ursula Kocher) of a volume on lying and fraud: *Lügen und Betrügen: Das Falsche in der Geschichte von der Antike bis zur Moderne* (Cologne: Böhlau, 2000), and the author of a book on electricity as a public science: *Öffentliche Wissenschaft. Elektrizität in der deutschen Aufklärung* (Göttingen: Wallstein, 2003). This award-winning book focuses on itinerant lecturers in the German enlightenment who made a living with their electrical shows.

Christine Lehman is physics teacher and author of a PhD on Gabriel François Venel, a French eighteenth-century chemistry professor. She is presently working on chemistry courses in eighteenth-century France.

Michael R. Lynn is Associate Professor of History at Agnes Scott College (Atlanta). He has a particular interest in the social and cultural history of early modern France, the history of the Enlightenment and the history of science and medicine. He is currently working on a book tentatively titled 'Shocked Monks and Savant Dogs: Popular Science in Enlightenment France.'

Liliane Pérez is a lecturer in the history of science, technology and industrial archaeology at the Conservatoire national des arts et métiers (Paris). She is the author of two books: *L'expérience de la mer. Les Européens et les espaces maritimes au XVIIIe siècle* (Paris, Seli Arslan, 1997) and *L'invention technique au siècle des Lumières* (Paris, Albin Michel, 2000). She co-authored (with D. Massourie and V. Serna) *Archives, objets et images des constructions de l'eau du Moyen Âge à l'ère industrielle* (Lyon, ENSH, 2002); (with A.-F. Garçon) *Les chemins de la nouveauté. Innover au regard de l'histoire* (Paris, CTHS, 2003); (with N. Coquery, L. Sallmann and C. Verna) *Artisans, industrie. Nouvelles révolutions du Moyen Age à l'époque contemporaine* (Paris, CTHS, 2004); (with M.-S. Corcy and C. Demeulenaere-Douyère) *Les archives de l'invention. Ecrits, objets et images de l'activité inventive des origines à nos jours* (Toulouse, CNRS, 2007). Her latest articles in English are: 'Dissemination of technical knowledge in the middle ages and the early modern history. New approaches and methodological issues' (with C. Verna), *Technology and Culture*, 47 (July 2006): 536–65; 'Technology as a public culture in the XVIIIth century: the artisans' legacy', *History of Science*, 45 (2) (2007): 135–53.

Jessica Riskin is Associate Professor in History of Science at Stanford University. Her research interests include Enlightenment science, politics and culture and the history of scientific explanation. She is the author of *Science in the Age of Sensibility: The Sentimental Empiricists of the French Enlightenment* (University of Chicago Press, 2002). She is the editor of *Genesis Redux: Essays on the History and Philosophy of Artificial Life* (Chicago: University of Chicago Press, 2007) and *Mind out of Matter: The Animal-Machine from Descartes to Darwin* (work in progress under contract with Basic Books).

Lissa Roberts is Associate Professor of the History of Science and Technology at the Center for Study of Science, Technology and Society, University of Twente. Her interests include eighteenth-century chemistry, instruments, and the claimed distinction between science and technology. She has published a number of papers on the cultural history of chemistry and on the Dutch Enlightenment.

Jonathan Simon is Maître de conférences (Lecturer) at Université Lyon 1, where he teaches the history and philosophy of science. With a PhD from the University of Pittsburgh, Jonathan has specialized in the history of pharmacy and chemistry in the eighteenth and nineteenth centuries, and the history of collections. He has published a book-length study of the chemical revolution, *Chemistry, Pharmacy and Revolution in France 1777–1809*, as well as several articles on both mineralogical and anatomical collections.

Larry Stewart is Professor of History at the University of Saskatchewan, Canada. He is the author of *The Rise of Public Science* (1992) and, most recently, with Margaret Jacob, of *Practical Matter. Newton's Science in the Service of Industry and Empire 1687–1851* (2004). He is currently writing a history of experimentation in the first Industrial Revolution.

Introduction

A Science Full of Shocks, Sparks and Smells

Bernadette Bensaude-Vincent and Christine Blondel

Enlightenment science was not something that could be confined to any narrow definition. Science, or natural philosophy as it was generally termed, could be practised for a variety of purposes in many different spaces, ranging from academies and learned societies to private cabinets and popular fairs, shops and boulevards. Scientific instruments were built and used not only for investigative and educational purposes but also for entertainment and popular shows. Air pumps, electrical machines, colliding ivory balls, coloured sparks, mechanical orreries, magic mirrors, speaking and defecating automata, and hot-air balloons constitute just a sample of the 'apparatus' used for public demonstrations. At the same time, public lecturers themselves mixed up social categories that were normally kept distinct, with aristocracy and clergy sitting side by side with merchants and university professors. Some of these public lecturers themselves succeeded in crossing national and social boundaries. Abbé Nollet, for instance, was a popular lecturer and writer who rose to become a professor and a member of the Paris Academy of Sciences.[1] As for the topics of public demonstrations, they ranged from mechanics, physics and chemistry, to anatomy. Everything – light, electricity, magnetism, water, gases, minerals, plants, cadavers and monsters – was apt to be displayed before the public. Between the culture of curiosities, which flourished in the seventeenth century, and the modern distinction between academic and popular science that emerged across the nineteenth century, Enlightenment science strikes us as a complex and multifaceted activity.[2]

Most of the clear-cut boundaries that serve to define today's science – divisions between academic institutions and the market place, between professionals and amateurs, between research and teaching, between work and leisure, between cognition and commerce – are irrelevant, precisely because many practices that were integral parts of science have subsequently been delegitimised and pushed

---

1   L. Pyenson and J.F. Gauvin (eds), *The Art of Teaching Physics: The Eighteenth-Century Demonstration Apparatus of Jean-Antoine Nollet* (Sillery, Québec: Septentrion, 2002).

2   W. Clark, J. Golinski and S. Schaffer (eds), *The Sciences in Enlightened Europe* (Chicago: University of Chicago Press, 1999); L. Stewart, *The Rise of Public Science* (Cambridge: Cambridge University Press, 1992). On the culture of curiosities see K. Pomian, *Collectionneurs, amateurs et curieux. Paris–Venise: XVIe–XVIIIe siècle* (Paris: Gallimard, 1987). On nineteenth-century popular science, see B. Bensaude-Vincent, and A. Rasmussen (eds), *La science populaire dans la presse et l'édition* (Paris: CNRS éditions, 1997).

to the margins of science. This volume – while itself full of sparks and smells – nevertheless raises broad issues about the ways modern science established its legitimacy and social acceptability through a process of 'purification' in which the 'scientific establishment' came, with ever greater authority, to condemn popular, entertaining and lucrative activities as non-scientific.

Our current notion of science may be a serious obstacle to understanding what was going on in cabinets, public courses and popular fairs. More generally, dealing with science in the early modern period requires making historiographic choices. The methodological precept – to forget about our present-day views of what science is or should be – applies in particular to eighteenth-century scientific activities. In order to capture their specificity, a pluralist notion such as 'scientific cultures' may be more appropriate than our modern monolithic and normative concept of science. We, as historians, need to resist the temptation of discriminating between 'real science' or its legitimate precursors and public spectacle. Thus, let us stroll about the streets of Paris with Michael Lynn and voyage through Germany with itinerant lecturers discovered by Oliver Hochadel. Let us have a look at the various demonstrations that disseminated science across multiple layers of society in the eighteenth century, thereby making an essential contribution to the construction of an 'enlightened public'.

Experiments in Shops, Streets and Cabinets

This volume arose from a conference held at the Cité des sciences et de l'industrie in Paris in 2003. The main purpose was to enlarge the scope of historical studies of eighteenth-century science so as to embrace the history of teaching institutions and the cultural history of consumption, especially that of entertainment and theatre.[3] With an almost exclusive focus on academic memoirs and publications, historians of science have been unable to see the wood for the trees. Alongside a few dozen illustrious academicians, there were hundreds of practitioners of science who made instruments, performed experiments, prepared medicines, and only occasionally published leaflets or a book. Exactly how many of these people were active in Europe in the eighteenth century? It is impossible to estimate their number, as something that most of them have in common is that they left little or no trace in the historical records that have come down to us.[4] Thus, one obvious reason for the traditional historical

---

3   See a similar enterprise for exploring the links between science, commerce and art in the sevententh-century, P. Smith and P. Findlen (eds), *Merchants and Marvels: Commerce, Science and Art in Early Modern Europe* (New York: Routledge, 2002).

4   However, recent historical investigation of archival materials provide local rough estimations. John Perkins and Christine Lehman have already identified more than 40 chemical lecturers in eighteenth-century France (see B. Bensaude-Vincent and C. Lehman, 'Public lectures of Chemistry in eighteenth-century France', in L. Principe (ed.), *New narrative in Eighteenth-Century Chemistry* (Dordrecht: Springer, 2007) pp. 77–97; John Perkins, 'Chemistry courses, the Parisian chemical community and the chemical revolution, 1770–1790', presentation at the 6th International Conference on the History of Chemistry, Leuven, Belgium, 28 August –1 September 2007.

focus on academic science is the accessibility of sources. Nevertheless, public demonstrators have left some traces, particularly as some of them delivered courses in institutional contexts such as local academies, learned societies or botanical gardens. In such cases, institutional archives can help to reconstruct their activities, but most of them were isolated entrepreneurs who did not belong to any guild or institution and often travelled from country to country. In these cases, we may occasionally come across such a figure by digging into local archives or browsing contemporary newspapers, but we are left to speculate as to what proportion such finds represent. Despite these practical difficulties, over the past decades scholars have brought to light an impressive number of picturesque but hitherto unknown figures, such as the Englishmen Stephen Demaimbray and Benjamin Martin, the Italians Laura Bassi and Giacomo Bianchi, or the Frenchman François Bienvenu, who are gradually becoming visible in the historical landscape.[5] These men and women travelled all over Europe, regularly crossing national boundaries, and occasionally adapting their names to fit the local language. Together with the essays published in the present volume, studies of such figures provide insights that can begin to limn the contours of a culture of scientific shows or performances that represents an essential element of a more adequate and complete image of eighteenth-century science.[6]

The roots of this scientific performance movement lie partly in teaching institutions, which gradually added experimental physics to the course of philosophy inherited from the scholastic curricula. As Laurence Brockliss has pointed out, a number of colleges in France developed experimental courses independent from philosophy teaching and most often open to the public.[7] Professors in European universities, such as s'Gravesande in Leyden, John Theophilus Desaguliers in London, Georg Christoph Lichtenberg in Göttingen, Alessandro Volta in Pavia and other, less well-known teachers in Dublin or Coimbra, gave public lectures in experimental physics. Public courses in chemistry and botany also attracted large audiences, made up of medical and pharmaceutical students as well as *philosophes* and *curieux*. Thus, teaching institutions became places for exchange between establishment and amateur scientists, as well as laymen and women.

---

5   On Demaimbray: A.Q. Morton and J.A. Wess, *Public and Private Science: The King George III Collection* (Oxford: Oxford University Press, 1993); on Bassi: P. Findlen, 'Science as a career in Enlightenment Italy: The strategies of Laura Bassi', *Isis*, 84 (1993): 441–69; on G. Bianchi: O. Hochadel, 'A Shock to the Public: Itinerant Lecturers and Instrument Makers as Practitioners of Electricity in the German Enlightenment (1740–1800)', in F. Bevilacqua and L. Fregonese (eds), *Nuova Voltiana. Studies on Volta and His Time*, vol. 5 (Pavia: Hoepli, 2003), pp. 53–68; on Bienvenu: P. Bret, 'Un bateleur de la science : Le «machiniste-physicien» François Bienvenu et la diffusion de Franklin et Lavoisier', *Annales historiques de la Révolution française*, 339 (octobre–décembre 2004): 95–127.

6   See the special issue on 'Science Lecturing in the Eighteenth Century', A. Morton (ed.), *British Journal for the History of Science*, 28 (1995), Part I.

7   Laurence Brockliss, 'Science, the Universities and Other Public Spaces: Teaching Science in Europe and the Americas', in R. Porter (ed.), *Eighteenth-Century Science, The Cambridge History of Science*, vol. 4, (Cambridge: Cambridge University Press, 2003), pp. 44–86.

Instrument makers were another major driving force in the emergence of experimental shows. Public demonstrations stimulated the design and manufacture of scientific instruments, covering not only classic instruments constructed for demonstrations of established phenomena but also instruments for scientific inquiry, as well as instruments for technical uses such as navigation. Indeed, many public lecturers were multifaceted, with Bianchi, Benjamin Martin and Sigaud de la Fond fulfilling the functions of builders, demonstrators, sellers, travellers, writers and participants in controversies.[8] These *hommes-orchestre* operated across social categories, playing a key role in the promotion of experimental science, contributing to its visibility in the public sphere.

Shops and workshops thus became favoured spaces for the display of machines and instruments. Here, customer-visitors could see science in action, discuss and compare the performances of instruments and order apparatus to equip their own personal laboratories. In England, shops were also meeting places where a form of reciprocal instruction became possible. The chapters by Larry Stewart and Liliane Pérez outline the role of merchants who cultivated profit and beauty and the emergence of a category of 'philosophical consumers' who moved from public to private spaces and developed a kind of tourism combining entertainment and learning.

Between Entertainment and Utility

As public demonstrations were often advertised as practical, sensational or even dramatic, this volume outlines two major features of the culture of science in the eighteenth century: entertainment and utility. Entertainment was a primary concern, but it does not mean that scientific demonstrations were not serious activities. Most essays in this volume show instead that entertainment went hand in hand with pedagogical purposes, as a number of lecturers claimed to offer access to knowledge by way of amusement. Experimental physics, for instance, initiated the tradition of science for fun. Jessica Riskin emphasizes the intermingling of tricks and true demonstrations. Amusing physicists played magicians while instructing their audience in natural philosophy. Chemistry lectures were apparently more didactic. In most cases they offered the only opportunity for medical students, apothecaries, miners and craftsmen to learn about chemical preparations. The chapter by Lehman on chemical lectures in Paris suggests that instruction was a prominent force behind the creation of public chemical demonstrations that, whether public or private, provided basic laboratory training for vocational purposes. They were also attended by artisans and women who needed to learn some chemistry for practical or domestic work.[9] However, Jan Golinski's presentation of Joseph Priestley's lectures and Lissa

---

8   On B. Martin: J.R. Millburn, 'The London evening courses of Benjamin Martin and James Ferguson: 18th-century lectures on experimental philosophy', *Annals of Science*, 40 (1983), 437–55 ; S. Schaffer, 'The consuming flame: Electrical showmen and Tory mystics in the world of goods', in J. Brewer and R. Porter (eds), *Consumption and the world of goods* (London: Routledge, 1993), pp. 489–526.

9   In the eighteenth century, women were often in charge of the fabrication of cosmetics, medicines and cleaning products. See C. Lanoe, 'Les jeux de l'artificiel. Culture, production

Roberts's presentation of Guillaume-François Rouelle's lectures show that, beyond all educational aspects, chemical lectures were also theatrical performances meant to impress the audience.

The crowds of people who attended public demonstrations and exhibitions were not all motivated by vocational interests. A number of essays in this volume emphasize the importance of commercial concerns associated with public demonstrations. Beyond merchants' displays in shops and workshops, public demonstrations served as a source of profit for instrument makers or pharmacists, who used to sell the products of their skills at the end of the lectures, wares often associated with a popular book or manual. As Larry Stewart and Liliane Pérez emphasize, public demonstrations fitted well with the burgeoning market ideology, triggering fierce competition between artisans and inventors, and helping to finance inventions, thanks to entrance fees or subscriptions paid in advance.

The best-paying customers were often members of the aristocracy who were searching for material to equip their private cabinets.[10] There were also many aristocratic amateur scientific practitioners in *ancien régime* France,[11] including Voltaire and Émilie du Chatelet, who acquired a large collection of physics instruments from the Abbé Nollet for 10,000 *livres*. Provincial academies, learned societies, amateur circles, and clubs provided many opportunities to perform experiments in front of either large or limited audiences, and thus to disseminate science and technologies.[12] Although we have no reliable evidence concerning scientific discussions that took place in Europe's salons, it is unlikely that amateur scientists refrained from discussing their experimental ventures in their evening conversations.[13] Experimental demonstrations even gained the favour of royal courts, with King George III of England owning a magnificent collection of scientific instruments. In France, Louis XV provided Abbé Nollet with an official appointment and ordered the performance of public experiments in the Hall of Mirrors at Versailles. Likewise, when Emperor Joseph II of Austria visited Paris in the 1780s, he invited his guests to attend the public demonstrations performed by Nicolas-Philippe Ledru.

---

et consommation des cosmétiques à Paris sous l'Ancien Régime XVIe–XVIIIe siècle' (PhD dissertation, University of Paris I, 2003).

10   J. Torlais, 'La physique expérimentale', in R. Taton (ed.), *Enseignement et diffusion des sciences au XVIIIe siècle* (Paris: Hermann, 1986), pp. 619–45.

11   The tax collector Dupin de Francueil had a private cabinet in Chenonceaux. In 1743, he appointed Jean-Jacques Rousseau to teach his son. See B. Bensaude-Vincent and B. Bernardi (eds), *Rousseau et les sciences* (Paris : L'Harmattan, 2003).

12   Simon Schaffer, 'Natural Philosophy and Public Spectacle in the 18th Century', *History of Science*, 21 (1983), 1–43; Michael R. Lynn, 'Enlightenment in the Public Sphere: The Musée de Monsieur and Scientific Culture in Late-Eighteenth-Century Paris', *Eighteenth-Century Studies*, 32 (1999), 463–76.

13   Antoine Lilti, *Le monde des salons. Sociabilité et mondanité à Paris au XVIIIe siècle*, Paris: Fayard, 2005.

The Epistemic Power of Sensationalism

The essays in the present volume suggest that public demonstrations not only served to disseminate science into society, but also contributed in various ways to the advancement of knowledge. Of course, the primary aim of such demonstrations was to attract as large an audience as possible; as Abbé Nollet confided to Benjamin Franklin:

> I am far from blaming those who, not sharing my views [...] are busy making brilliant or even terrifying experiments, and sustaining the admiration of the *curieux* who take part in these discoveries [...]; electricity becomes more interesting as the number of amateurs increases.[14]

Public demonstrations encouraged experimental practices outside the limits of academic institutions. Instrument makers became key actors on the scientific stage and some of them enjoyed academic recognition. In support of this claim, we can cite Abbé Nollet in France, George Adams in England and Amici in Italy, all of whom were raised to academic status following a career as public lecturers.

Public demonstrations helped legitimize experimental knowledge. As Louis-Sébastien Mercier, a keen observer of Paris culture, noted at the end of the eighteenth century: 'The reign of humanities is over, physicists replace poets and novelists, the electrical machine takes the place of a theatre play.'[15] The long-standing negative image of laboratory experimenters as manual workers, sweating over their long and physically demanding labour, was gradually being replaced by an alternative rhetoric that attacked scholars pontificating in their doctoral robes and praised laboratory work.

Advocates of experimental practices flourished in the 1750s, especially in the circle of the *philosophes*. Here, it is sufficient to cite Diderot's assault on the speculative and abstract knowledge of those who were only able to 'reflect', but who 'have many ideas and no instruments', in his *De l'interprétation de la nature*. In the same year, 1753, Gabriel François Venel's heroic portrayal of the chemist as an 'artist' in the article 'chymie' of the *Encyclopédie*, echoed Diderot's defence of experiment.[16] Venel saved his praise for the true chemist, who was ready to take off his gown and base his knowledge on practical work. Since experiments required much money and courage, experimenters were 'citizens who deserve all our thanks'. The traditional clichés about the power of experimental evidence and the no-less-

---

14   'Je suis bien éloigné de blâmer ceux qui, ne pensant pas comme moi, [...] s'occupent à rendre les expériences brillantes ou même effrayantes, et à soutenir l'admiration des curieux qui prennent part à ces découvertes [...]; l'électricité devient par là plus intéressante, le nombre des amateurs augmente.' Nollet, Jean-Antoine, *Lettres sur l'électricité*, Paris, 1753, p. 29.

15   L.S. Mercier, 'Le règne des lettres est passé, les physiciens remplacent les poètes et les romanciers, la machine électrique tient lieu d'une pièce de théâtre', in Jeremy D. Popkin (ed.), *Panorama of Paris*, , (University Park: Penn State University Press, 1999).

16   Simon Julia, *Mass Enlightenment: Critical Studies in Rousseau and Diderot* (Albany: State University of New York Press, 1995).

common attacks on the 'esprit de système' were rooted in the robust soil of the daily demonstrations that introduced laymen to the secrets of natural philosophy.

Jessica Riskin argues that visual experience was considered a major source of knowledge and that the advancement of knowledge presupposed empirical training. Despite his oppostion to Nollet's Cartesianism, Voltaire confessed that 'one learns more from Abbé Nollet's experiments than from all the books of Antiquity.'[17] The power of visual experience was legitimized by the prevailing empiricist philosophy, which claimed that all ideas originated in sensation. If knowledge entered the mind through the senses, then public demonstrations were the best form of pedagogy. Watching the experimental performance was a way to re-enact the generation of ideas on the *tabula rasa* of the child's mind that is at the origin of our ideas. And the demonstrator's commentary or the book sold at the end of the show helped to build up more complex notions. Vision was the most important sense in the Enlightenment period. What kind of knowledge could be acquired by blind people was a standard philosophical issue discussed in works ranging from Locke's *Essay on Human Understanding* (1690) to Diderot's *Lettre sur les aveugles* (1749). For most philosophers, visual experience was not only the origin of ideas but also the key to all intellectual processes.

While sensation was the necessary basis of all knowledge, sensibility also formed part of the epistemic strategies of the Enlightenment.[18] Admiration and repulsion, the sense of the sublime and the sense of horror, all such aesthetic emotions aroused by tragedy were occasionally mobilized by public demonstrators. With the coming of pneumatic chemistry, Jan Golinski argues, chemical lectures developed an aesthetic sensibility to the terror of the forces of nature that confined the culture of 'sublime', in fine arts and literature. Aesthetic sensibility was also part of the exhibitions of anatomical specimens. As Jonathan Simon's chapter on Honoré Fragonard convincingly argues, the anatomical specimens made for teaching purposes were also meant to impress the public. Affects and emotions were not banished from science learning.

Theatres of Nature

With the use of theatrical performances to display natural phenomena, science was participating in eighteenth-century aesthetics. As Lissa Roberts's contribution emphasizes, theatrical settings, with the audience sitting around a stage upon which experiments were performed or models exhibited, were supposed to display nature itself. It was of no consequence that the stage was covered with artefacts such as vessels, instruments or wax models. This apparatus simply helped to unveil nature, to magnify its aspects or emphasize its processes. Furthermore, such theatrical

---

17 Xenophanes 'on apprend plus dans les seules expériences de l'abbé Nollet que dans tous les livres de l'antiquité' (www.voltaire-integral.com/20/xenophanes.htm).

18 Riskin has convincingly argued that the French *philosophes* encouraged the use of the emotions for understanding nature, rather than excluding them as epistemological obstacles J. Riskin, *Science in the Age of Sensibility. The Sentimental Empiricists of the French Enlightenment* (Chicago, London: Chicago University Press, 2002).

demonstrations can be understood as indirect descendants of the theatre metaphor used to depict natural philosophy, although its meaning shifted dramatically across the eighteenth century. For Louis Bernard Bovier de Fontenelle, who is often considered the founding father of science communication, nature was a spectacle performed on a theatre stage.[19] Fontenelle ridiculed the naive audience sitting in the stalls, uncritically satisfied with the visual experience provided by the performance, and praised the natural philosopher, whose place was behind the stage, trying to grasp the mechanisms at work. Far from undermining the beauty of nature, going beyond the appearances in order to understand the hidden causes was interpreted as a way of augmenting the dignity of nature. By contrast, in the mid-eighteenth century, the best-seller *Le spectacle de la nature* written by Abbé Noel-Antoine Pluche developed the same metaphor, but this time clearly favouring the visual experience of the audience in the stalls. He did not care that 'the mechanisms of the machines be opened' as his object was to retain 'what is visually striking'.[20] Pluche and other public lecturers who reasoned in the same way were not, however, encouraging a passive and lazy attitude on the part of the audience. Rather, they wanted the focus to be placed on what could be made apparent, that is, on the 'phenomena' in the etymological meaning of the term, because the spectacle was aimed at stabilizing phenomena rather than penetrating to their hidden causes. Far from confining the audience to the passive contemplation of nature's wonders, public demonstrations encouraged the construction of devices and instruments, and the replication of experiments. In this respect they not only stimulated the practices of science in various social contexts but also contributed to the stabilization of phenomena and advancement of knowledge. Hundreds of replications of the same experiments generating sparks or explosions transformed occasional events into regular phenomena, thus reinforcing the conviction that artificial devices could reveal nature itself. Moreover, these phenomena were observed and commented on by hundreds of spectators, making them integral parts of culture and prompting fierce debates touching on philosophical and religious issues. For clergymen such as Nollet, Priestley or Haüy, public demonstrations were also a way of displaying God's magnificence. From this perspective, the natural philosophers could accompany their exhibitions of the wonders and marvels of light, electricity and the vacuum with disquisitions on their theological and moral implications serving to edify their audience. Thus, they acted as mediators, acting out the role of ministers celebrating religious services in a different context.

Enlightening the Public

Following the pioneering work of Jürgen Habermas on the emergence of the public sphere, the tremendous impact that the emerging public sphere had on the political

---

19   L.B. Bovier de Fontenelle, *Entretiens sur la pluralité des mondes habités*, 1686 (republished Paris: Fayard, 1991).

20   N.A. Pluche, *Le spectacle de la nature ou entretiens sur les particularités de l'histoire naturelle* (Paris, chez la veuve Estienne), vol. 1, 1749, p. x.

life of a number of European countries has been well documented.[21] It is equally well established that the public played a significant part in the emergence of modern experimental science, as has been shown in a number of exemplary case studies.[22] Nevertheless, the public considered in such studies is mostly restricted to the upper classes. By contrast, a number of essays in the current volume testify to the fact that the public interested in science and technology covered a far wider social spectrum. People from the lower classes were also provided with food for thought by public performers, and were no less qualified than the social elite to appreciate the wonders of nature and deconstruct experimental tricks. Furthermore, the heterogeneity of the audience for science had a significant impact on its authority in society, with the witnessing of sparks, light and smoke by ladies, clergymen, artisans, doctors and *philosophes* helping to make such evidence more compelling. These 'epistemological dramas' also contributed to the promotion of science and reason above the traditional authority of religion in modern societies, with Cartesians and Newtonians using these phenomena as a means to spread their respective gospels through popular publications, public lectures and public demonstrations. The heterogeneous audiences for scientific demonstrations were crucial for making the bridge between scientific culture and common sense. They thus helped make non-intuitive scientific propositions – such as inertia or the movement of the earth – more real than the convictions generated by untutored daily observation.

The crowds that attended the public lectures delivered all over Europe also generated the famous 'public taste for science (*goût public des sciences*)' that was recognized as a major feature of the period by many contemporary commentators such as Mercier, or the chemist Pierre-Joseph Macquer. As scientific spectacles became integral parts of urban social culture, public lecturers spread their ideology, world-views and values through material phenomena. Robert Darnton has argued that the crowds that gathered to look at hot-air balloons or to participate in the adventures of Mesmer's magnetic tub helped to discredit the order of the *ancien régime* and contributed to the origins of the French revolution.[23] Without venturing into causal explanations of historical events, one can reasonably conclude that the multiple cultures of sciences favoured rational world-views that competed with religious belief and traditional notions of political order. Scientific spectacles created

21   J. Habermas, *The Structural Transformation of the Public Sphere*, trans. Thomas Burger (Cambridge: MIT Press, 1989). See also Arlette Farge, *Dire ou mal dire. L'opinion publique au XVIIIe siècle* (Paris: Seuil, 1992), English transl., *Subversive Words. Public Opinion in Eighteenth-Century France* (Philadelphia: Penn State Press, 1995).

22   S. Shapin and S. Schaffer, *Leviathan and the Air-pump. Hobbes, Boyle and the Experimental Life* (Princeton: Princeton University Press, 1985); E. Eisenstein, *The Printing Revolution in Early Modern Europe* (Oxford: Oxford University Press, 1993).

23   R. Darnton, *Mesmerism & the End of the Enlightenment in France* (Harvard University Press: Cambridge, Mass., 1968); C.C. Gillispie, *The Montgolfier Brothers and the Invention of Aviation, 1783–1784* (Princeton: 1983). Recent historical studies include J.M. Hunn, 'The Balloon Craze in France, 1783–1799: A Study in Popular Science', (unpublished PhD dissertation: Vanderbilt University, 1982); M. Thebaud-Sorger, '"L'air du Temps". L'aérostation: savoirs et pratiques à la fin du XVIIIe siècle (1783–1785)' (unpublished PhD thesis, Paris, École des hautes études en sciences sociales, 2004).

a niche for public debate – along with cafés and newspapers – located in between the official sphere of national or provincial academies and the private sphere of the family and the salons.

Thus, science gained sufficient credit in the public sphere that it was considered perfectly legitimate for governments to finance and organize scientific research in the early nineteenth century and to introduce science teaching in education systems. But before science and scientists retired into their academic ivory towers and a new generation of teachers took on the task of transmitting science to students, there was a time – in the early nineteenth century – when scientific reputations were enhanced by a capacity to present science in public performances. Many scientists, such as Humphry Davy or Michael Faraday at the Royal Institution in London, maintained for some time the tradition of spectacular demonstrations.[24]

By means of their dazzling performances, public lecturers thus managed to engage various fractions of civil society in science. In this respect their experimental culture – between the age of curiosity and the age of popular science – constitutes a genre of its own that could be labelled 'civil science'

We are grateful to Jonathan Simon for the translations and rewritings into the English language. We also thank the Centre de recherche en histoire des sciences et des techniques (CNRS-Cité des sciences et de l'industrie) for the organisation of the workshop which initiated this volume.

---

24   David M. Knight, 'Getting Science Across', *British Journal for the History of Science*, 29 (1996), 129–38; 'Scientists and their publics: Popularisation of science in the nineteenth century', in Mary-Jo Nye (ed.), *The Cambridge History of Science, volume 5, The Modern Physical and Mathematical Sciences* (Cambridge: Cambridge University Press, 2003), pp. 72–90.

Chapter 1

The Laboratory, the Workshop, and the Theatre of Experiment

Larry Stewart

One of the great myths with which experiments have been often burdened is that they either have proved self-evident (and thus readily reproducible) or, at crucial moments, have even appeared fundamental to our comprehension of the world. Such 'eureka' notions are inherently rhetorical. In the course of their replication and display these epistemological dramas served, in the early-modern world, to provide authority to an exercise that was, at its heart, one of translating the burden of truth away from faith and authority to evidence, through experimental observation. In this essay, I wish to explore the diffusion of the spectrum of experimentation that appeared so compelling to eighteenth-century observers of the scientific scene such as Voltaire or Diderot. It is my contention that experiment and dramatic demonstrations, driven especially by the promise of the practical, established an effective framework for the spectacular operating far beyond the esoteric confines of natural philosophical theory – most especially, through the use of curious and fabulous instruments.

The emphasis on method – specifically on the evolving link between experiment, public replication and demonstration – would magnify the role of the philosophical consumer. In Britain, for example, public debates frequently followed the publication of the *Philosophical Transactions of the Royal Society*. Inherently, private and public were realms much less distinct than the structures of early scientific societies implied. Consequently, the spectacle and the promotion of laboratory experience would matter as much, if not more, than the library. Authority and audience converged – notably, in the eighteenth century, in the theatre of demonstration, replication and dispute. For some philosophers, giving public lectures might even take precedence over their commitments to the imprimatur that had emanated from the heights of the Royal Society or of the Académie des Sciences. John Theophilus Desaguliers, Newtonian and demonstrator to the Royal Society, was once rebuked by Newton in 1725 for failing to present sufficient experiments to the Society. Desaguliers's undiplomatic reply was to offer demonstrations of experiments he had already happily provided to paying audiences at his public lectures.[1] For three decades he successfully exploited interest in the latest discoveries and disputes of natural philosophy, whether concerning the problematic optical notions of Newton or arguments with Leibniz over occult attractions across void space. Many of these

---

1   L. Stewart, *The Rise of Public Science. Rhetoric, Technology, and Natural Philosophy in Newtonian Britain, 1660–1750* (Cambridge and London: Cambridge University Press, 1992), pp. 132–3.

conflicts involved problems related to unseen and hotly contested forces such as gravity, magnetism or electricity.

The urgency of utility was the foundation of many a public demonstration. Thus, by mid century, debates over the nature and, ultimately, even the usefulness and efficacy of electrical phenomena were especially popular as well as immensely controversial. Benjamin Franklin would expose this in famous disputes over the shape of the lightning rod.[2] Usefulness had become a powerful rhetorical device. For example, as Paola Bertucci has reported, in 1747 a Mr Booth of Dublin, who had seemingly cured a paralytic arm by applying electric shocks, inquired of the experimentalist Benjamin Wilson whether he should send his account to the illustrious Royal Society for their approbation or to the much more widely circulated *Gentlemen's Magazine* (which, in any case, commonly reported on matters revealed in the *Philosophical Transactions*).[3] For the philosophically inclined, there were increasingly many venues other than the Royal Society. Philosophical controversies explicitly invited a public adjudication. And there could be little drama without an audience. The widening gyre of forms of experimentation ultimately represented a challenge to the seeming impermeability of early modern social as well as philosophical boundaries.

Experimental Spaces

To justify experiment may now seem a peculiar necessity. But in the early-modern world, experimental method was far from unproblematic. The relation between experiment and demonstration was blurred by experimental accounts intended more to assert nature's facts than to reveal the route to discovery. Demonstrations thus became ever more significant for seemingly crucial experiments – for the aristocratic and diplomatic visitors to the Royal Society as much as for subscribers at many a public lecture. The appearance of the king or nobility at Desaguliers's trials of strength by mechanical means both eliminated mystery and secured Newton's laws.[4] But, more importantly, the influence of a Newtonian rhetoric became profound in the eighteenth century. One would find in the works of the practical chemists, notably in Robert Dossie's *Institutes of Experimental Chemistry* (1759), an utter aversion to

2   J. Riskin, *Science in the Age of Sensibility. The Sentimental Empiricists of the French Enlightenment* (Chicago and London: University of Chicago Press, 2002). T.A. Mitchell, 'The Politics of Experiment in the Eighteenth Century: The Pursuit of Audience and the Manipulation of Consensus in the Debate over Lightning Rods,' *Eighteenth-Century Studies*, 31 (1998): 307–31.

3   P. Bertucci 'The Electrical Body of Knowledge: Medical Electricity and Experimental Philosophy in the Mid Eighteenth Century,' in P. Bertucci and G. Pancaldi (eds), *Electric Bodies. Episodes in the History of Medical Electricity*, Bologna Studies in History of Science, 9 (Bologna: CIS, Dipartimento di Filosofia, 2001), pp. 43–68, esp. 54. See also P. Bertucci, 'Domestic Spectacles: Electrical Instruments between Business and Conversation', Chapter 5 in this volume.

4   J.T. Desaguliers, *A course of experimental philosophy* (London: 1734) pp. 255–72.

system makers that was worthy of any of Newton's disciples. Dossie declared the need for 'induction from facts'.[5]

The spectrum of experiment meant geographic dispersal as well. Demonstrations were far from a cosmopolitan affair, although such vast metropoles as London or Paris, easily the largest cities in Europe in the eighteenth century, certainly provided the desired audiences for the experimentalists. When, in the early part of the century, the Reverend William Whiston came down from Cambridge and the Reverend John Theophilus Desaguliers from Oxford, they had the latest Newtonian experience in their pockets. The result was careers that spanned over four decades and impetus to a new industry of lectures, which became hotly contested by many interlopers in the provinces as well. But it was likewise notable that the Reverend Stephen Hales, one of the auditors of the first Cambridge Professor of Chemistry Giovanni Francesco Vigani, set upon exploring chemical reactions even after Hales, too, had removed from Cambridge in 1709 to take up duties as minister of the Thames market town of Teddington.[6] Newtonian clergymen scattered their creed widely and on fertile ground. Now anonymous in many cases, those who did the laboratory work actually did matter.[7] Credible replication required skill and demanded an audience. Showmen and witnesses needed each other for experiment to matter.

Newton's gospel was far beyond Cambridge and London. The disciples of Descartes or Leibniz who stubbornly disputed Newton's doctrine of forces held an apparently hopeless position in the face of the overwhelming tide of Newtonian demonstrators. Willem s'Gravesande imported Newton's philosophy into the Netherlands after having attended Desaguliers's lectures in London in 1716. Desaguliers likewise ventured across the North Sea in 1731 and 1732 as he undertook lecture tours of the Netherlands. But it was also in France, in the aftermath of Voltaire's proselytizing *Letters concerning the English nation* (1733), that lecturers shaped the theatre of experiment. In the 1750s, the Abbé Nollet adapted his electrical researches to provide public displays as part of his protracted dispute with Benjamin Franklin over the causes of electricity. Electricity prompted quite extraordinary displays throughout Western Europe: boys could be suspended by silk threads to create a static attraction, as was done in London by Stephen Gray or in Paris by Charles Dufay or Nollet; shocks might be dispersed through a line of guards or priests, or even applied to unsuspecting country folk on bridges crossing the Thames.[8]

---

5   Quoted in F.W. Gibbs, 'Robert Dossie (1717–1777) and the Society of Arts', *Annals of Science*, 7 (June 1951): 149–72, esp. 156.

6   S. Schaffer and L. Stewart, 'Vigani and after: chemical enterprise in Cambridge 1680–1780', in Mary Archer and Christopher Haley (eds), *The 1702 Chair of Chemistry at Cambridge. Transformation and Change* (Cambridge: Cambridge University Press, 2005), pp. 31–56.

7   S. Pumfrey, 'Who did the work? Experimental philosophers and public demonstrators in Augustan England', *British Journal for the History of Science*, 28 (1995): 131–56.

8   Riskin, *Science in the Age of Sensibility*, pp. 76ff, 88–90 ; and J. Riskin, 'Amusing Physics', Chapter 3 in this volume; Bertucci, 'The Electrical Body of Knowledge', pp. 40–9 and Chapter 5 in this volume. J.L. Heilbron, *Electricity in the 17th and 18th Centuries. A Study in Early Modern Physics* (Berkeley and Los Angeles: University of California Press, 1979), pp. 246–343; M. Ben-Chaim, *Experimental Philosophy and the Birth of Empirical Science.*

Experiment evolved into spectacle. If, to many an audience, serious philosophy was submerged in fleeting entertainment, this nonetheless had also profound implications for the everyday practice of experiment. Replication of the dramatic enticed as much as entertained. Thus, by 1800, in the 'Fantasmagorie' of Etienne Gaspard Robertson in Paris, electrical sensations could be produced by friction machines or voltaic piles in displays involving 'more than fifty people'.[9] And even a sense of practical consequence was not to be excluded by the spectacular. This was particularly well demonstrated when, in a dispute over pointed or blunt ends for lightning rods, Benjamin Wilson built a massive conductor 155 ft in length in London's Pantheon to represent a cloud discharging before a carefully selected audience including George III. He was also the director of the private theatre of the Duke of York. Wilson knew the value of the dramatic, even if the immediate and more mundane issue was the protection from lightning of the king's armouries.[10]

During the eighteenth century, and often since, the dramatic was all too readily dismissed as shallow entertainment, pandering to a pedestrian market for magic shows and village strongmen. To have let such a rigid notion stand belies a critical goal of expanding the understanding of physical principles. But the distinction between the private laboratory and the public audience may be misleading. As David Gooding suggests, the investigation of nature in the laboratory was, in any case, dependent on a public philosophical discourse. The apparent isolation of the laboratory bench from the notions received among a widening audience was largely artificial.[11] In the early eighteenth century audience magnified the credibility of natural philosophy. There was, therefore, a market place where natural philosophy was more than commodity; it was a place where experimental philosophy triumphed. Just as reports in the public press diluted the exclusivity of fellowship in private societies, philosophical displays became as essential as private experiments. Audiences were the mirror in which replication was confirmed. For this reason alone, demonstration devices became as crucial as the apparatus on a private bench. Moreover, public knowledge and practical benefit was a link not always to be broken.

Apparatus

Many makers ensured the laboratory did not remain an exclusive preserve. Not all instruments were either supremely accurate or sophisticated. Controversy soon arose over the efficiency and the accuracy of many instruments, especially those that might be used on a private laboratory bench or in the field, such as those of

---

Boyle, Locke and Newton (Aldershot: Ashgate, 2004), pp. 25–42; W. Watson, 'A Collection of Electrical Experiments Communicated to the Royal Society', *Philosophical Transactions of the Royal Society*, 45 (January 1747–48): 49–120, esp. 53.

9   G. Pancaldi, *Volta. Science and Culture in the Age of Enlightenment* (Princeton: Princeton University Press, 2003), pp. 218–19; T.L. Hankins and R.J. Silverman, *Instruments and the Imagination* (Princeton: Princeton University Press, 1999) pp. 63–4.

10   Mitchell, 'The Politics of Experiment', pp. 320–2.

11   D. Gooding, *Science and Philosophy. Experiment and the Making of Meaning* (Dordrecht, Boston, London: Kluwer Academic Publishers, 1990), esp. pp. 76–85.

the instrument maker George Graham, used by Maupertuis to determine the shape of the earth.[12] Moreover, careers were made by those able to contrive apparatus for the delights of electrical or magnetic display – such as that of Gowin Knight, who invented a device for creating artificial magnets, or those of the later electrical instrument maker Edward Nairne. Some devices were much in demand, even at considerable expense, but others opened experimental doors at a much cheaper rate. Yet, it is obvious that makers such as Graham, Knight and later Nairne and Blunt might have a substantial custom, however costly some of their apparatus.[13] Of course, skills in experimental and instrumental design were widely sought, but instruments also served various purposes such as magnifying a curiosity or even invoking a mechanical, or medical, benefit. Indeed, the Swedish engineer Marten Triewald had reported to the Royal Society on his electrical experiments and evidently amassed one of the largest collections of demonstration devices in Europe prior to 1750. This was likewise later true of the vast armoury of Martinus van Marum in Haarlem. Even the engineer John Smeaton, elected to the Royal Society in 1753 as a 'maker of Philosophical Instruments', had so impressed Joseph Priestley that he used Smeaton's improved air pump for experiments on specific gravities of air.[14] As Bertucci has revealed, Nairne could supply devices designed by the electrician Tiberius Cavallo, the inventor William Nicholson and the Italian gentleman Alessandro Volta.[15] The boundaries between maker, designer, merchant and user were not often precise.

The international trade in apparatus expanded rapidly in the eighteenth century. Certainly by the 1770s, few intent experimenters would be limited by the local instrument market. Leading natural philosophers and public lecturers trolled the same experimental networks and instrument makers' shops. Hence, the Portuguese instrument maker, and probable industrial spy, Jean Hyacinthe de Magellan, sold instruments from London, sending Gowin Knight's fashionable magnetic apparatus to courts in Spain and Portugal and numerous instruments to his contacts in France and the Netherlands. One can, for example, trace Magellan buying Wedgwood thermometers for his own trade and export.[16] Similarly, the continuous rancour between Franklin and Nollet encouraged many to buy instruments in an attempt to replicate their hotly contested experiments. The international pace of these researches gathered even further momentum at the end of the century as a consequence of Italian reports of the voltaic pile and the spread of galvanism.[17] And it was Alessandro Volta who, in his own attempt to build an array of experimental weaponry for the electrical

---

12 M. Terrall, *The Man Who Flattened the Earth, Maupertuis and the Sciences in the Enlightenment* (Chicago and London: University of Chicago Press, 2002), pp, 102, 105, 136.

13 P. Fara, *Sympathetic Attractions. Magnetic Practices, Beliefs, and Symbolism in Eighteenth-Century England* (Princeton: Princeton University Press, 1996), pp. 41ff.

14 J.L. Heilbron, *Electricity in the 17th and 18th Centuries*, pp. 80, 292; Royal Society MSS, Certificates, 2, 1751–56, Nos 442 and 7.

15 P. Bertucci, 'A Philosophical Business: Edward Nairne and the Patent Electrical Machine (1782)', *History of Technology*, 23 (2001): 41–58, esp. 54–5.

16 Keele University, Wedgwood MSS, L26-4427-4432, 1786–1787.

17 Fara, *Sympathetic Attractions*, pp. 22, 43; J. Delbourgo, 'Electrical Humanitarianism in North America: Dr. T. Gale's Electricity, or Ethereal Fire, Considered (1802) in Historical Context', in Bertucci and Pancaldi (eds), *Electric Bodies*, pp. 117–56; see also M. Pera, *The*

wars, likewise purchased instruments from Magellan and built his battery upon hints originally received from William Nicholson in London. Interestingly for the traffic in industrial goods and instruments, Nicholson may well have served the pottery manufacturer Josiah Wedgwood as his commercial representative in Europe before settling in London as publisher, teacher and inventor.[18]

Philosophical conflict was a growth industry in the eighteenth century. To a large degree, these were instrumental wars. Furore arose, for example, between Magellan and his rival Cavallo over magnetism and the effectiveness of eudiometers to measure the salubrity of airs. During the 1770s, Magellan was assisting Priestley in the analysis of gases. In 1777 Priestley requested the industrialist Matthew Boulton, in Birmingham, to get for his experiments some 'air as it is actually breathed by the different manufacturers in this kingdom and hope you will be so obliging as to procure me the proper samples from Birmingham'.[19] Industrialism and urbanism induced a new climate of experimental urgency. And Dr. Thomas Beddoes of Bristol, the celebrated democrat and collaborator of James Watt, deplored the 'new poisons arising daily in London'.[20] Beddoes went on to be one of the greatest exponents of pneumatic medicine, through the application of new airs in the controversial treatment of endemic diseases such as consumption. Instrumental simplicity was fundamental here, both in the preparation of these new airs and in the manufacture of a portable device that made it possible for ill patients to breathe the gases, and for numerous country surgeons and physicians to prescribe them. Instruments were increasingly central to public philosophical practice.

Thus practical apparatus, usable by novices, was as much in demand as those for the most profound and experienced experimentalists. If expensive devices limited participation in philosophical debate, elaborate ones further sowed confusion, privileging instrumental skill while obscuring comprehension. It was for this reason that instrument makers such as Nairne and Blunt in London could gather a following among those whose curiosity increasingly turned to the laboratory bench. The expanding array of apparatus transformed instruments into devices of the dramatic. Nairne's catalogue of goods and prices enabled the curious to see beyond his patented electrical machine, used increasingly in medical circles, to the more standard apparatus of the experimenter such as Nicholson's doubler, Cavallo's multiplier, Hadley's quadrants and Nairne's portable laboratory.[21] But apparatus did not always have boundaries.

Ambiguous Frog. The Galvani-Volta Controversy on Animal Electricity, trans. Jonathan Mandelbaum (Princeton: Princeton University Press, 1992).

18   Pancaldi, *Volta. Science and Culture*, pp.198ff; H. Chang, *Dictionary of National Biography* (Oxford: Oxford University Press, 2004) sv. Nicholson.

19   R.E. Schofield (ed.), *A Scientific Autobiography of Joseph Priestley* (Cambridge, MA and London: MIT Press, 1966), pp. 161–2.

20   D.A. Stansfield, *Thomas Beddoes M.D. 1760–1808. Chemist, Physician, Democrat* (Dordrecht: D.Reidel, 1984), pp. 141, 150.

21   Bertucci, 'A Philosophical Business,' p. 54; W. Hackmann, 'The Medical Electrical Machines of John Wesley and John Read', in M. Beretta, P. Galluzzi and C. Triarico (eds), *Musa Musaei. Studies on Scientific Instruments and Collections in Honor of Mara Miniati*, Biblioteca di Nuncius, Studi e Testi, 49 (Firenze: Instituto e Museo di Storia Della Scienze, 2003), pp. 261–77.

Nairne's electrical machine was advertised as 'constructed with a particular View to the Purposes of Medicine, yet it will be found equally applicable to philosophical Uses'.[22] This was only part of a world in which hot-air paper balloons could be bought at Christie's auction rooms and portable breathing machines might be found alongside stylish furniture at Chippendale's.[23]

But how did buyers respond? Drawn initially by drama, much, of course, depended on the extent of curiosity and a commitment to the exploration of nature. For example, experimental apparatus was clearly regarded as essential to the innovative sons of Lunar industrialists. Thus, Tom Wedgwood, who took as tutor in Edinburgh the later professor of natural philosophy John Leslie, laid plans to establish a house that Leslie would occupy, in a plan hatched by Tom and his brother John. This involved a scheme 'To buy some different apparatus for natural Philosophy, such as an Electrical machine – an air pump & different things, & so to go through the different sciences in an experimental manner.'[24] Instrument makers held the key. In these widening networks, the brilliant experimentalist Humphry Davy effectively became London agent for the Wedgwood sons. They set up an account with Blunt and Nairne from which Davy could purchase apparatus on their behalf.[25] Nairne's expertise as an electrical instrument maker was notably sufficient to attract a great deal of attention from a wide circle of medical practitioners of an experimental frame of mind, even unto devising methods of treatment, as revealed in the recommendations of the surgeon Miles Partington.[26]

Such practical approaches to apparatus argue strongly that the boundaries between medical practice and experimentation were greatly eroded at the end of the century. The epistemology of the bench, which the spectacular displays of the public lecturers revealed, had profound implications. Instrumental improvement and simplification, for example, lay behind the success of the Dutch instrument maker Martinus van Marum.[27] Simple and affordable instruments enhanced participation, concluded Priestley in 1778. They also induced ideological speculation. As once with the printing of prayer books and cheap gospels, the spread of apparatus amid a world of rapid economic transformation insinuated the abolition of mystery and ceremony inherent in ecclesiastical authority and social hierarchy.[28] This epistemological reform was induced by the seductions of

---

22   Wellcome Institute, MS1175, T.B. Birkbeck, 'Miscellanea Electrica', p. 5.

23   British Library, Add. MSS 22897, fol. 17, Cavallo to James Lind, 14 February 1784; and fol. 23, 10 October 1784; Birmingham Central Library, James Watt Papers, W/9/11, Cavallo to Lind, 15 January 1798.

24   Keele University, Wedgwood Mosely Collection, WM 21, Tom Wedgwood to Jos. Wedgwood, 27 April 1790.

25   Keele University, Wedgwood Mosely Collection, WM 21, Tom Wedgwood to Jos. Wedgwood, 12 April 1800. On Davy see David Knight, *Humphry Davy. Science and Power* (Oxford and Cambridge, MA: Blackwell, 1992).

26   Wellcome Institute, MS 1175, T.B. Birkbeck, 'Miscellanea Electrica'.

27   L. Roberts, 'The Death of the Sensuous Chemist: The "New" Chemistry and the Transformation of Sensuous Technology', *Studies in the History and Philosophy of Science*, 26 (1995): 503–29, esp. 517, 524–5; T.H. Levere, 'Measuring Gases and Measuring Goodness,' unpublished typescript (1999).

28   S. Schaffer, 'Priestley's Questions: An Historiographical Survey', *History of Science*, 22 (1984), 151–83, esp. 174. S.F. Mason, 'Jean Hyacinthe de Magellan, F.R.S. and the

the spectacle. Priestley, and his contemporaries, understood the force of replication in an emerging scientific culture much broader than that sustained by the incrustations of status and exclusivity. For the Unitarian Priestley and associates, such as James Watt, junior, a social and republican reformation lay at stake. Likewise, in the 1790s the democrat Thomas Beddoes once wrote, about his own chemical courses at Bristol, that he was glad of the public interest. Amid political turmoil, he thought his lectures might be useful in 'preventing some acts of barbarity' that demands for social reformation and rising expectations could produce.[29] Reformist ideology, instruments and industry had occasionally much in common. The rhetoric of utility had tied the laboratory to the drama of steam and forge.

Laboratory and the Workshop

The anonymity of most private laboratory practice has proved a considerable hurdle to historians breaching the limits of printed, and much-polished, accounts of the products of the bench. But there exist traces, in print, in manuscript and in business records, of practitioners who demonstrably traversed many social and epistemological categories. Among the most revealing commentators on the eighteenth-century laboratory are those whose explicit intention was to reach the literate artisan and entrepreneur. Practical lectures on chemistry had existed in London from the end of the seventeenth century and Cambridge was no exception, where apothecaries and physicians encountered the new Professors of Chemistry after 1702. The distinctions presumed to exist between colleges and commerce dissolve before the evidence.[30] For example, Robert Dossie, the son of an apothecary, reflected the long-established connections between chemistry and pharmacy existing not only in universities but in market towns as well. Dossie apparently was himself apprenticed to an apothecary and was exposed to chemistry and physics while attending one of the many courses of experiments with which the century abounds.[31] Similarly, his contemporary William Lewis was the son of a brewer in Richmond and a neighbour to the celebrated Stephen Hales. Lewis's father, also William, was sufficiently well off to send his son to Christ Church, Oxford, and by his late 20s the younger Lewis was already giving chemical lectures in his Laboratory in New Street, Fetter Lane, London, 'with a View to the Improvement of Pharmacy, Trades, and the Art itself'.[32]

Chemical Revolution of the Eighteenth Century', *Notes and Records of the Royal Society*, 45 (1991): 155–64, esp. 156; Fara, *Sympathetic Attractions*, pp. 43, 61, 87; J. Golinski, *Chemistry and Enlightenment in Britain, 1760–1820* (Cambridge: Cambridge University Press, 1992), pp. 122–3.

29   Birmingham Central Library, James Watt Papers, W/9/7. Beddoes to Watt, 21 April [1796?].

30   A.E. Musson and E. Robinson, *Science and Technology in the Industrial Revolution* (Toronto: University of Toronto Press, 1969), pp. 25–6; Schaffer and Stewart, 'Vigani and after', pp. 31–56.

31   Gibbs, 'Robert Dossie', pp. 150–1.

32   Gibbs, 'William Lewis', p. 124, quoting *The Daily Post*, 11 January 1737.

Such endeavours, of course, reflect the general trend toward public demonstrations that we find in the generation after Newton's death. Newton's disciples, such as Desaguliers, had included many sensational mechanical contrivances in their lectures. But Lewis was intent that his efforts would reach beyond the more elaborate and often expensive shows of some experimental demonstrators. When, by 1748, he planned a *Commercium Philosophico-Technicum*, he attracted subscribers to a 'foundation of philosophical and experimental history of arts'. The intent was to expand laboratory trials of new materials through 'a small, commodious, and easily manageable apparatus, procurable at a moderate expense'.[33] The spread of public lectures was reflected as well in a parallel development of private laboratories such as that of George Fordyce, MD, a pupil of William Cullen in Edinburgh, and who came to London in 1759 to start a course on *materia medica*. Fordyce established a laboratory in Theobald's Court off the Strand, where Dossie also probably undertook attempts to find a method of purifying otherwise putrefying whale and cod oil for use in trades. In their visits to tradesmen, both Dossie and Lewis received many an impetus for further experiments in the workshops and factories of London.[34]

The presumed barriers between scholars and craftsmen, between philosophers and artisans, need therefore to be considered carefully.[35] Indeed, there were many in the eighteenth century who thought these distinctions to be both unnecessary and harmful to the philosophical enterprise. Evading such social or intellectual boundaries proved critical to the knowledge economy that characterizes both enlightenment and industry. Here the dramatic did the job. Of course, the enlightened ideal of the dissemination of knowledge was famously reflected in the *Encyclopédie* in mid century.[36] But this was also revealed in the intentions of experimentalists such as Dossie and Lewis as well as of illustrious industrialists such as James Watt, Josiah Wedgwood and their sons. In 1759 Dossie, in his *Elaboratory Laid Open*, began with a description of a large number of industrial practices, many of which had attracted patents, such as the manufacture of sulphuric acid at the Great Vitriol Works of Joshua Ward in Twickenham. By then Dossie had settled in Berwick Street, Soho, which was not only becoming fashionable but which was soon also an area riddled with schools of natural and experimental philosophy.[37] Here electrical fire and anatomical displays competed for audiences by way of the practical and the theatrical. Dossie's works were among those much in demand. In 1759 he also began his anonymous *Institutes of Experimental Chemistry* with a general plan for making

---

33 Gibbs, 'William Lewis', pp. 126–7.

34 Gibbs, 'William Lewis', p. 136–7; Gibbs, 'Robert Dossie', p. 162.

35 L. Stewart, 'Science, Instruments, and Guilds in Early-Modern Britain,' *Early Science and Medicine*, 10 (2005): 392–410.

36 J. Mokyr, *The Gifts of Athena. Historical Origins of the Knowledge Economy* (Princeton and Oxford: Princeton University Press, 2002); R. Yeo, *Encyclopaedic Visions. Scientific Dictionaries and Enlightenment Culture* (Cambridge and London: Cambridge University Press, 2001).

37 Gibbs, 'Robert Dossie', pp. 152–3; L. Stewart, 'Putting on Airs: Science, Medicine and Polity in the Late Eighteenth Century', in T. Levere and G.E. Turner (eds), *Discussing Chemistry and Steam. The Minutes of a Coffee House Philosophical Society 1780–1787* (Oxford and New York: Oxford University Press, 2002), pp. 207–55, esp. 222, 230.

experimental philosophy a method useful in trades. Notably, Dossie then believed that this approach had already been promoted by the French government, which had 'diffused such a judgment and taste in design, among all classes of artisans, as render France ... the source of nearly all invention of fashions ...'. Here he anticipated the plan of Diderot and d'Alembert. And Dossie's method attracted the attention of the *Critical Review*, which remarked:

> In this age of dissipation and scribbling, it is with satisfaction we see the ingenious author of the *Elaboratory laid open*, resume the pen, in order to draw the attention of the public from the lighter amusements, now called learning, to the more severe and useful study of philosophy on the just principles of experiment.[38]

Notice was served of the shift from the sensational to the functional. In many cases in the eighteenth century, epistemological differences in education and training may seem to have distinguished experimental and natural philosophers from artisans and craftsmen. But this is largely a historiographical contrivance. Separate spheres of knowledge or of method were not adopted with equanimity. When Lewis published his *Philosophical Commerce of Arts* in 1763, he did so with the unequivocal intention of reaching skilled artisans, mechanics, instrument makers and entrepreneurs in an emerging industrial enlightenment.[39] Half a century of lecturers had shown that philosophic spectacle could attract an audience. But for Lewis, much of the everyday life in the laboratory consisted of testing materials routinely employed in trades, such as much sought-after preservatives for ships, inks, sealing-wax and endless other substances. Yet, it would be mistaken to see Lewis's as accounts simply of trials of materials.

Laboratory experience also emphasized the search for overarching explanation. Lewis was equally concerned with developments in phlogiston theory, printing a translation, probably completed by his assistant Alexander Chisholm, of the works of the German Professor Caspar Neumann in 1759. Even more significantly, Lewis was an adept experimentalist and his method was to carefully reproduce his own experiments on saltpetre, on behalf of the Society of Arts. Lewis tested Virginian saltpetre by establishing as a control substance the very finest nitre purchased in London shops. Notably, he assessed the reactions by weight to determine the value of the residue after filtration with fixed vegetable alkaline. In this regard, Lewis was actually carrying further the work of Dossie but at a higher level of chemical sophistication. Both Dossie and Lewis were charged by the Society of Arts with the responsibility for examining the methods employed in America in assaying potash, which the Society was intent on promoting. By 1767, the assessment of solutions and the results of filtration were replaced by the distinct measurement of the capacity to saturate acids in comparison to the purest alkali then available. Two important means were employed: first the measurement of the quantity of the acid not by vague volumetric measures such as drops or teaspoons, 'but by weight'. Moreover, Lewis assessed the saturation point by 'the change of colour produced in certain vegetable

---

38   Quoted in Gibbs, 'Robert Dossie', pp. 154–5.
39   Gibbs, 'William Lewis', pp.132–3.

juices, or on paper stained with them'.[40] The spectacle was submerged in precision measurement.

The Manufacturer's Inheritance

Joseph Wright of Derby painted the light of both the forge and the experiment as the theatre of the early-modern world. In his canvases, laboratory and manufactory were equally enlightened.[41] Likewise, many of those adept at experiment sought employment in early industrial concerns. Alexander Chisholm is of particular interest insofar as he bridged the world of the experimental demonstrator and the industrial chemist. At mid century, Chisholm had come out of Marischal College, Aberdeen to become an assistant to Lewis in London chemical lectures. Upon Lewis's death in 1781, Chisholm was immediately employed by Josiah Wedgwood and together they recorded thousands of experiments and trials built upon Chisholm's work with Lewis.[42] Chisholm proved critical to the production of Wedgwood's pottery. But he also exchanged a broad international correspondence on issues then at the centre of the chemical revolution. It is especially revealing that Chisholm and Lewis, both products of the academy, made a specific effort to engage the manufactory as well. In the surviving traces of Lewis's and Chisholm's early work, many of which ultimately fell into the hands of Josiah Wedgwood, there were numerous reports of first-hand journeys to manufacturing sites, along with many extracts of published chemical works, especially from Europe.

The Wedgwoods' interest in experiments was part of the long tradition of practical chemists. James Keir sought their expertise concerning samples of white lead he had sent to Wedgwood's works at Etruria in Staffordshire, while speculating on its potential in manufacturing. Keir repeated Tom Wedgwood's experiments made 'in your joint capacity as chemist & potter' and concluded that it was hardly likely that a new method of making it should improve the manufacturing prospects. Keir's report on samples is of particular note because he was responding also to having been sent a paper on heat, one of the very problems that confounded the phlogiston dispute. In Keir's view, to contemplate such important, and then pressing, difficulties was proof that Tom Wedgwood as well as the entrepreneurial Josiah 'may be considered truly deserving the name which the old chemists took to themselves, of 'Philosophers by Fire'.[43] This was not mere flattery. Keir's interest in using white lead in glazing obviously piqued possibilities in Wedgwood's own pottery as much as elevating Keir's own prospects.

It made sense to turn to the Wedgwoods for reasonable advice, if only because it was Josiah Wedgwood who was supplying Keir with the very tubes

---

40   Gibbs, 'William Lewis', pp. 130, 140–2.

41   D.H. Solkin, 'Joseph Wright of Derby and the Sublime Art of Labor', *Representations*, 83 (Summer 2003): 167–94.

42   Musson and Robinson, *Science and Technology* (reprint, London: Gordon and Breach, 1994), pp. 53–4, 78.

43   Keele University, Wedgwood MSS, E1-697, James Keir to Thomas Wedgwood, 19 April 1792.

and retorts he was using in his own Tipton laboratory near Birmingham.[44] It was in this context that Keir and Tom Wedgwood exchanged opinions on how best to proceed in chemical investigations. Keir told the young Wedgwood in the autumn of 1791 that he was delighted 'to find there is any one in this Country who has courage & ability to attempt such delicate & difficult experiments as those you intend'. They were looking for what Keir called the 'foundation of reasoning on chemical combinations'. Keir was anxious to recommend that the investigation of physical properties include the refraction of liquids and various mixtures, pointing out that 'It was by observing the great refractive powers of the diamond that Newton conjectured its affinity to inflammable bodies long before any experiments had given that idea.' He compared this to his experience with nitrous acid in 'its phlogisticated & dephologistigated states, & their consequent comparison ...'. From highly volatile experiments on metallic solutions by acids he proposed that Tom Wedgwood 'may render your plan of experiments more extensive & interesting by not confining them to liquids, but also to comprehend such solids as can be dissolved in any of your liquids, as metals, salts, &c'.[45] Such collaborations between industrial chemists were extensive. The noisome everyday world of production magnified the interest in broader theoretical issues. Above all, many of our industrialists revealed a profound knowledge of debates in chemistry in which they too sought a role.

It has long been known that experimental and industrial interests converged in the eighteenth century. However, experiment imposed a burden on its practitioners. Like Priestley, Thomas Beddoes in Bristol was concerned to broaden public knowledge. Practical utility would be merged with method and display. Indeed, in 1797 Beddoes found that the subscription to his own lectures had been well received 'unless, this Buonaparte should knock all other thoughts out of Bristol heads'.[46] By that time, experimental lectures had such a following that Thomas Garnett of Anderson's Institution in Glasgow proposed to deliver courses throughout Britain, to be illustrated 'by working machines, and the various processes of the arts would be performed before the audience'. Garnett's notion clearly had every chance of following upon the success he already had in Manchester, Liverpool, Birmingham and Glasgow, 'having created a taste in the rising generation for Chemistry by showing them its utility and connection with the different manufactures'.[47]

The spectrum of exploratory experiments, demonstrations, and of trial and error was refracted through the demands of everyday life. It is particularly significant that this was recognized by those who relied heavily on the daily

---

44   Keele University, Wedgwood MSS, E1-698, James Keir to Thomas Wedgwood, 26 December 1787.

45   Keele University, Wedgwood MSS, E1-692, James Keir to Thomas Wedgwood, 27 October 1791.

46   Birmingham Central Library, JWP, W/9/17, Beddoes to James Watt, 13 November 1797.

47   Musson and Robinson, *Science and Technology* (1969), pp. 146, 181; Birmingham Central Library, JWP, W/9/30, J. Carmichael to James Watt, 9 February 1797.

experience of workmen in manufactures. The evolution of experimental method responded to the advance of chemical theory, adventures in nomenclature and the constant demands for practical consequence. Thus, Keir exchanged a series of letters with young Tom Wedgwood, himself an accomplished experimentalist, on the matter of phosphorescence. The brilliant phosphoric light in the production of vitriolated tartar, which had then attracted attention in philosophic journals, Keir pointed out, 'has been well known to the workmen at my manufactory for many years past', especially noticeable at night when crystallized on the side of iron vessels.[48] Keir acknowledged the workshop as a valuable fount of information regarding the chemical reactions he and the Wedgwoods explored. Undoubtedly, many of these experiences took on greater meaning in the context of disputes between Lavoisier and phlogistonists. But, it is important to recognize, chemical experiments involved material manufacturing practice as well, especially where the theatre of the laboratory and commonplace industrial experience melded together. Whoever did the work mattered as much as who contemplated light emanating from a crucible. James Watt's own experience in matters chemical reflects that of the Wedgwoods. Certainly, by the 1790s when he was still exploring possibilities in pneumatic chemistry, Watt was prepared to state categorically that 'Knowing the insufficiency of theory & the incompetence of the human mind to embrace every circumstance of a complicated subject of any kind, *I am a great friend to experiment.*'[49] Those who understood the workshop transformed the experimenter's bench.

These laboratory networks kept expanding, notably to include numerous physicians in the new industrial towns such as Manchester and Birmingham. And the democratic doctor Thomas Beddoes, removed from Oxford to Bristol, entered into a project in pneumatic chemistry, assisted by Watt's design of a breathing apparatus. Innovative physicians took up the cause, produced oxygen and nitrous oxide in their own laboratories, so that by the middle of the 1790s Beddoes received reports from hundreds of practitioners who, he believed, were adopting Watt's breathing device in the treatment of disease.[50] Not only did innovations suggest new uses, but vast possibilities for laboratory exploration were clearly an attraction. Thus, for example, Beddoes proclaimed to a friend in 1792 that 'You will hear soon of Mr Volta's &c expts – I think to be able to apply [them?] so as to excite a new system of medicine.'[51] Many an experimental innovation attracted them, and especially a new piece of experimental apparatus such as

---

48   Keele University, Wedgwood MSS, E1-694, Keir to Thomas Wedgwood, 17 March 1792. See Wedgwood, 'Experiments and Observations on the Production of Light from Different Bodies, by Heat and Attrition', *Philosophical Transactions*, 82 (1792): 28–47; Wedgwood, 'Continuation of a Paper on the Production of Light and Heat from Different Bodies', *Philosophical Transactions*, 82 (1792): 270–82.

49   Birmingham Central Library, James Watt Papers, 4/65/19, Watt to Thomas Percival, 24 November,1794. My italics.

50   Keele University, Wedgwood Mosely collection, WM 35, Beddoes to Thomas Wedgwood, [22 February 1795?].

51   Cornwall Record Office, Davies Gilbert Correspondence, DG 41/54, Thomas Beddoes to Davies Gilbert [Giddy], 8 October 1792.

Volta's battery. Whether balloons or bell jars, the rising of hot-air adventurers over the fens or the shocking of the lame in London surgeries, the experimental enterprise produced a drama that drew many to spectacle of industry and nature.

Chapter 2

Technology, Curiosity and Utility in France and in England in the Eighteenth Century

Liliane Pérez

Of the beauty, which the appearance of utility bestows upon all the productions of art.

Adam Smith.[1]

In the eighteenth century, with the commercialization of leisure and elite tourism, shows, museums and exhibitions developed. Many guides were published inviting people to enjoy walking in the street,[2] shopping, and visiting big cities as part of a new type of Grand Tour.[3] They would list shops and workshops where fashionable wares could be purchased.[4] From rococo trade cards to inventions displayed in plate-glass windows, visual devices were used in attempts to stimulate desires for consumer goods.[5] As the emerging consumer society relied strongly on non-verbal

---

1   A. Smith, *The Theory of Moral Sentiments* (1759); D.D. Raphael and A.L. Macfie (eds), *Glasgow Edition of the Works and Correspondence of Adam Smith* (Indianapolis: Liberty Fund, 1982), vol. 1, p. 179.

2   J. Stobart, 'Shopping streets as social space: leisure, consumerism and improvement in an eighteenth-century country town', *Urban History*, 25–1 (1998): 3–21; P. McNell and G. Riello, 'The art and science of walking: gender, space, and the fashionable body in the long eighteenth century', *Fashion Theory*, 9–2 (2005): 175–204.

3   R.D. Altick, *The Shows of London* (London, Cambridge, MA: The Belknap Press, 1978); R. Porter and M.M. Roberts, *Pleasure in the Eighteenth Century* (London: Macmillan, 1996); A. Bermingham, and J. Brewer (eds), *The Consumption of Culture, 1600–1800* (London: Routledge, 1997); S. Van Damme, *Paris, capitale philosophique de la Fronde à la Révolution* (Paris: Odile Jacob, 2004); G. Chabaud, E. Cohen, N. Coquery and G. Penez (eds), *Les guides imprimés du XVIIᵉ au XXᵉ siècle. Villes, paysages, voyages* (Paris: Belin, 2000); D. Roche, *Humeurs vagabondes. De la circulation des hommes et de l'utilité des voyages* (Paris: Fayard, 2003); C. Walsh, 'Shopping et tourisme: l'attrait des boutiques parisiennes au XVIIIe siècle', in N. Coquery (ed.), *La boutique et la ville. Commerces, commerçants, espaces et clientèles XVIe–XXe siècle* (Tours, CEHVI-Université François-Rabelais, 2000), pp. 223–38.

4   N. Coquery, 'Qu'est-ce que le "remarquable" en économie ? La boutique dans le paysage à Paris d'après les guides du XVIIIᵉ siècle', in Chabaud et al (eds), *Les guides imprimés*, pp. 419–28.

5   C. Walsh, 'Shop design and the display of goods in eighteenth-century London', *Journal of Design History*, 8 (1995): 157–76; C. Walsh, 'The design of London goldsmiths'

language,[6] shops became sites of polite culture, not entirely dissimilar to museums.[7] A variety of display techniques, such as exhibitions, public shows and demonstrations of goods in showrooms was used. Thus, visual rhetoric played a major part in urban culture and in the emergence of a public milieu.[8] Tasteful strategies of display and entertainment fostered new aesthetics of curiosity that were more socially open and that accompanied the commercialization of leisure and pleasure.[9]

In this chapter, I will explore the interaction between display and commerce, in a context where utility became the chief criterion of cultural practices, where new ranges of tools and labour- or capital-saving devices spread in trade and manufacture, where 'credibility and worthiness' in machines emerged as a major factor in promoting enterprise.[10]

Between Curiosity and Utility

On the one hand, inventions belonged to the realm of curiosity. They were based on excellence, on skilfully made and ingenious works, on exceptional care taken in the creation of singular articles, in imitation of Nature and of marvellous effects in defiance of natural laws.[11] Far from disappearing, the concept of invention as ingenuity was reinforced by commercial strategies that emphasized novelty, variety and spectacular shows.

---

shops in the early eighteenth century', in D. Mitchell (ed.), *Goldsmiths, Silversmiths and Bankers: Innovation and the Transfer of Skill, 1550–1750* (Stroud: Alan Sutton Publishing, Center for the Metropolitan History, 1995), pp. 96–111; C. Velut, 'Le monde intérieur de la boutique: les boutiques de papiers peints à Paris, 1750–1820', in N. Coquery (ed.), *La boutique et la ville*, pp. 277–94.

6   M. Berg and H. Clifford, 'Commerce and the commodity: graphic display and selling new consumer goods in 18th-century England', in M. North and D. Ormrod (eds), *Art Markets in Europe, 1400–1800* (Aldershot: Ashgate, 1998), pp. 187–200; C. Walsh, 'The advertising and marketing of consumer goods in eighteenth-century London', in C. Wischermann and E. Shore (eds), *Advertising and the European City. Historical Perspectives* (Aldershot: Ashgate, 2000), pp. 79–95; K. Scott, 'Archives and collections. The Waddesdon Manor trade cards: more than one history', *Journal of Design History*, 17 (2004): 91–108.

7   M. Berg, 'Inventors of the world of goods', in P. K. O'Brien and K. Bruland (eds), *From Family to Corporate Capitalism. Essays in Business and Industrial History in Honour of Peter Mathias* (Oxford: The Clarendon Press, 1998), pp. 21–50.

8   L. Hilaire-Pérez, 'Les boutiques d'inventeurs à Paris et à Londres au XVIIIe siècle. Jeux de l'enchantement et de la raison citoyenne', in N. Coquery (ed.), *La boutique et la ville*, pp. 171–89.

9   B.M. Benedict, *Curiosity: A Cultural History of Early Modern Enquiry* (London, Chicago, University of Chicago Press, 2001).

10   B. Marsden and C.Smith, *Engineering Empires. A Cultural History of Technology in Nineteenth-Century Britain* (Basingstoke: Palgrave Macmillan, 2005), p. 7.

11   A. Pacey, *The Maze of Ingenuity. Ideas and Idealism in the Development of Technology* (Cambridge, MA: MIT Press, 1992); A. Pacey, *The Meaning of Technology*, (Cambridge, MA: MIT Press, 1999); S. Schaffer 'The show that never ends: perpetual motion in the early eighteenth century', *British Journal for the History of Science*, 28 (1995): 203–27.

On the other hand, inventions were advertised as the keys to standardizing production, of the profit motive and of reforming policies in the utilitarian ideology that prevailed among Newtonian 'entrepreneurs of science'.[12] Codes of entertainment changed, 'technological tourism' emerged.[13] Tools, mechanisms and processes were exhibited and workshops were opened to potential investors and privileged customers. Entrepreneurs devised strategies based on the seductive capacity of technological rationality, displayed by means of models, tests and performances.[14]

Was there any tension between curiosity and utility? James Watt was cautious about how his steam engines were advertised and was shocked that the Albion Mill could be seen as 'an Object of Curiosity'. This, he thought, could endanger 'the credit of the Company'.[15] But the boundaries were blurring: commercial displays aimed to be useful and agreeable, as much as instructive and entertaining.[16] Moreover, fine arts and techniques, aesthetics and profit, were brought together in European societies of arts that tried to open up open social networks to support inventive activity.[17] The success of curiosities played a part in the aesthetics of utility.

In 1759, Adam Smith confronted the relationship between curiosity and technology in his *The Theory of Moral Sentiments*. One section was devoted to 'the effect of utility upon the sentiment of approbation'. The author analysed 'the beauty which the appearance of utility bestows upon all the productions of art'. Smith understood 'art' as craft skills and the capacity to contrive devices. At the core of his argument was the concept of fitness for purpose:[18]

> That the fitness of any system or machine to produce the end for which it was intended, bestows a certain propriety and beauty upon the whole, and renders the very thought and contemplation of it agreeable, is so very obvious that nobody has overlooked it. [19]

---

12   L. Stewart, *The Rise of Public Science: Rhetoric, Technology, and Natural Philosophy in Newtonian Britain, 1660–1750* (Cambridge: Cambridge University Press, 1992); S. Schaffer, 'Natural philosophy and public spectacle in the eighteenth century', *History of Science*, 21 (1983): 1–43.

13   Marsden and Smith, *Engineering Empires*, p. 227.

14   'The advertising, instructions, and repair manuals that come with the new machines are meant to be convincing documents. The images in them suggest their technological sophistication and, more important, their technological rationality,' S. Lubar, 'Representation and power', *Technology and Culture*, 36–2 (1995): suppl. S54–S81, on p. S69; J.A. Bennett, 'Shopping for instruments in Paris and London', in P.H. Smith and P. Findlen (eds), *Merchants and Marvels. Commerce, Science, and Art in Early Modern Europe* (New York, London: Routledge, 2002), pp. 370–95.

15   Marsden and Smith, *Engineering Empires*, p. 60.

16   I.R. Morus, 'Manufacturing nature: science, technology and Victorian consumer culture', *British Journal for the History of Science*, 29 (1996): 403–34.

17   L. Hilaire-Pérez, *L'invention technique au siècle des Lumières* (Paris: Albin Michel, 2000).

18   N. De Marchi, 'Adam Smith's accommodation of "altogether endless" desires', in M. Berg and H. Clifford (eds), *Consumers and Luxury. Consumer Culture in Europe 1650–1850* (Manchester, New York: Manchester University Press, 1999), pp. 18–36.

19   Smith (1759), p. 179.

More than the efficiency of the object itself or the benefit deriving from its use, what mattered was the arrangement of the machine and its capacity to fulfil the purpose of the person who had conceived it: 'the exact adjustment of the means for attaining any conveniency or pleasure, should frequently be more regarded, than that very conveniency or pleasure'. Through the concept of fitness for purpose, Smith was conceiving of technique as 'purposive action'.[20] Means mattered more than ends. Although Smith used the words 'machine' and 'system', the examples he chose to explain his theory were consumer goods, semi-luxury wares: watches and 'trinkets', 'baubles', 'toys'. 'What pleases these lovers of toys is not so much the utility, as the aptness of the machines which are fitted to promote it.' In the eighteenth century, such artefacts were also called curiosities, novelties and inventions. As economic debates in Europe focused on luxury,[21] Smith provided an original approach, linking frivolous toys to the aesthetics of utility. Curiosity was no longer opposed to utility: both belonged to a 'history of doing'.[22] Smith could then reconcile profit with beauty, accumulation with social utility.[23]

But to what extent did Smith's views reflect the contemporary understanding of taste? First, I will examine how, in shops, fairs and showrooms, curiosities opened the way to the aesthetics of utility. Second, I will argue that workshops and manufacturing sites became new places of entertainment and wonder, reshaping both aesthetic codes and the understanding of technology.

Toyshops and 'Technical Curiosities'

In London, from the beginning of the eighteenth century, shops that sold curiosities played a major part in urban visual culture. They were known as 'toyshops', as in the title of Robert Dodsley's popular play *The Toy-shop*, which translates into French as *Le magasin de curiosités*.[24] Toys and trinkets, although criticized as frivolous by moralists and economists, were prominent among Enlightenment consumer goods. The term 'toy', which in the sixteenth century meant finery or stratagem in love,[25] referred in the eighteenth century to a multitude of articles – light metalwares, buckles, buttons, snuffboxes, penknives, boxes with secret components, jewels,

---

20   R. Laudan, 'Natural alliance or forced marriage? Changing relations between the histories of science and technology', *Technology and Culture*, 36–2 (1995): S17–S28, on p. S26; H. Vérin, *La gloire des ingénieurs. L'intelligence technique du XVIe au XVIIIe siècle* (Paris: Albin Michel, 1993).

21   M. Berg and E. Eger (eds), *Luxury in the Eighteenth Century* (Basingstoke: Palgrave Macmillan, 2003); M. Berg, *Luxury and Pleasure in Eighteenth-Century Britain* (Oxford: The Clarendon Press, 2005).

22   Roberts, L., 'A world of wonders, a world of one', in Smith, Findlen, P. (eds), *Merchants and Marvel*, pp. 309–411.

23   Benedict, *Curiosity: A Cultural History*, p. 77.

24   R. Dodsley, *The Toy-shop. A Dramatick Satire* (London: Lawton Gilliver, 1735), reprinted in H.M. Solomon (ed.), *The Toy-shop (1735). The King and the Miller of Mansfield (1737). Robert Dodsley* (Los Angeles: University of California Press, 1983).

25   J.A. Simpson and E.S.C. Weiner (eds), *The Oxford English Dictionary* (Oxford: The Clarendon Press, 1989).

as recorded in trade dictionaries.[26] The semantic evolution from tricks to trinkets accompanied the rise of markets for semi-luxury goods, on which Birmingham built its success – in the words of Edmund Burke, 'the Great Toyshop of Europe'.[27]

Toys were eighteenth-century curiosities *par excellence*, combining variety, innovation and the imitation of noble metals with the operation of miniaturized and hidden mechanisms. Their manufacture demonstrated a high level of skill and ingenuity, relying on advanced processing techniques such as rolling, plating and polishing, and new materials such as cast steel, alloys and varnishes, combined with a profusion of models, shapes and designs. These objects belonged to an economy of display, to conspicuous consumption and social 'strategies for showing'.[28] They were 'crucial elements within a developing non-verbal language'.[29] Toyshops provided new opportunities for visual entertainment. Articles for sale caught the eye of consumers and passers-by. Pleasure and profit were united. Artful mechanisms and optical instruments were prominent. Toymen, such as George Wildey and the Pinchbecks, were often watchmakers, spectacle makers and jewellers and they subcontracted work to large networks of highly skilled artisans. The exhibition of technical skills played a major part in the curiosities they offered to the public. There was a direct link between toyshops and the emergence of exhibitions of technology.

Over two generations, the Pinchbecks ran toyshops in London where they sold trinkets and displayed curious clockworks.[30] Christopher Pinchbeck (1670–1732) set up as a clockmaker and toyman around 1700 in St George Court (West Smithfields), and later on (1721) in Fleet Street at the 'Astronomical Musical Clock'. Formerly a pastry cook, he used small characters of elaborate clockwork to decorate Twelfth

---

26 'Toys' are translated into 'Bijoux, breloques, colifichets' in D. Lobo, *A Nomenclature or Dictionary, in English, French, Spanish, and German, of the Principal Articles manufactured in this Kingdom...* (London, printed for the editor, 1776), p. 160.

27 M. Berg, 'Commerce and creativity in eighteenth-century Birmingham', in M. Berg (ed.), *Markets and Manufactures in Early Industrial Europe* (London: Routledge, 1991), pp. 173–204.

28 M. Pointon, *Strategies for Showing. Women, Possession and Representation in English Visual Culture, 1665–1800* (Oxford: Oxford University Press, 1997).

29 H. Clifford, 'In defence of the toyshop: the intriguing case of George Willdey and the Huguenots', *Proceedings of the Huguenot Society*, 27 (1999): 171–88, on p. 173; R. Smith, 'James Cox (1723–1800): a revised biography', *The Burlington Magazine* (June 2000): 353–61, on p. 358.

30 I am very grateful to Alex Werner for providing references in The National Archives and his unpublished paper entitled 'The "ingenious" Mr. Christopher Pinchbeck (1670–1732)', delivered at the *Skilled Workforce Project Workshop*, 8 November 1992, Museum of London. R. Shenton, *Christopher Pinchbeck and his Family* (Ashford: Brant Wrights Associates Ltd, 1976); S. Lumas and J. Cox, 'False gold in Fleet street. The Pinchbeck metal', *Country Life* (24 September 1981): 1049–50; Altick *The Shows of London*, pp. 23–8, 57–62, 86.

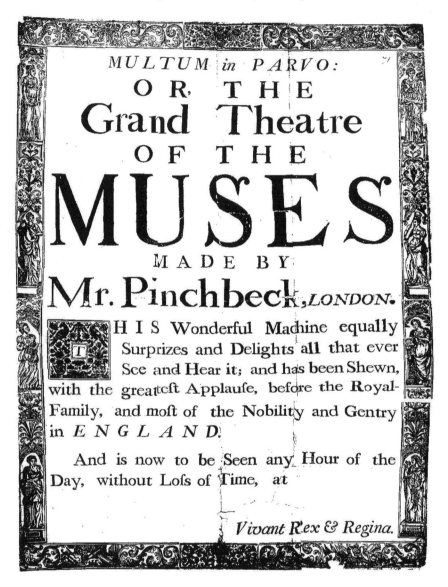

Figure 2.1   Multum in Parvo. British Library: 1850.c.10 (71). © British Library.

Night cakes sold by his wife in the shop next door. His business was successful.[31] He grew in reputation by demonstrating his musical clocks and other curiosities in partnership with the conjuror Isaac Ffawkes. In 1729, he advertised an itinerant 'Grand Theatre of the Muses' or *Multum in Parvo*, a musical clock equipped with two moving pictures that played Handel's music and imitated bird songs (Figure

---

31   According to Sun Fire Insurances archives (Guildhall Library, London), his assets increased from £500 in 1722 to £1,000 in 1729.

2.1). This 'entertaining piece of art' migrated from Southwark and Bartholomew Fairs to coffee-houses, including George's in Stocks Market, Hyde Park Corner, The Black Lyon in Ludgate Hill, South Sea Coffee House in Bishop Gate Street, and a private house in Cow Lane during Bartholomew Fair.[32] Pinchbeck charged one shilling for entrance, while James Cox charged half a guinea. From 1731, the clock was on view in Pinchbeck's shop in Fleet Street.

Adverts in the press listed toys, watches and jewellery sold in the shop, plus a model of the Chelsea waterworks. Pinchbeck's probate inventory included a huge range of tools for watch making and working metals.[33] Pinchbeck also invented an alloy of copper and zinc oxide (powder of tutty) that could pass for an imitation of gold ('similor'). He used it for polishing and as 'a material useful in numerous trades'. The musical clock, the alloy, together with snuffboxes, buckles and buttons belonged to the same line of business based on marketing the taste for curiosities and ingenious contrivances. Imitation, artful devices and skills brought entertainment and delight to the senses. The consumer was drawn in as a spectator.

Following Pinchbeck's death in 1732, the business was taken over by his sons. Christopher (1710–1783) and Edward (1713–1766) continued clock making, shows and the toy trade in two shops in Fleet Street. Each ran a distinctive shop in Fleet Street but Christopher initiated a new trend. At 'Pinchbeck's Head', he contrived a new musical machine, the 'Panopticon', that, besides giving concerts, displayed a shipyard, a founder's shop, 'a Stone Mason's Yard; with men sawing, polishing, chiselling' and 'a Smith's Shop; with Men forging, grinding, sawing, planishing'.[34] The repertory of curiosities was coming to encompass scenes of industry. In parallel, Christopher Pinchbeck occupied new premises, in Cockspur Street, close to the fashionable Hay Market, where Jacques Vaucanson's automata were exhibited in 1742.[35] Pinchbeck advertised two rooms on the top floor: one was for auction sales, conferences and 'select concerts'; in the other, he set up a repository of curiosities, pictures, jewellery, porcelain, clocks and scientific instruments, which he retailed on commission.[36] He added an exhibition of mechanical models 'pleasing and instructive' (for sale): a safety crane rewarded by the Society of Arts; a machine for driving piles (used to attract investors for Westminster and Blackfriars bridges); machines for preventing the fall of weights, especially in coal mines; a curious clock; and screw drivers by which screws were made invisible. Christopher Pinchbeck junior offered to buy out 'Models, Inventions, or Real Curiosities of any sort'. He took out three patents for toys, was an active member of the Society of Arts, and

---

32 BL, 74.1889.B10

33 The National Archives [hereafter TNA]: PROB 31/141/364. See also Werner, 'The "ingenious" Mr. Christopher Pinchbeck'.

34 BL: 74.1889.B10.

35 A. Doyon and L. Liaigre, *Jacques Vaucanson, mécanicien de génie* (Paris: Presses universitaires de France, 1966).

36 BL: D. Lysons, *Collectanea*, vol. II, folio 181: 1881.b.6; C.191.c.16. The repository could be compared to the Hôtel Jabach in Paris at the same period, although machines were not exhibited in Hôtel Jabach; J.D. Augarde, 'Noël Gérard (1685–1736) and le Magasin Général à l'Hôtel Jabach', in R. Fox and A. Turner (eds), *Luxury Trades and Consumerism in Ancien Régime Paris* (Aldershot: Ashgate, 1998), pp. 169–89.

Figure 2.2 Pinchbeck Senr. Clock, Watchmaker, and Toyman, At Pinchbeck's Head in Fleet Street. Daniel Lysons' Collectanea, British Library: 1881.b.6 vol. 2 (2) fo. 182. © British Library.

became the president of the Society of Engineers (Smeatonians). Objects displayed in his repository could also be seen in workshops, such as the 'patent alarm' for stopping carriages, exhibited in the premises of the famous coachbuilders Owen O'Keefe in Long Acre and Joseph Jacob in Saint Mary Axe.[37]

Christopher Pinchbeck's shops thus offered a multifaceted show, combining curious musical clocks, representations of work, toy ware and mechanical models. Just as in James Bisset's toyshop and museum in Birmingham nearly a century later, just as in the Society of Arts, which exhibited paintings and machines from 1761, or just as in John Theophilus Desaguliers's house in Channel Row (which was full of machines and antiques bequeathed by the architect William Talman in 1719),[38] several cultural practices intersected in Pinchbeck's shop: demonstration, entertainment, instruction, appreciation of art. The aims were to sell, purchase and resell. However, the mechanical exhibition, called '*Utile & dolci* or the minor Mechanical Exhibition', expressed a new code of curiosity that blurred the boundaries between utility and pleasure, between fine arts and technology, and between culture and profit.

Later on, Pinchbecks' advertisements were collected and arranged by Daniel Lysons (1762–1834). A member of the Society of Arts, a fellow of the Royal Society and an antiquarian who toured England, Lysons made up enormous folios of adverts and tracts relating to inventions and curiosities (Figure 2.2).[39] He focused on operations, movements and processes, thus opening the way to the aesthetics of utility epitomized in the 'Grand Theatre of Muses' or the allegory of trades. Curiosities, inventions and mechanisms belonged to the 'pleasures of the imagination', as Adam Smith suggested in his *Theory of Moral Sentiments.*[40]

Pinchbeck the eldest was acquainted with the showman and clockmaker James Cox, famous for his museum of automata in Spring Gardens (1772). Pinchbeck expressed his admiration in a letter to him. He referred to Pinchbeck's repository as the 'minor' exhibition, hoping that his 'few rude models and machines … have some merit'.[41] Cox's automata were made for luxury markets and performed artful movements. But utility was also at stake: 'The chronoscope, the automaton that plays upon the flute, the use made of natural mechanic powers in several of these pieces, offer surely ideas *useful* and *philosophical* enough to defend themselves from the reproach of being only glittering gewgaws'. Cox also claimed to have

found means to make the labour and industry of so great a number of the most ingenious Artists concur to its perfection. The Painter, the Goldsmith, the Jeweller, the Lapidary, the Sculptor, the Watchmaker, in short almost all the liberal arts have found employ in it …

---

37 BL: 74.1889.B10.

38 TNA: PROB 3/19/45.

39 BL: D. Lysons, *Collectanea*: 1881.b.6; C.191.c.16.

40 J. Brewer, *The Pleasures of the Imagination. English Culture in the Eighteenth Century* (London: HarperCollins, 1997).

41 Guildhall Library (London): PAM 6546, J. Cox, *A Collection of Extracts for the London Publications relative to the Museum in Spring Gardens* (London: printed for the editor, 1772), p. 17.

which, in virtue of their acknowledged connections, are so well disposed for mutual aid, in lending splendor to each other. [42]

Curiosity met utility in several ways. It conveyed symbolic and philosophical meanings; it provided employment to skilled workers, and it fostered connections between trades.[43] Cox described his pieces in much technical detail, as one would describe a machine. The workman who contrived the Peacock was praised '*as another nature*', because 'not so much as a single screw is to be seen in the whole construction'.[44] In using the language of curiosity, Cox's automata echoed Adam Smith's definition of beauty as perfect fitness for purpose. His collaborators and successors were the mechanics Jean-Joseph Merlin and the Jaquet-Droz (father and son).[45]

Such shops were not unique to England, they existed also in France.[46] In the 1770s, the mercer Granchez attracted customers at the Petit Dunkerque in Paris by advertising 'mechanic game tables, which play by themselves; snuffboxes containing a water jet with wind, others with moving pictures. Soothsayer mermaids, mysterious dials, small wells providing candies that one may desire, ... three-colour cases, mysterious spectacles, other small jewels and New Year's gifts'.[47] Contrivances representing workplace scenes also appeared in the 'Musée bijou' designed by the Périer brothers for Madame de Genlis, the tutor of the duke of Orleans's children.

Toyshops belonged to the world of projectors, of patentees and entrepreneurs of science.[48] In the 1720s, Pinchbeck's shop was also the office of the newspapers launched by the Newtonian projector Richard Bradley, the *Weekly Miscellany*, which advertised trifles, useful knowledge and company shares.[49] A similar example in France would be Vaucanson. He exhibited curious automata in Paris and London, he designed physiological models, mechanical inventions and improved machinery

---

42   Bodleian Library (Oxford): Catalogue of lotteries, 1773: 73226.

43   M. Pointon, 'Dealer in Magic: James Cox's Jewelry Museum and the Economics of Luxurious Spectacle in Late-Eighteenth-Century London', in De Marchi and Goodwin (eds), *Economic Engagements with Art*, pp. 423–51.

44   Y. Zek and R. Smith, 'The Hermitage Peacock. How an eighteenth century automaton reached St Petersburg?', *Antiquarian Horology* (2005): 699–715, on p. 704.

45   *John Joseph Merlin. The Ingenious Mechanick* (exhibition catalogue) (Kenwood House: The Iveagh Bequest, 1985); R. Smith, 'The Swiss connection. International networks in some eighteenth-century luxury trades', *Journal of Design History*, 17 (2004): 123–39; R. Smith, 'James Cox (1723–1800): a revised biography', *The Burlington Magazine* (June 2000): 353–61, on p. 358..

46   C. Sargentson, *Merchants and Luxury Markets. The Marchands Merciers of Eighteenth-Century Paris* (London: Victoria and Albert Museum, 1996).

47   M. Thomas, *Almanach général des marchands, négocians et commerçans de la France et du reste de l'Europe* (Paris: Valade, 1772), p. 621.

48   C. MacLeod, *Inventing the Industrial Revolution. The English Patent System, 1660–1800* (Cambridge: Cambridge University Press, 1988); C. MacLeod, 'The 1690s patents boom: invention or stock-jobbing?', *Economic History Review*, 39 (1986): 549–71.

49   R. Bradley, *Weekly Miscellany for the Improvement of Husbandry, Trade, Arts and Sciences* (London, 1727). The newspaper was also sold by Mr Fowler, mathematical instrument maker in Swiching's-Alley near the Royal Exchange.

as an inspector of manufactures, in the Hôtel de Mortagne, which became the first national repository of machines after his death (1783) and provided the core collection of the Conservatoire des arts et métiers (1794.)[50] Automata opened the way to a science of movements, operations and processes.

The main driving forces were state economic reformism and private business, for profit did not depend solely on entrepreneurs. In France, the idea of creating connections between artists, craftsmen, scientists and contractors belonged to reforming and revolutionary initiatives, such as the Salon de la Correspondance by Pahin de la Blancherie (1777) and the Lycée des Arts by Gaullard-Desaudray (1792). Formerly a manufacturer of toy ware, who stayed a while in Birmingham, Desaudray set up his Lycée in the Palais-royal, a major site of luxury trades, curiosities and technical attractions.[51] Desaudray's institution provided support to inventors, exhibitions of machines, public experiments, courses in technology, and numerous leisure activities. For him, 'sciences and the arts go forward hand in hand, they lend one another mutual assistance.[52] As serious occupations 'should be balanced by leisure and resources provided by agreeable talents', the Lycée provided a ballroom, a concert hall, a cabinet of physics and curiosities, a billiard saloon, a coffee room and a restaurant. Its aim was to attract the public through 'easy enjoyments' (*'jouissances faciles'*). Delight, games and fancy could be provided by inventions, since they were conceived of as products of fantasy and imagination, echoing the range of toys Desaudray had manufactured, with varying shapes, models and brilliancies ad infinitum.[53]

A new culture of curiosity was enhanced by the rise of consumption and by the success of display techniques in urban culture. Curiosities, inventions, novelties opened the way to the aesthetics of utility understood as fitness, based on the praise of design, project and purpose. As workshops and manufactures gradually became tourist sites of exhibition, a new understanding of machinery emerged.

---

50 R. Benhamou, 'From *curiosité* to *utilité*: the automaton in eighteenth-century France', *Studies in Eighteenth-Century Culture* 17 (1987): 91–105; D. Puymèges, 'Les anatomies mouvantes', *Milieux*, 7/8 (1981–1982): 62–6; D. de Place, 'Le sort des ateliers de Vaucanson, 1783–1791, d'après un document nouveau', *History and Technology*, 1 (1983): 79–100.

51 L. Hilaire-Pérez, 'Des entreprises de quincaillerie aux institutions de la technologie: l'itinéraire de Charles-Emmanuel Gaullard-Desaudray (1740–1832)', in J.-F. Belhoste, S. Benoît, S. Chassagne and P. Mioche (eds), *Autour de l'industrie, histoire et patrimoine. Mélanges offerts à Denis Woronoff* (Paris: Comité pour l'histoire économique et financière de la France, 2004), pp. 547–67.

52 C.E. Gaullard-Desaudray, *Nouvelle constitution des sciences, arts et métiers, avec le projet de décret présenté à l'Assemblée nationale...* (Paris, 1792), pp. 14–15.

53 M. Berg, 'French fancy and cool Britannia: the fashion markets of early modern Europe', *Proceedings Istituto Internazionale di Storia Economica F. Datini* (Prato, 2000), pp. 1–36.

Workshops and Technical Shows

At the end of the eighteenth century, workshops and manufactories joined the range of curiosities to be visited. One major reason for this was related to marketing strategies. Sites of production played a major part in the modes of communication used to advertise inventions and promote enterprises. This trend echoed a growing interest in machinery among different sections of the public. It also initiated formalization of practical and technological.

In many respects displays of machines were considered useful and pleasant entertainments that had a place among urban curiosities. Numerous guides and almanacs testified to the renewal of genteel culture. Alongside monuments, museums and cabinets, engines and workshops were integrated into the range of economic curiosities. In the guides edited by Luc-Vincent Thiéry, the Périer brothers' steam engines, set up in Chaillot in 1781, under contract with Watt, deserved special attention, as well as their factory, which also supplied engines in 1786 for the Gros-Caillou pumps. Their workshops were 'curious to see because of their number of workers and their two ingenious machines for different works'.[54] The opening ceremony of the Gros-Caillou waterworks was recorded by memorialists, and many engraved plates of the Périers' waterworks illustrate the new industrial architecture.[55] Depictions of the pumps entered art markets as picturesque views, supported by the aesthetics of the sublime.[56]

Tourist guides mentioned shops and workshops offering shows and exhibits. For instance, Thiéry's *Guide des Amateurs* gave special notice to Réveillon's wallpaper factory, praising its 'vast and splendid workshops, where nearly 400 workmen are occupied; they are open to the public and to foreigners and are worth seeing'. The most detailed guide of its kind was printed in Lyons in 1818. In a paragraph devoted to silk throwing, the author explained that:

> The mechanism for the throwing of silk must interest the curious and foreigners. A horse on the fourth floor turns a wheel that operates several others in the lower rooms and these make several thousands of bobbins to spin and they are furnished in an instant. The famous Vaucanson is credited with the invention of this machine, which, by simplifying the work, makes the preparation of the organzine threads a more perfect and less costly.[57]

---

54   L.-V. Thiéry, *Almanach du voyageur à Paris, contenant une description intéressante de tous les Monuments, Chefs-d'œuvre des Arts, & Objets de curiosité que renferme cette Capitale* (Paris, 1781); L.-V. Thiéry, *Guide des amateurs et des étrangers voyageurs à Paris...* (Paris: Hardouin & Gattey, 1786–1788); L.-V. Thiéry, *Le Voyageur à Paris, Extrait du Guide des Amateurs et des Etrangers Voyageurs à Paris* (Paris: Gattey, 1789, repr., Paris: Bernard Coppens, 1989).

55   P. Smith, 'Les pompes à feu. Le dossier iconographique', *L'Archéologie industrielle en France*, 35 (1999): 53–62.

56   On the aesthetics of the sublime in public demonstrations of chemistry see Jan Golinski's chapter in this volume.

57   Chambet, Charles Joseph (1818), *Guide de l'étranger à Lyon ou description des curiosités, des monuments et des antiquités que cette ville renferme...* (Lyon: Chambet, 1818), pp. 121–2.

In the following pages, the author mentioned Jacquard's 'extremely ingenious' looms, a 'superb workshop for the manufacture of tulle' by Mr Bonnard, 'skilful machines to stamp buttons', a manufacture of golden brass, a great founder's shop and a 'brewery situated in Saulnier house, behind Ainay church. Foreigners might watch there with interest the mechanical means devised for the operations of brewing.'[58] Techniques of production were entering the culture of pleasure and entertainment.

Although trade cards and bill headings often pictured sign boards, commodities or the retail environment rather than industrial scenes, industrial premises and workers were not forgotten.[59] Two categories of cards stand out: those of artisans and of manufacturers. Artisans' cards tended to idealize work in a period when it was increasingly performed by subcontracted outworkers, behind the scenes, in yards and garrets.[60] The manufacturers' cards promoted their goods by referring to artisan work practices, or by beautifying the factory, as in the case of Howard's foundry in 1838. Machines, such as the milling machine for tobacco and snuff advertised by Benjamin Pearkes, ca. 1760, acquired an emblematic status as the vision of the workshop gained in stylistic abstraction.[61]

Customers as Experts: a New Commercial Strategy

In a more realistic genre, artisans and manufacturers opened their premises to the public for technical demonstrations, as part of their marketing strategies. Consumers were gradually wooed as experts and potential users, even though they were still regarded mainly as amateurs seeking pleasure and entertainment. In Thiéry's *Guide pour les Amateurs*, the scientific-instrument maker François Bienvenu combined demonstrations in the warehouse ('*magasin*') and visits to the workshop.[62] Thiéry wrote that he 'demonstrates on Tuesday evenings, in the free assemblies which he holds in his warehouse, the various phenomena of electricity and physics' but also:

> These various instruments are manufactured at home, in a workshop on the same floor as his store; amateur purchasers will be able to watch the production of the objects which they will wish to order. If, by chance, some fault happen to escape the scrupulous inspection that he makes of each piece before delivering it to the purchaser, he is duty-bound to change it or it repair it without charge.[63]

---

58 Chambet, Charles Joseph, *Guide de l'étranger*, pp. 131, 134, 155.

59 Berg and Clifford, 'Commerce and the commodity', p. 197.

60 G. Riello, 'Strategies and boundaries. Subcontracting and the London trades in the long eighteenth century', *History and Enterprise* (forthcoming). I am very grateful to the author for allowing me to see this unpublished paper.

61 Bodleian Library: John Johnston Trade Cards, 28 (26).

62 P. Bret, 'Un bateleur de la science: le "machiniste-physicien" François Bienvenu et la diffusion de Franklin et Lavoisier', *Annales historiques de la révolution française*, 338 (2004): 95–127.

63 Thiéry, *Guide des amateurs*, p. 220.

Purchasers were addressed as judges and experts, a strategy aimed at securing the transactions by reducing the asymmetry of information between maker and customer. This development, which departed from the traditional delight and mysteries of the culture of curiosities, was fostered by public experiments conducted in towns. Desaguliers's garden in Channel Row was famous as a place for demonstration of inventions. Some of them were lavishly advertised, such as Joshua Haskins' Plunging Engine for Raising Water, as a means to legitimize his invention and to support his request for a patent: 'It is not an Imposition to the Publick to offer such an Invention, in such a Manner, as may draw in the Unwary to be concern'd in. And how can it be made appear to the Government to merit a Patent.'[64] As spectators were too numerous, Haskins had to deliver tickets to 'Persons of Honour, Physicians and others of Judgement and Reputation' in Lisbon Coffee House. The authority of expert witnesses was more powerful than public audiences in building up the credibility of inventions.

In France, proof ceremonies were a major procedure in the granting of privileges, rewards and official certification. Whereas proofs of utility often took place in closed areas such as administrators' offices, the Academy of sciences and the Hôtel de Mortagne, experiments were also conducted in public places, such as the Tuileries for Philippe de Lasalle's silk machinery and the Luxembourg Gardens for testing crucible and cast steel from the Amboise manufactory.[65] French inventors benefited from a tradition of public experimentation in which efficiency was as much at stake as curiosity. They easily integrated public shows into their strategies, along with tracts, instructions, and advertisements announcing the performances.

Inventors consciously built up their public sphere, their markets and their reputation by using advertisements in the press, in almanacs and in leaflets. They contrived networks of displays while they colonized the press. The mechanic Arnoux, an inventor of a plough, advertised public experiments at Saint-Cloud Park that were reported in the *Journal de Paris*, and offered to perform new tests in the Capucins' enclosure. [66] The invitation was handwritten on the tract, which served as a ticket. Although entrance was free, Arnoux set up a minimal control. Inventors carefully selected their public according to their social status. In 1784, the projector Renaux distinguished three groups among the public, according to their financial or symbolic credit: subscribers to his inventions and academicians would have free access, others would pay three *livres* for the two-hour show.[67]

---

64   BL: Collection of ballads, broadsides etc., C.116.i.4, items 16 and 17.

65   Pérez, *L'invention technique*. In London also, experiments took place in gardens. Hugh Roberts advertised a model of waterworks, first in Saint James's Park and then in the Long Gallery, between the two Houses of Parliament (BL: Collection of ballads, broadsides etc., C.116.i.4, item 132).

66   Arnoux, *Prospectus de la charrue cabestanière* (Paris: Bibliothèque nationale de France, 1785) [hereafter BnF]).

67   Centre historique des Archives nationales [hereafter CHAN]: O/1/1293; Hilaire-Pérez, *L'invention technique*, p. 400.

Technical demonstrations were also promoted by the rise of the capital goods sector.[68] Engine makers devised display strategies to sell their wares, while seeking guarantees to avoid counterfeiting, such as patents and subscriptions. Initial capital could be raised by subscriptions, which also helped to control the diffusion of innovations. Only subscribers and licensees would be allowed to watch the operation of the machines. One Laforest, in 1822, offered subscribers 'a public demonstration' of his flax-beating machine and promised to them 'to operate it themselves on samples of hemp and flax'.[69] Watching and using were the privilege of investors. Although working the machines was not sufficient to understand them, it was a first step.

Visual information became part of sophisticated business strategies, as illustrated by the Parisian pump manufacturer François-Xavier d'Arles de Linières, who tried to market his complex and costly articles in the rue Neuve Saint-Gilles (Marais area) in the 1760s.[70] De Linières published several tracts and booklets offering explanations and detailed experiments.[71] Customers were treated as potential operators of the pumps. Convinced that clients needed 'real sensations' (*sensations extérieures*), de Linières promised that 'he will operate [*fera jouer*] in the manufactory the pumps fit for each use' every Tuesday, to persuade people who 'claim that the immensity of their advantages ... is absolutely impossible'.

Although demonstrations were aimed at publicizing techniques, secrets were guarded. For instance, on the occasion of an official visit by Parisian expert architects of the Building Law Court (*Chambre des bâtiments*) in 1769, de Linières did not permit them to see certain pieces of the machinery. Instead of watching the complete engines in operation, they were offered a demonstration of six 'experimental pumps' ('*pompes d'expérience*') displayed in the yard of the manufactory.[72] They did not have access to a 'cabinet of models', with small-scale machines, for the use of the '*directeur géomètre*'. Thus, within the factory, there was a cautious discrimination between what to conceal and what to put on show. The strategic knowledge that had to be kept secret concerned the technical functioning of the complete machine. De Linières feared that practical demonstration of his machines would permit their mechanisms to be understood, and consequently copied. From the individual parts, one could not figure out how the machine performed a set of functions. The aim of the small-scale models was to make the processes visible. For their part, the experts claimed that they could not evaluate the machine tools because they had not witnessed their efficiency.[73]

---

68 C. MacLeod, 'Strategies for innovation: the diffusion of new technology in nineteenth-century British industry', *Economic History Review*, 45 (1992): 285–307.

69 Laforest, *Souscription aux modèles gravés de la broie mécanique* (1822), Paris: BnF: 8°W2 4532.

70 De Linières also belongs to the tiny group of inventors who received an exclusive privilege in France and a patent in England.

71 Bibliothèque municipale de Lyon: 116902, 116903; CHAN: F/12/2324.

72 CHAN: Z/1J/933/2.

73 In the same way, modern managers would not allow workers to see the complete picture of machines, but only drawings of pieces, to prevent workers' 'use their independent judgement' Lubar, 'Representation and power', p. 72.

Not only profit was at stake in technical displays. In France, demonstrations were pedagogical, aligned to the standardization of disclosure procedures. The French government set up a network of technical centres based on innovative manufactories that held privileges, and repositories among which machines circulated together with skilful artisans. 'Visual thinking', addressed to the 'mind's eye' was crucial in replicating equipment, training students and teaching entrepreneurs.[74] In Paris, an important centre was established in the hospital of Quinze-Vingts, located rue de Charenton, in the eastern craft district. The Quinze-Vingts established innovative workshops for spinning cotton and a manufactory for cast steel razors.[75] Experiments, copying of models, comparative tests, training a workforce, demonstrating machines in conjunction with the Hôtel of Mortagne (rue de Charonne) made the *Quinze-Vingts* a major component in civic ambitions for a technology based on disclosure, tests and teaching. In 1791, the administrator Jean-François Tolozan justified the maintenance of the Quinze-Vingts workshops 'to show people who would wish to set up similar factories, the result of the operations, by speaking to their eyes'. Operational knowledge was the basis of a reform in technical training that would lead to the emergence of engineering science. In the school of design at the Conservatoire des arts et métiers,[76] '*lavis*' design and 'descriptive geometry' were taught as the best way to represent machines in operation.[77] According to Claude-Pierre Molard, the first demonstrator, 'speaking to the eyes is the best means to reach the mind'.[78] In Lyons, the leading city of invention, in 1801 the inventor de Lasalle taught about his new looms by comparing them in the Grand-Collège with other looms in use in the town.[79] Demonstration based on analogies, protocols and formalized procedures was gradually emerging, which aided understanding of operations, processes and actions.

What political aims prompted the institutionalization of demonstrations? Pahin de la Blancherie explained the revolutionary potential of operational knowledge when he proposed to conduct 'free demonstration of an art, at each meeting' of his society:

---

74   E. Ferguson, *Engineering and the Mind's Eye* (Cambridge, MA: MIT Press, 1992); E. Ferguson, 'The mind's eye: nonverbal thought in technology', *Science*, 197 (1997): 827–36; Lubar, 'Representation and power', p. S56.

75   L. Dolza, L. Hilaire-Pérez and Z. Weygand, 'Les institutions d'assistance aux XVIIIe et XIXe siècles à Paris et à Turin: des ateliers entre rentabilité, réforme et expérimentation', in M. Hamon (ed.), *Travail et métiers avant la révolution industrielle* (Paris: CTHS, 2006).

76   C. Fontanon, 'Conviction républicaine pour une fondation', in C. Fontanon, M. Le Moël and R. Saint-Paul (eds), *Le Conservatoire National des Arts et Métiers au cœur de Paris* (Paris: CNAM, 1994), pp. 60–8.

77   A. Mercier, 'Les débuts de la "petite école". Un apprentissage graphique, au Conservatoire, sous l'Empire', *Cahiers d'Histoire du CNAM*, 4 (1994): 27–56.

78   S. Chassagne, *Le coton et ses patrons, 1760–1840* (Paris: EHESS, (1991), p. 251.

79   Archives municipales de Lyon: 77 WP 001. As the guild officials put it, 'here the eye can judge, swiftly, what the mind takes a long time to grasp even in the clearest and most methodical reports'.

We think that the communication which will occur by this means between artists of different kinds, who will learn the operations particular to arts which adhere one to another, while apprenticeship and guild privileges compose them as separate classes, will produce very favourable effects for the progress of the arts.[80]

Demonstrations helped to move beyond the boundaries inherited from the guilds.[81] The concept of operation was the keystone of technology considered as a science aimed at fabrication. Johann Beckmann, in his *General Technology* (1806), defined technology as the science of 'operations of art', 'whatever the materials [used] and the goods manufactured'.[82] Beckmann's general notion resulted from 'thinking of analogies based on the observation of trades'. But Pahin's originality lay in not separating 'technological' demonstration from pleasure: 'at the same time ... amateurs will be able to acquire very-pleasant knowledge of an infinity of things which they could not learn in the workshops'. Demonstrations were addressed to 'artists' and amateurs. Thus, alongside the culture of entertainment, they contributed to blurring the boundaries between science, curiosity, art and techniques.

Conclusions

Eighteenth-century technical shows renewed the codes of curiosity, in connection with the rise of consumption and the commercialization of leisure. Curiosities such as clocks, toys and automata opened the way to Adam Smith's aesthetics of 'fitness for purpose', praising the 'appearance of utility' – that is, the machine's capacity to achieve its function, no matter how frivolous it might be. This association of beauty with project and design fostered a growing interest in the demonstration of machines. Workshops became places of display.[83]

Two major trends have been identified in this chapter. On the one hand, entertainment blurred the boundaries between mechanical arts and polite arts, between pleasure and instruction, between progress and profit. On the other, demonstrations emphasized operations, processes, beyond distinctions of trades. From both a new concept emerged: the synthetic understanding of techniques, in light of 'purposes of fabrication', either revealing the 'unity of conception', the project lying behind

---

80   *Nouvelles de la République des Lettres et des Arts*, 16 mars 1779, p. 48.

81   For debates on guilds and cross-skills, see Turner, *Luxury Trades and Consumerism*, pp. 63–96. L. Hilaire-Pérez, and C. Lanoë, 'Pour une relecture de l'histoire des métiers: les savoirs des artisans en France au XVIIIe siècle', in D. Margairaz and P. Minard (eds), *Mélanges en l'honneur de Daniel Roche* (Paris: Collège de France, 2008).

82   A. Picon, 'Matière et travail. La classification des arts et métiers de l'*Encyclopédie*', in S. Albertan-Coppola and A. M. Chouillet (eds), *La Matière et l'homme dans l'Encyclopédie* (Paris: Klincksiek, 1998), pp. 235–46; A. Picon, 'Gestes ouvriers, opérations et processus techniques. La vision du travail des encyclopédistes', *Recherches sur Diderot et sur l'Encyclopédie*, 13 (1992): 131–47; H Vérin, 'La technologie comme science autonome', paper delivered at the conference on *Rénovation et mutations des savoirs, 1795–1805*, Paris (I am grateful to Hélène Vérin for access to this unpublished paper).

83   D. Woronoff (ed.), *Les images de l'industrie, de 1850 à nos jours* (Paris: CHEFF, 2003).

artefacts or enhancing fabrication as a chain of transverse operations, running across materials. The synthetic view of techniques would become the aim of the science of machines later called technology. This new discipline, promoted by scientists and economists in courses, dictionaries and treatises, originated in the practical world of shops and in workshops.

Acknowledgements

I am very grateful to Bernadette Bensaude-Vincent, Maxine Berg, Patrice Bret, Helen Clifford, Christine MacLeod, Giorgio Riello and Roger Smith for their comments on the manuscript.

Chapter 3

Amusing Physics[1]

Jessica Riskin

'Roses from which the thorns have been carefully removed': thus the author of a 'manual of amusing physics' advertised its contents.[2] The dethorned rose of popular science took root in the decades around 1700 and this essay investigates its first flowerings. Public science was meant to be 'not dull, tedious, disgustful, not rugged and perplexing, not austere and imperious, but facile, bland, delightful, alluring, captivating'.[3] Philosophical amusements were 'remedies invented to revive the depressed spirits;'[4] they were suited also 'to decorate the mind'.[5] Never to tax, pain or bewilder; instead to charm and seduce, adorn and enliven – *physique amusante* must amuse. Early lecturers' efforts to amuse were dramatically successful. Fashionable people thronged to see nature's ways laid bare. At the same time, however, amusement was a serious business informed by epistemological, pedagogical and social principles that, by the end of the eighteenth century, were well established. What follows is an examination of how the inventors of public science understood

---

1   The material on which this essay is based is drawn partly from my book *Science in the Age of Sensibility: The Sentimental Empiricists of the French Enlightenment* (Chicago: University of Chicago Press, 2002) and partly from a series of articles that I wrote for the *Storia della scienza*, edited by Sandro Petruccioli (Roma: Istituto della Enciclopedia Italiana), vol. VI, 2002): 'Dimostrazioni e intrattenimento', pp. 139–43; 'Gli amusements aeriformi, Gli amusements imponderabili, Gli amusements automatici', pp. 261–8; and 'I parafulmini', pp. 275–88.

2   J.S. Julia de Fontenelle, *Manuel de physique amusante, ou Nouvelles récréations physiques* (Bruxelles: 1829), p. 10. 'Amusing physics' is a literal translation of *physique amusante*, the term that French popular lecturers generally used to describe their subject. There was no English equivalent; the English (and Dutch) lecturers simply called their courses 'Experimental Philosophy' or 'Natural Philosophy' with no explicit mention of popularity.

3   W. Hooper, *Rational recreations: in which the principles of numbers and natural philosophy are clearly and copiously elucidated, by a series of easy, entertaining, interesting experiments: among which are all those commonly performed with cards* (London: 1787), vol. 1, p. iv.

4   L.H. Despiau, *Select amusements in philosophy and mathematics: proper for agreeably exercising the minds of youth*, trans. Charles Hutton (London: G. Kearsley, 1801), p. 2.

5   E.G. Guyot, *Nouvelles récréations physiques et mathématiques: contenant ce qui a été imaginé de plus curieux dans ce genre & ce qui se découvre journellement: auxquelles on a joint leurs causes, leurs effets, la manière de les construire, & l'amusement qu'on en peut tirer pour étonner & surprendre agréablement* (Paris: 1772–1775), vol. 1, p. x.

their mission and how this mission took on, not only a philosophical and cultural, but also a political importance.

Early public lecturers were the first systematically to address the question of how science and civic life should engage. This question is just as old as its two chief elements: modern natural science and modern public life. Starting around the middle of the seventeenth century, each of these, the nascent 'public sphere'[6] and the new body of scientific practices, helped crucially to constitute the other. By 1700, the study of nature was becoming a public project in both the political and the commercial sense. The earliest royal academies of science had been founded in London and Paris in the 1660s. Meanwhile experimenter-entrepreneurs – driven by the expense of new apparatus such as air pumps and, later, electrical generators – had taken to giving public demonstrations, selling subscriptions to courses of lectures and marketing popular texts. These produced a paying public for natural knowledge and, simultaneously, a public programme in the study of nature.[7]

Among the first to teach popular courses of experimental physics were Isaac Newton's propagandists: Francis Hauksbee, John Keill and John Theophilus Desaguliers.[8] But on the continent, Descartes's publicists were already at work. Jacques Rohault, Pierre-Sylvain Régis and Pierre Polinière each presented Paris with a Cartesian physics, starting in the late seventeenth century.[9] Public lecturers were of various classes. Some, such as Hauksbee, Keill and Desaguliers, were instrument builders, demonstrators and lecturers associated with learned societies. Others, such as the Dutch Newtonian popularizer Wilhelm Jacob s'Gravesande, were university

---

6   For a review and revisionist critique of the literature on the Enlightenment origins of the forms of modern life, see S. Toulmin, *Cosmopolis: The Hidden Agenda of Modernity* (Chicago: The University of Chicago Press, 1990). On Jürgen Habermas's influential notion of a bourgeois 'public sphere', see J. Habermas, *The Structural Transformation of the Public Sphere: An Inquiry into a Category of Bourgeois Society*, trans. Thomas Burger (Cambridge, MA: MIT Press, 1991); and C. Calhoun, *Habermas and the Public Sphere* (Cambridge, MA: MIT Press, 1993).

7   Most of the literature on the origins of popular science treats Britain. See J. Golinski, *Science as Public Culture: Chemistry and Enlightenment in Britain, 1760–1820* (Cambridge: Cambridge University Press, 1992); S. Schaffer, 'Natural Philosophy and Public Spectacle in the Eighteenth Century', in *History of Science* 21 (1983): 1–43; L. Stewart, *The Rise of Public Science: Rhetoric, Technology and Natural Philosophy in Newtonian Britain, 1660–1750* (Cambridge: Cambridge University Press, 1992). For views beyond Britain, see T.L. Hankins and R.J. Silverman, *Instruments and the Imagination* (Princeton: Princeton University Press, 1995); J.L. Heilbron, *Electricity in the Seventeenth and Eighteenth Centuries* (New York: Dover, 1999); B. Stafford, *Artful Science: Enlightenment Entertainment and the Eclipse of Visual Entertainment* (Cambridge, MA: MIT Press, 1996); and G.V. Sutton, *Science for a Polite Society: Gender, Culture and the Demonstration of Enlightenment* (Philadelphia: Westview, 1995).

8   On early Newtonian popularization, see Betty Jo Teeter Dobbs and Margaret C. Jacob, *Newton and the Culture of Newtonianism* (Atlantic Highlands: Humanities Press, 1995), ch. 2; Stewart, *The Rise of Public Science* (1992).

9   On early continental and Cartesian (as well as British and Newtonian) popularization, see Heilbron, *Electricity*; and Sutton, *Science for a Polite Society*.

professors. Still others were private entrepreneurs. An example is Jean Antoine Nollet, though he later became a lecturer in colleges and technical schools.[10]

Early teachers of popular courses were thus a mixed bunch: English, French and Dutch, Newtonian and Cartesian, academic and independent. Despite these differences, they formed an intimate crew. Both the Newtonian s'Gravesande and the Cartesian fellow-traveller Nollet modelled their courses on those of Desaguliers', who boasted during the 1730s that he had personally trained eight of the dozen or so public lecturers in the world.[11] Together, then, a handful of people from several countries, with diverse philosophical commitments and varied social positions, worked to establish a public curriculum in natural science.

How did these inventors of public science jointly envision their object? Nollet emphasized that, in designing his course, he had sought a delicate balance between 'spectacles of *pure* amusement' on the one hand, and 'too serious a study' on the other. He intended 'everyone', persons 'of all ages, sexes and conditions', to feel 'free to instruct themselves, without being reproached for a childish recreation' on the one hand or a forbidden 'curiosity' on the other, 'in a word, to accommodate both the decorum suited to the sciences and the delicacy of the Auditors'.[12] If recreational science were truly to have no social limits, its intellectual limits must be carefully drawn. Stripping the thorns from the flower of physics was a delicate business.

Striking effects that dramatized the various elements of natural philosophical theory comprised the core of popular science. This was partly for theatrical and commercial reasons, but there was also a pedagogy at work. The English popular lecturer and writer Joseph Priestley announced its informing principle in a call for a national education in natural science:

the curiosity and surprise of young persons should be excited as soon as possible; nor should it be much regarded whether they properly understand what they see, or not. It is enough, at the first, if striking facts make an impression on the mind, and be remembered. We are, at all ages, but too much in haste to *understand* ... the appearances that present themselves to us.[13]

An insistence upon simply *seeing* permeated the amusing physics curriculum. Indeed, this emphasis was implicit in the very word 'amusing', whose meaning transformed over the half century during which amusing physics became popular but always retained the visual aspect of its original connotation. Both the French verb 'amuser'

---

10   Heilbron, *Electricity*, Part I, ch. 2.

11   Heilbron, *Electricity*, pp. 13–19; J. Torlais, *Un physicien au siècle des lumières, l'abbé Nollet* (Paris, 1954), p. 31; J.T. Desaguliers, *A Course of Experimental Philosophy* (London, 1734–44), vol. 1, preface.

12   J.A. Nollet, *Programme, ou, Idée générale d'un cours de physique expérimentale, avec un catalogue raisonné des instruments* (Paris, 1738), pp. xi–xii. Nollet also distinguished the 'curiosity of an Amateur' from the 'study of a Philosopher'. On Priestley's lectures, see Golinski 'Joseph Priestley and the Chemical Sublime in British Public Science', Chapter 8 in this volume.

13   J. Priestley, *Experiments and Observations Relating to Various Branches of Natural Philosophy* (London, 1779–1786), vol. 1, p. x.

and the English word 'to amuse' originated in the early seventeenth century from a combination of French roots that meant 'to put into a stupid stare', and early uses of the word generally involved visual captivation and trickery: 'To cause to "muse" or stare; to confound, distract, bewilder, puzzle', to 'divert the attention; to beguile, delude, cheat, deceive'.[14]

Late in the seventeenth century, the nuance began to shift. 'Amuser' is defined in the 1694 *Dictionary of the French Academy* as 'to detain uselessly', but 'amusant' now means 'one who amuses agreeably, who diverts'.[15] And by the middle of the following century, the sense of amusement had reversed. Etienne Bonnot de Condillac, in his 1754 *Dictionary of Synonyms*, distinguishes the 'amusing' from the 'agreeable' as the more substantive category of pleasures. He writes: 'one is amusing by the resources of one's mind. The agreeable mind says well what it says, the amusing mind always has something to say'.[16] Thus, the English popularizer Adam Walker could write: 'the philosophic mind can draw amusement from every object that passes before it'.[17] Over the course of the eighteenth century, amusement – the captivation and manipulation of the visual sense – had acquired an intellectual purpose.

That purpose derived from the prevailing sensationist pedagogy, founded on the axiom that knowledge entered the mind through the senses. To teach natural science to a general audience, therefore, one must display otherwise hidden properties and principles as strikingly as possible, translating theory into physical sensations. One area popular lecturers ruled out of bounds, not surprisingly, was the mathematical. But mathematics was not the only area they excluded. The reason the lecturers assumed mathematics would be unpopular was that it was 'abstract'.[18] Desaguliers and others assumed that the public could grasp, and would be amused by, the tangible and the sensible. So the newer meaning of 'amusing' resembled its original meaning in its basis in sensory manipulation. The task of an amusing physicist was to translate not just the mathematical, but all that was abstract in natural philosophy, into sensory experiences. Thus, s'Gravesande said he would 'set the very Mathematical

---

14   *Oxford English Dictionary* (Oxford: Oxford University Press, 1989), entry 'amuse'.

15   *Dictionnaire de l'Académie française* (Paris, 1694), vol. 2, p. 105.

16   Etienne Bonnot de Condillac, *Dictionnaire des synonymes* (1758), in Georges Le Roy (ed.), *Oeuvres philosophiques* (Paris, 1947–51), vol. 3, p. 33.

17   Adam Walker, *Analysis of a Course of Lectures on Natural and Experimental Philosophy* (London, 1822), p. v.

18   The experimental method of teaching was 'most satisfactory, where Persons have not a *Genius*, or *Leisure* sufficient to come up to the abstracted Demonstration of the Geometrician'. Isaac Greenwood, *An experimental course of mechanical philosophy: Whereby such a competent skill in natural knowledge may be attained to (by means of various instruments, and machines, with which there are above three hundred curious, and useful experiments performed) that such persons as are desirous thereof, may, in a few weeks time, make themselves better acquainted with the principles of nature, and the wonderful discoveries of the incomparable Sir Isaac Newton, than by a years application to books, and schemes* (Boston: Bartholomew Green, 1726).

Conclusions [of Newtonian philosophy] before the Reader's Eyes' by the method of experiments.[19] Similarly, Desaguliers wrote:

> Tho' [the] Truth [of the Newtonian Philosophy] is supported by Mathematics, yet its Physical Discoveries may be communicated without. The great Mr. Locke was the first who became a Newtonian Philosopher without the help of Geometry, for having asked Mr. Huyghens, whether all the mathematical Propositions in Sir Isaac's Principia were true, and being told he might depend upon their certainty, he took them for granted ... and became Master of all the Physics.[20]

Newtonianism without geometry was now available to '[p]ersons of all ranks and Professions, and even the Ladies ... by way of Amusement'. Desaguliers's subscribers' list supports this claim, including countesses and viscounts, a bricklayer, a glass stainer, a bookseller and a merchant as well as 'His and Her present Majesty'.[21] The new accessibility rested upon 'machines' designed to 'explain and prove experimentally what Sir Isaac Newton demonstrated mathematically'.[22] This was not to suggest that demonstration equipment could replace geometry. On the contrary, Desaguliers allowed that one must sometimes 'make Use of Ways of demonstrating as are not mathematically true'.[23] The experiments in his public course, he warned, 'may not always prove, but sometimes only illustrate a Proposition'.[24] An example was Desaguliers's illustration of the difference between motion and velocity. A bent spring would give the same amount of motion, but twice the velocity, to a weight of X as to one of 2X – roughly. 'N.B'., Desaguliers added, 'This experiment is made use of rather to illustrate this Matter than to prove it'.[25] Priestley compared the illustrative or demonstration experiment and its corresponding equipment, such as orreries and planetary machines, to 'work[s] of fiction', as distinct from 'true history'.[26]

Illustrative experiments reversed the trajectory of explanation generally cited by natural philosophers during the early eighteenth century. Experimenters continually emphasized the importance of an empirical basis for knowledge, arguing that theory must be founded in experience. But as popular lecturers, they retranslated the resulting theory into experimental depictions, bringing empiricism full circle, making sensory experience the end as well as the beginning of popular natural knowledge. In so doing, amusing physicists taught their pupils to be thorough phenomenologists. Nollet, for example, reported that he found it 'preferable to ... make less use of words

---

19   W.J. s'Gravesande, *Mathematical elements of natural philosophy confirmed by experiments, or An introduction to Sir Isaac Newton's philosophy*, trans. J.T. Desaguliers, (London: J. Senex, 1721–26), vol. 1, pp. xvii–xviii.

20   Desaguliers, *A Course of Experimental Philosophy* (1734–44), vol. 1, preface.

21   Desaguliers, *A Course*, vol. 1, preface.

22   s' Gravesande, *Mathematical elements* (1731 [4th edn]), vol. 1, p. v.

23   Desaguliers, *A Course*, vol. 1, preface.

24   s'Gravesande, *Mathematical elements* (4th edn), vol. 1, p. v.

25   Desaguliers, *A Course*, vol. 1, p. 144.

26   Priestley, 'Lectures on History and General Policy' (1761), in J.T. Rutt (ed.), *The Theological and Miscellaneous Works of Joseph Priestley*, 25 vols (London, 1817–31), vol. 24, pp. 27–8.

than of demonstrations'.[27] He promised never to 'pass beyond a sensible physics' and to apply himself 'particularly to revealing the relations among the phenomena'.[28] He and other popular lecturers expected their students' attitude toward the physics they were taught to be much like the one Desaguliers attributed to John Locke: with the help of demonstration experiments, the students would grasp what was being claimed while accepting on faith that there were good reasons why.

Some examples follow of how popular lecturers worked out this phenomeno-logical form for popular science early in the eighteenth century. Next come some instances of a fully developed public science after mid century, once the demonstration experiment had become familiar and begun to influence the practice of expert science as well. The chapter concludes in the last decades of the century, with some results of the newly formed public stance toward natural science.

Sensationist Science

Early popular physics courses were organized on sensationist principles in terms of the sensible properties of matter and were divided into two broad sections: the general and the particular properties. The general properties of the first section included both Cartesian and Newtonian elements: extension, resistance, divisibility, attraction and repulsion. All were abstractions of the sort lecturers assumed would be problematic to the general public and would require illustration. In his first experiment, Nollet exploited a chemical process for coin-clipping to illustrate the divisibility of matter. He ignited sulphur around a coin to separate out one of its alloys as a sulphide. The coin appeared undiminished. The alloy, whose disappearance made no visible difference, represented to the senses the insensibly tiny parts of matter, making divisibility tangible and thereby amusing.[29]

Attraction was dramatized in the opening lecture of s'Gravesande's course by the merging of two drops of liquid that 'as soon as they touch one another ever so little ... immediately run together into one larger Drop'.[30] Similarly, Desaguliers raised a red fluid in a row of capillary tubes of graduated width, showing that it mounted the highest in the smallest tube, in which it was in closest contact with the glass. Here was a pretty portrait of the attractive property of matter. As a further manifestation of attraction, Desaguliers revealed that a glass tube, when rubbed, attracted a feather to its surface. The tube then repelled the feather, allowing Desaguliers to illustrate the repulsive tendency of matter. Finally, he used magnetic attraction and repulsion as depictions of attraction and repulsion in general. The causes of motion were distinct, Desaguliers assumed, in each of the three cases.[31] But he set aside the question of causation and, indeed, any attempt to explain the phenomena. These experiments

---

27   Nollet, cited in Torlais, *Un physicien au siècle des lumières*, p. 47.

28   Nollet, *Leçons de physique expérimentale* (Amsterdam: Arkste'e & Merkus, 1754), vol. 1, pp. 237, xx.

29   Nollet, *Leçons de physique expérimentale* (1754), vol. 1, p. 14.

30   s'Gravesande, *Mathematical elements* (4th edn), vol. 1, p. 12.

31   Desaguliers said, for example, 'as Magnetism is a particular Virtue that affects only Load-stones and Iron and Steel, we shall refer a fuller Account of it to another Place; because

were 'made use of rather to illustrate ... than to prove'. Desaguliers's students were simply meant to see the phenomena and so to witness that 'Attractions, and Repulsions ... do really exist'.[32]

We are offered a glimpse of Desaguliers's students' attitude toward this use of illustration in place of proof. In his fifth lecture, Desaguliers used a machine designed to demonstrate the composition of velocities. A gear combined a vertical with a horizontal motion along two rulers, making a pencil attached to it trace a diagonal line.

Some objected that this contraption, though it made the pencil move diagonally, 'did not prove that Nature acted that way'.[33] This reservation, echoing the contemporary controversy among natural philosophers over the source of motion in a moving body, suggests that at least some of Desaguliers's students were alert to the hidden philosophical complexities of his illustrations. As long as these complexities remained hidden, Desaguliers and his colleagues could agree upon illustrations even where they did not agree upon explanations and so design courses in unison.

Similarly, Nollet side-stepped the question of what causes a moving body to continue in motion when he illustrated the conservation of momentum in elastic collisions. He used rows of ivory balls suspended from pegs.

Dropping the first ball against the second, he made the last in the row fly up; when it dropped back, the first flew up again. He told his students that, having 'abstained' from examining the nature of movement in general, they would not 'stop to discuss how the speed passes from one body to the other'. Instead, by dropping balls of different sizes and in different combinations with one another, they would simply see that elastic bodies transmit speed in such a way as to preserve the product of mass and velocity. This, Nollet taught, was an observable feature of the property of elasticity, like the feature that made the ivory balls transmit an impact from the first to the last ball in line.[34]

Philosophical definitions, like general properties of matter, needed to be rendered visible. Desaguliers illustrated the difference between motion and velocity by a spring that shot forward two weights, one twice the size of the other. Although the spring was equally bent in each case, implying that the same quantity of motion must be transmitted, the smaller weight travelled twice as far as the larger one.

Finally, mathematical laws must be depicted. Desaguliers illustrated the inverse-square law – that 'qualities' originating in a point decrease as the square of the distance – by means of an experiment. Shining a candle through a pinhole in a piece of pasteboard, he held up a one-inch cube at a distance of 1 foot from the candle. He then showed that its shadow covered the face of a 2-inch cube at a distance of 2 feet

we are now only considering general Properties of Bodies'. Desaguliers, *A Course*, vol. 1, pp. 10–18.

32 Desaguliers, *A Course*, vol. 1, pp. 44, 21.

33 Desaguliers, *A Course*, vol. 1, p. 289.

34 Nollet, *Leçons de physique expérimentale* (1754), vol. 1, pp. 321, 359, 367–9.

from the candle. The second cube's face was four times that of the first 'as appears by applying the first Cube upon the last'.[35]

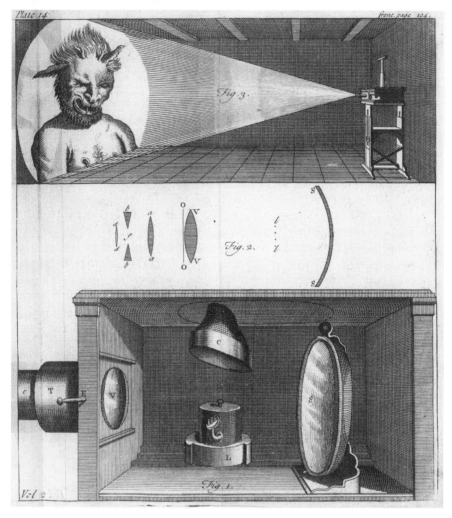

Figure 3.1   s'Gravesande's magic lantern.

Translating a mathematical law into a sensible property, Desaguliers replaced geometrical justification with empirical demonstration, even to the extent of empirically showing the ratio of the two cubes' surfaces. Imagine a student in the course wondering why the inverse-square law held. The available explanation, because this candle casts the shadow of this 1-inch cube over the whole face of this 2-inch cube, epitomizes Desaguliers's continual pedagogical return to the tangible particular.

---

35 Desaguliers, *A Course*, vol. 1, pp. 10–11.

Figure 3.2 Nollet's polemoscope. Jean-Antoine Nollet, *Leçons de physique expérimentale*, Paris, vol. 5, 1764, Leçon XVII, planche 6.

The second half of the popular science curriculum, on particular properties of matter, also included mathematical laws requiring translation into sensory experiences. Mathematical optics was the leading example. Desaguliers devoted a full third of the curriculum of his first public course to amusing optics, dramatizing the geometry of light rays. The most successful item of amusing optics was the Magic Lantern.

This was a box with an oil lamp inside, the light from which was focused by a combination of lenses and mirrors onto a painted glass slide set into the side of the box. A set of lenses on the other side projected the slide's image onto an external screen. The Magic Lantern had originated as an instrument of natural magic. s'Gravesande brought it into the amusing physics curriculum during the second decade of the eighteenth century, while in search of interesting 'machines made by the combination of mirrors and lenses which afford useful and pleasant appearances' that would illustrate the laws of geometrical optics.[36] The Magic Lantern was included in virtually all popular courses and compilations of amusing physics thereafter.[37]

A similar optical amusement was featured in Nollet's course: the polemoscope. This instrument conveyed an image along a tortuous route through a pipe to a viewer. In addition to furnishing their houses with microscopes and telescopes, Parisians began to install polemoscopes in their windows to identify unexpected visitors and to carry portable polemoscopes useful for spying on a neighbour while appearing to gaze philosophically into the distance.[38]

Along with optics, the second half of the popular physics curriculum, on particular properties of matter, originally included pneumatics and hydrostatics. Hydrostatics was a rose whose thorns were difficult to strip. But there was one successful and widely repeated hydrostatical amusement. It was called Tantalus's Cup and demonstrated the relations of water and air pressure in the working of a siphon.

A siphon inserted through the bottom of a cup was hidden by a hollow figure of Tantalus, his chin just over its bend. Once the cup was filled to above the siphon's bend, the demonstrator showed that the siphon would drain the cup down to the botton. Fill the cup just to Tantalus's chest and it would hold water for any length of time. But try compassionately to fill the cup high enough for him to drink, and it would drain dry.[39]

Amusement in the Air

The amusement potential of pneumatics was much greater than that of hydrostatics, for one reason: the air pump. Here was an amusing machine complete with a sensible property, the spring of the air, and an apparatus for creating any number of illustrations of this property. Air-pump experiments dominated the half of the early popular courses devoted to particular properties of matter (Figure 3.3). A favourite

---

36 s' Gravesande, *Mathematical elements* (1721–26), vol. 2, p. 98–9.
37 See Hankins and Silverman, *Instruments and the Imagination*, p. 49–50.
38 Torlais, *Un physicien au siècle des lumières*, p. 167.
39 Desaguliers, *A Course*, vol. 2, pp. 148–9.

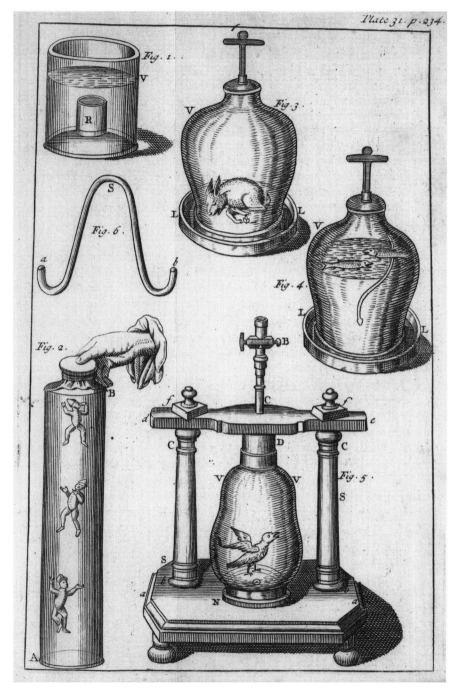

Figure 3.3   s'Gravesande's airpump experiments.

experiment was the rejuvenation of an elderly apple by means of the spring of the air. Desaguliers described it as follows: 'Take an Apple, as much shrivelled as can be had, and lay it on the Pump, set a Receiver over it, as you exhaust the Receiver the Apple will appear as smooth as one fresh gathered.'[40]

Desaguliers performed fifty air-pump experiments in his course, many of them adapted from Robert Boyle's original experiments and almost all of them presented as simple 'illustrations' of the spring or pressure of the air. He burst an empty bottle under the receiver and exhausted a mug of beer, afterwards inviting his students to confirm by taste that it was 'quite dead'. He made several 'pleasant fountains' by allowing an evacuated receiver to communicate with a basin of water or mercury through a spout. He inconvenienced fish, making them rise and fall in a vessel of water by altering the air pressure over it and then did the same with hollow glass figures. He placed the bottom half of an eggshell in the receiver and restored it to the appearance of a whole egg by the expansion of the air in the bubble between the inner skin and the shell.[41]

There were exceptions to the rule of simple illustration among Desaguliers's air-pump experiments – experiments that, rather than merely manifesting the spring of the air, instead expressed an argument about its cause or function, or related it to another property, or tested its extent under various conditions. In one example, Desaguliers showed that a syringe would not work in an exhausted receiver, in order to argue 'that all the Phaenomena of Suction and Pumps, are not owing to the Abhorrence of a Vaccuum in Nature, but to the Pressure of the Air'.[42] However, most of what the students in Desaguliers's public course learned about air pressure was, simply, to see it again and again. A machine that made visible an otherwise abstract theoretical principle, the air pump was the ultimate amusement.

Hydrostatical amusements multiplied with the Chemical Revolution of the 1770s and '80s, which transformed the singular Aristotelian element of air into a plurality of airs distinguished by dramatic differences in their behaviour.[43] Hydrogen, for example, was marked by its flammability. Place some pieces of iron or zinc in a small phial and pour over them a solution of sulphuric acid, then cork the phial, but pierce the cork with a narrow pipe. The steam that rises from the pipe will be hydrogen gas. You will know it by applying a candle to the steam, which will immediately catch fire. Oxygen, meanwhile, was distinguished by its necessity to respiration and combustion. This was amusingly demonstrated by feeding the various gases into closed vessels containing candles and, more poignantly, mice and birds.

---

40   J.T. Desaguliers, *Physico-mechanical lectures, or, An account of what is explain'd and demonstrated in the course of mechanical and experimental philosophy, given by J.T. Desaguliers, M.A., F.R.S.: wherein the principles of mechanics, hydrostatics and optics, are demonstrated and explain'd by a great number of experiments: design'd for the use of all such as have seen, or may see courses of experimental philosophy* (London, 1717), pp. 39–40; and William Vream, 'A Description of the Airpump', in Desaguliers, *Physico-mechanical Lectures*.

41   Desaguliers, *A Course*, vol. 2, pp. 374, 379–86.

42   Desaguliers, *A Course*, vol. 2, pp. 384–5.

43   For a different perspective on the demonstrations using newly discovered gas in the 1770s, see the chapter by Jan Golinski in this volume.

Scientific amusements involving the airs were the driving force behind the development of balloon travel during the 1780s.[44] Balloons were largely the result of the search for good illustrations of the airs' properties: expansiveness, lightness, flammability. Even more importantly, they were the product of a mode of scientific teaching founded in those properties and their illustrations. The inventors of aviation were the products and purveyors of amusing physics.

Joseph Montgolfier, the originator of the idea of balloon air travel, was an autodidact. His informal education in the new chemistry of gases came largely, though indirectly, from popular lectures in that field. His cousin Matthieu Duret had, in preparation for medical studies, attended public courses with the leading Parisian chemistry lecturers: Jean Baptiste Bucquet, Antoine François Fourcroy, Guillaume François Rouelle, Pierre Joseph Macquer and Jean Darcet.[45] Montgolfier closely questioned Duret and, from these interviews, adopted the notion that heat was itself a kind of gas, the 'igneous gas'. Being an expansive and elastic fluid, heat could be harnessed to perform mechanical work. Among other uses, it could be combined with atmospheric air to make a new gas having a buoyant tendency, a lifting force.[46]

Together with his brother Etienne, Montgolfier put this notion to the test. The trick was to capture the igneous gas in a sealed container. The first *montgolfière* was a taffeta bag filled with the igneous gas by a brazier of shredded wool and straw and lined with paper for better containment. The balloon took flight from Annonay, home of the Montgolfier family's paper factory, on 4 June 1783. The *Réveillon*, an improved version funded by the Ministry of Finance, lifted off from Versailles the following 19 September. It was modified, chiefly in that the taffeta was varnished rather than lined, and cheerfully decorated in the style of contemporary wallpaper, having been designed in collaboration with the wallpaper manufacturer Jean-Baptiste Réveillon and built at his factory in Paris. Spectators filled the grounds, windows and rooftops of the château to see the *Réveillon* carry the first air-travellers – a sheep, a rooster and a duck – aloft in a suspended cage. They landed 2 miles away in good health.[47]

The next *montgolfière* would carry human passengers, beginning with Etienne Montgolfier and the Montgolfiers' collaborator, Jean François Pilâtre de Rozier. Pilâtre de Rozier had also gained his education in public science courses in the capital and he himself ran a court-patronized popular science outfit in the Palais Royal. Here he spoke amusingly on topics in physics and chemistry and demonstrated electrical and chemical phenomena. Pilâtre de Rozier had the unfortunate distinction of being the first air fatality. His hapless inspiration was to combine two designs into one, the igneous gas balloon and the 'inflammable air' (hydrogen) balloon, hoping to achieve

---

44   The following account of the origins of balloon air travel is informed by Charles Coulston Gillispie, *The Montgolfier Brothers and the invention of aviation, 1783–1784: with a word on the importance of ballooning for the science of heat and the art of building railroads* (Princeton: Princeton University Press, 1983).

45   On these public lecturers see Lehman's 'Between Commerce and Philanthropy: Chemistry courses in Paris', Chapter 7 in this volume.

46   Gillispie, *The Montgolfier Brothers*, p. 15.

47   Gillispie, *The Montgolfier Brothers*, pp. 21–4, 37–43.

the best of both, the quick rise of inflammable air and the easy ascents and descents of hot air.[48]

Although the Montgolfiers recommended against this plan, Pilâtre de Rozier's reasoning was in keeping with their own first principle of balloon design, namely, that the task was to harness all fluids having a buoyant property. Indeed, Joseph Montgolfier understood his own hot-air balloon to work not simply by heat but by an amalgam of buoyant fluids whose expansive properties were displayed in the courses his cousin Duret had attended – aqueous and oily vapours and inflammable airs, produced by combustion, and electricity, picked up by the balloon as it mounted. [49]

The hydrogen balloon, meanwhile, had been the invention of an exemplary amusing physicist, Jacques-Alexandre-César Charles. His professional purpose, according to a contemporary, was 'to perfect the art of experimentation to such a degree that it would convey the truths of physics to the eye in as exact a manner as mathematics does to the mind'.[50] Charles taught the most fashionable course of lectures in experimental physics in Paris. In it, he liked to convey to the eyes of his students the buoyant properties of inflammable air (hydrogen), using the gas to blow soap bubbles that bobbed straight to the ceiling. He could then display the flammability of the gas by lighting the bubbles to create small explosions. The Montgolfier brothers had kept the design of their balloon a secret during the summer of 1783, following the Annonay ascent. But Charles wanted to reproduce their performance in Paris, where his constant audience was willing to support him in ballooning, as in his public course, through a subscription list.[51]

Thinking of his inflammable-air-filled soap bubbles, Charles designed a balloon of taffeta and India rubber. He filled it with inflammable air by a generator composed of oil of vitriol (sulfuric acid) poured into a barrel of iron filings. The *charlière* took flight on the evening of 27 August 1783 from the Champ de Mars.

Subscribers filled the grounds and windows of the neighboring Ecole militaire; others occupied the surrounding rooftops, the opposite bank of the Seine and carriages congesting the road from Versailles. The show was brief: within two minutes, the balloon had climbed to 1,500 feet and disappeared from view.[52]

Electrifying Science

By the middle of the eighteenth century, the illustrative mode of teaching natural science had begun to influence research as well, shifting physics away from the general properties of matter, which had to be demonstrated in terms of the particular properties of matter, and toward the more immediately demonstrable particular properties themselves. In this shift, new areas of both research and amusement gained prominence. The leading example was electricity. Although electricity appeared in the first half of Desaguliers's course as an illustration of the general properties of

---

48   Gillispie, *The Montgolfier Brothers*, pp. 44–56, 118–20.
49   Gillispie, *The Montgolfier Brothers*, pp. 140–1.
50   Gillispie, *The Montgolfier Brothers*, p. 28.
51   Gillispie, *The Montgolfier Brothers*, pp. 28–9.
52   Gillispie, *The Montgolfier Brothers*, pp. 29–31.

attraction and repulsion, it was mostly absent from the second half of his course, nor did it appear in s'Gravesande's course. But, as the particular properties half of the amusing physics curriculum expanded in breadth and importance around mid century, electrical displays exploded onto the scene. Key discoveries in electricity, several of which were made by popularizers, rapidly advanced that science during the 1740s and made electrical demonstrations the flashiest part of the lecturer's portfolio.[53]

Figure 3.4   William Watson's electrical displays

Desaguliers's assistant, Stephen Gray, was a pioneer in the use of the glass baton, which he rubbed to generate electricity. Gray made leaves of brass dance beneath the baton and electrified feathers and cork. He also invented the human capacitor by electrifying a boy suspended from the ceiling by silk cords. Meanwhile, a professor of natural philosophy at the University of Wittenberg named Georg Matthias Bose was inventing a better generator. In Bose's generator, a glass globe was spun on a wheel and the charge was communicated to a 'prime conductor', an iron rod or gun barrel, suspended over the machine by silk cords. Bose devised many amusements with the help of this machine, including running a wire from the prime conductor to within reach of his seat at his dinner table. He could then grasp the wire while touching the table with his other hand and cause sparks to fly from his guests' forks. In another

---

53   I. Bernard Cohen and John Heilbron have each investigated the role of public lecturers in advancing the study of electricity in the eighteenth century. Cohen describes, for example, how a popular lecturer, Abraham Spencer, introduced Benjamin Franklin to electrical science by offering a course of lectures in 'experimental philosophy' in Boston and Philadelphia in the early 1740s. See Cohen, *Benjamin Franklin's Science* (Cambridge, MA: Harvard University Press, 1990), ch. 4. See also Heilbron, pp. 158–68.

trick, Bose forced a man to drop a coin held between his teeth by discharging the prime conductor on it. Benjamin Franklin (1706–1790) performed a lady's version of this trick, the electrified kiss.[54]

Following the invention of the Leyden jar in 1746, even better amusements were possible. The Leyden jar was a grounded glass container of water charged by a wire running into it from the prime conductor. Completing a circuit from the inside to the outside, for example by holding the jar and touching the wire at the same time, produced an impressive and powerful commotion. The London demonstrator William Watson discharged the bottle by means of a circuit that ran through a wire across Westminster Bridge, then back through the river itself, shocking chains of people on each bank and igniting a bowl of spirits.[55] Nollet also shocked crowds. According to the memoirs of the Academy of Sciences for 1746, he shocked 180 people simultaneously before the King at Versailles. He also shocked over 200 Cistercian monks in their monastery in Paris.[56]

Innovation was strained in the fervour to produce variants on the Leyden shock; in one try, two people completed the circuit by presenting each other raw eggs.[57] Franklin used metal foil and glass to make condensers in the form of framed pictures. One depicted the king with a removable crown. A person holding the frame in one hand while removing the crown with the other, would complete the circuit and be punished for his treason. Franklin also made a spider out of burnt cork and linen threads, that danced back and forth between the charged Leyden jar and a wire conductor.[58]

The Thunder House used the Leyden jar to depict the power of lightning. A small wooden model house with an iron rod rising the length of one wall and extending above the roof, the Thunder House was developed by the lecturer and instrument maker Joseph Aignan Sigaud de la Fond. A section of the rod halfway up the wall was removable. When the section was in place and the continuity intact, one could discharge a Leyden jar onto the rod with no effect. When the section was removed, however, the discharge caused an explosion. Moreover, Sigaud contrived the little house with hinges such that the explosion would raise the roof and separate the walls.[59] The display forcefully showed that the electrical fluid was both volatile and conductible, as did the electrical pistol, made by discharging a Leyden jar through a cartridge of gunpowder.

Nollet used little squares of pewter to form images and written messages and then discharged a Leyden jar through them to produce flaring electrical paintings and written messages in the dark. (He similarly had the idea, which he never carried

---

54   Heilbron, *Electricity*, pp. 230–48.

55   Torlais, *Un physicien au siècle des lumières*, p. 172.

56   *Histoire de l'Académie royale des sciences avec les mémoires de mathématique et de physique tirés des registres de cette Académie* (Paris, 1751 [year 1746]), *Histoire* 7–8, *Mémoires* 18; Heilbron, *Electricity*, pp. 318–20.

57   Nollet, *Leçons de physique expérimentale* (1748), cited in Heilbron, *Electricity*, p. 319.

58   Franklin, *Experiments and Observations on Electricity* (London, 1751), pp. 28, 17.

59   J.A. Sigaud de la Fond, *Description et usage d'un cabinet de physique expérimentale* (Paris: chez Gueffier, 1784), vol. 2, p. 404.

out, of channelling the charge from a stroke of lightning into a house and using it to write 'you will die' in fiery letters on the wall.) The Leyden jar ultimately became the whoopie cushion of the 1740s. They were installed, like polemoscopes, over the front doors of houses, in such a way that a person stepping on the mat while ringing the doorbell would complete the circuit and receive a shock. They were built in the shape of canes and left lying innocently in a rack until someone picked one up and ... received a shock.[60]

People thereby became intimately familiar with the properties of electricity: its attractive and repulsive capacities, its communicability, its different behaviour in different substances, its fiery nature. In Nollet's and other popular courses they also learned that an extensive and rich experience of electrical phenomena constituted knowledge of them. They had seen electricity create spectacular effects; they had become accustomed to explaining such effects by the capacity of electricity for creating them, which capacity they understood because they had seen it. Experiencing the effects became its own explanation.

The assimilation of extraordinary experiences as natural knowledge, ironically, would come by the end of the century to exasperate purveyors of amusing physics. One would write:

> There are people to whom the most astonishing effect seems unworthy of their attention, once they can, with a single word, assign it a cause, true or false; I've seen, for example, a man who didn't want to see the trick of the number-box because, he said, *that trick is generally understood by everyone*. What! he was asked, you know by what means one can know in advance the arrangement of numbers that a man must then create at random? ... Yes, of course, he replied, IT'S BY ELECTRICITY.[61]

Amusing physics had engendered a general willingness to attribute extraordinary effects to unexplained natural properties of matter. A physics lecturer writing in 1799 expressed frustration that his students 'wished to see physics, not to learn anything about it'. They had been taught over the past century that those were the same thing.

The phenomenological public stance toward natural knowledge carefully crafted by the inventors of popular physics was well established by the end of the eighteenth century and began to shape the politics of natural science. Three examples follow of the political ramifications of popular physics, drawn from French developments of the 1780s and '90s.

Public Science and Politics

The first example involves electricity. After the successful test of the lightning rod at Marly-la-Ville in May 1752, people began to install lightning rods on their houses,

---

60   Torlais, *Un physicien au siècle des lumières*, pp. 47, 173–74.

61   H. Decremps, *Codicile de Jérome Sharp: professeur de physique amusante: où l'on trouve parmi plusieurs tours dont il n'est point parlé dans son Testament, diverses récréations relatives aux sciences & beaux-arts: pour servir de troisième suite à la magie blanche dévoilée* (Paris: F.J. Desoer, 1791), p. 5.

often to the great consternation of their neighbours, who worried, not unreasonably, that the things might be dangerous. A great controversy took place in the spring of 1783 in the French provincial town of Saint-Omer.[62] One M. de Vissery de Bois-Valé, lawyer and amateur physicist, had alarmed his neighbours by erecting a lightning-rod on his chimney. His neighbours had petitioned the town magistrates to have him remove it, which they duly did. Vissery engaged the help not only of a senior and established Arras lawyer, but also of several scientific academies and members of the Royal Academy of Sciences in Paris. The lawyer, who was himself an amateur natural philosopher, wrote a hefty memoir and then handed the lesser work of oral argument over to an unknown and junior member of the Arras bar, Maximilien Robespierre. Robespierre, whose own amateur love of experimental physics had won him the nickname 'Barometer', won the case. He received enthusiastic mentions in the *Mercure de France* and in *Causes célèbres*, a popular journal devoted to legal highlights, that excerpted long passages from his pleas. He was then elected to the Academy of Arras, a first step, according to his biographer, toward 'the Estates General, and into history'.[63]

And what about Robespierre's winning argument? In the scientific part, he invoked a now-familiar sensible property of electricity, namely, its 'predilection' for metal, which made it 'impossible' for electrical matter to jump from a metal bar to a wooden house. This, he said, was no miracle, but an 'ordinary phenomenon'. Public science had taught Robespierre what *not* to explain. When the Saint-Omer magistrates asked how to conceive that such a vast quantity of volatile material could enter such a small point, he chastised: 'How to conceive this phenomenon? ... It matters little how to conceive it, if experience attests that it exists. If it were inexplicable, it would have that in common with most other effects that nature presents to us.' Lightning, he continued, would escape from a conductor when rivers climbed mountains, when iron fled the magnet, when dropped rocks forgot to fall, and theirs was not to reason why.[64]

In the jurisprudential part of his argument, Robespierre abandoned the original lawyer's strategy. He had argued that the town magistrates should have deferred to the Academy of Dijon, which had given Vissery's lightning rod its seal of approval. Robespierre instead took the opposite tack. This matter, he said, was well within the purview of the magistrates. Lightning rods were not a subject of 'specialized study in Physics'. They were public science: experience had demonstrated their efficacy to anyone with 'common sense and eyes'.[65] Robespierre's winning strategy was to argue that experiential knowledge of natural phenomena was the appropriate basis for public decisions and expertise was unnecessary. It was a strategy he would

---

62 I have discussed this episode more fully in J. Riskin, *Science in the Age of Sensibility: The Sentimental Empiricists of the French Enlightenment*, ch. 5: 'The Lawyer and the Lightning Rod'.

63 A. Counson, *Franklin et Robespierre* (Paris: H. Champion, 1930), p. 8.

64 M. Robespierre, *Plaidoyers pour le Sieur de Vissery de Bois-Valé, appellant d'un jugement des Echevins de Saint-Omer, qui avoit ordonné la destruction d'un Par-à-Tonnerre élevé sur sa maison* (Arras, 1783), pp. 31–5, 35–6, 56–7, 61–6.

65 Robespierre, *Plaidoyers*, pp. 17, 83, 78.

pursue ten years later, when, at the helm of the Jacobin-led National Convention, he abolished scientific academies.

Next, consider an episode that took place the following year, in the summer of 1784.[66] That was the summer that Louis XVI appointed two commissions, one from the Academy of Science and Faculty of Medicine and the other from the Society of Medicine, to examine the practice of Franz Anton Mesmer. For five years Mesmer had not only amused but ostensibly cured a growing segment of Parisian society by channelling their animal-magnetic fluids with a metal wand. Mesmer's central claim was that people were filled with a universal fluid, flowing into a north pole in their heads and out via a south one in their feet. This was perfectly in keeping with contemporary natural science, especially as presented in popular lectures, where the so-called 'imponderable' fluids – electricity, magnetism, heat, light – played starring roles. Mesmer and his followers, moreover, offered strong empirical evidence of their own fluid's existence. By channelling it through their patients, they were able to provoke powerful crises not unlike the Leyden commotion: fits of writhing and fainting. Popular physics had prepared the public to be interested in a new fluid and its impressive properties. Mesmer's clinic, established upon his arrival in Paris in 1778, was an immediate success. Unable to treat all the ailing Parisians who arrived at his door, Mesmer was forced to magnetize a tree near the *porte Saint-Martin* to accommodate the overflow.

Mesmerism borrowed from popular physics not only the theoretical framework of imponderable fluids, with their now-familiar behaviours, but also its foundation in sensationist epistemology. Animal magnetism was itself, according to its mesmerists, a 'sixth sense', which explained why it could be neither described nor defined. Senses were prior to ideas and could only be experienced. Moreover, Mesmer did something even better than offering a fluid that could be known only and absolutely by the experiencing of it. He presented a fluid that was itself the basis of experience. He claimed that the animal magnetic substance was the cause of all sensation, 'an agent acting on the ... the nerves of the animal body'.[67] Mesmer's disciple Armand Marie Jacques de Puységur, who invented the technique of hypnotism during his investigations of animal magnetism, wrote: 'it is concerning our *sensations* that he has come to enlighten us', and therefore 'his doctrine tends to lend support to all the truths that, until now, spoke only to the *mind*'.[68] Because animal magnetism was a sense, Puységur affirmed, it had to be experienced to be understood. He and Mesmer both invoked the Enlightenment's favourite epistemological metaphor: they could no more explain the magnetic sense to one who had never felt it than they could explain colour to a blind person.

---

66 The following discussion is drawn from Riskin, *Science in the Age of Sensibility*, ch. 6: 'The Mesmerism Investigation and the Crisis of Sensibilist Science'.

67 F.A. Mesmer, 'Dissertation by F.A. Mesmer, Doctor of Medicine, on His Discoveries' (1799), in George Bloch (ed. and trans.), *Mesmerism, A Translation of the Original Scientific Writings of F.A. Mesmer* (Los Altos: William Kaufman, 1980), pp. 89–130, on pp. 89, 93, 127.

68 H.J. de Chastenet, marquis de Puységur, *Mémoires pour servir à l'histoire et à l'établissement du magnétisme animal* [1786], edited by Georges Lapassade and Philippe Pédelahore (Bordeaux: Editions Privat, 1986), pp. 73–4 and 147–8.

When both royal commissions denied the existence of Mesmer's magnetic fluid, attributing the effects he elicited instead to an even more mysterious power, the power of imagination, mesmerists and their many followers were incredulous. The Academicians had undermined the very premise upon which public knowledge of natural science had been founded. 'You have ... seen facts, facts that surprised you, extraordinary facts ... – [and] *You ignored them*,' exclaimed one.[69] Another wrote that if the imagination had the power to enact such effects, then 'there will no longer be anything certain, either in our ideas or in our sensations'.[70] The commissions confronted a public conviction that knowledge of natural phenomena was founded in dramatic, sensible manifestations of otherwise hidden principles. By denying mesmerism, and especially by attributing its effects to imagination, the commissioners challenged the epistemological authority of sensation, but did not easily undermine it. Mesmerism persisted into and through the nineteenth century. The mesmeric Society of Universal Harmony, which closed in 1789, was re-established in 1815 by Puységur as the Society of Mesmerism. Revolutionaries such as Pierre Samuel Dupont de Nemours, Louis Sébastien Mercier and Jean Louis Carra cited universal fluids acting upon inner senses, representing the union of physical and moral forces, and so the hope for a naturalized politics of universal harmony.

A final example of the public stance toward natural science at work at the end of the eighteenth century is the correspondence of the French Revolutionary Committee on Public Instruction.[71] The Committee was formed in 1791 and was assigned the task of establishing a system of civic education. It received a flood of mail from concerned citizens. Virtually every educational plan presented in the Committee's correspondence reflected the sensationist pedagogy of amusing physics. A manifesto on public instruction recommended that educators 'give rise to sensations before ideas'. It was 'clearly demonstrated', the author announced, 'that all ideas derive from sensations'. Therefore the 'whole art of instruction' must be in the 'linking of sensations'.[72] A plan for a 'Republican secondary school' argued against using the 'language [of] the *Savants* ... [which] was not that of nature; that of observation and experience, for which it suffices to have senses'.[73] A report on the newly established *Conservatoire des arts et métiers* (Conservatory of Arts and Crafts) urged, as the proper ideals for the young institution, teaching students '*the science of facts*'

69   J.B. Bonnefoy, *Analyse raisonnée des rapports des commissaires chargés par le Roi de l'examen du magnétisme animal* (Lyon, 1784), p. 53.

70   Deslon, *Supplément aux deux rapports de MM. Les commissaires* (1784), pp. 54–5, cited in Schaffer, 'Self Evidence', in J. Chandler, A.I. Davidson and H. Harootunian (eds.), *Questions of Evidence: Proof, Practice, and Persuasion across the Disciplines* (Chicago: University of Chicago Press, 1993), pp. 56–91, on p. 87.

71   For a more in-depth analysis of the correspondence of the Committee on Public Instruction along these lines, see Riskin, *Science in the Age of Sensibility*, ch. 7.

72   E.B. Manuel, *Étude de la Nature en général et de l'homme en particulier, considérée dans ses rapports avec l'instruction publique* (Paris, 1793), pp. 13, 15–16.

73   Anonymous, 'Programme du Lycée républicain' (Paris, n.d.), p. 6.

rather than *'the science of talk'*, and '[making] them see' rather than 'making them speak'.[74]

The principle that ideas originate in sensations, having been an epistemological axiom and a method of teaching natural science, rapidly took on a larger meaning, becoming a moral doctrine of the sensory origins of virtue, and a political doctrine of the source of good citizens. The Comte de Lacépède argued that political stability would grow from a national programme of education founded in 'facts'.[75] Another theorist of civic education, preaching to the Committee on Public Instruction, proclaimed: 'it is by way of the senses that the virtues enter the heart ... [and] vices enter by the same door'.[76] A third suggested that moralists seek the source of social ills in the physical sensations that first gave rise to harmful ideas. He decreed that 'physics [should] be always the guide of morality', and demanded, 'let a course of experimental physics ... serve as an introduction to moral education'.[77]

By the 1790s, then, the informing principles of amusing physics were entrenched in an enthusiastic public's deepest intuitions regarding nature and natural knowledge. More, amusing physics was well on its way towards establishment, not only as the official science, but as the moral safeguard for a new citizenry.

74 *'The science of facts'* rather than *'the science of chatter'*, Alquier, 'Rapport sur une résolution du Conseil des Cinq-Cents' (27 nivose an 6 [17 January 1798]), p. 10. AN, AD/VIII/29, pièce 12.

75 E.B. de La Ville, comte de Lacépède, *Vues sur l'enseignement public* (Paris, 1790) vol. 2, p. 25.

76 N. Raffron, 'Troisième discours'(1793), in Comité d'instruction publique, *Procès-verbaux du Comité d'instruction publique de l'Assemblée législative*, ed. James Guillaume (Paris, 1889), vol. 2, p. 233.

77 Manuel, *Etude de la nature*, pp. 15–16, 36.

Chapter 4

Experimental Physics in Enlightenment Paris: The Practice of Popularization in Urban Culture

Michael R. Lynn

Louis-Sébastien Mercier began his *Tableau de Paris* with a bird's-eye view of Paris and noted that, as you walk through the streets, 'everywhere science calls out to you and says, "Look"'.[1] Were we, like Mercier, able to walk around eighteenth-century Paris and narrate what we saw, the presence of science might soon overwhelm our description. In a *cabinet de physique* on the rue St Jacques we could see a specialist in electricity apply a shock to a group of men and women, all holding hands so that they might feel the current pass through their bodies. While strolling near the Palais-royal we might meet shop owners hawking scientific equipment and offering free demonstrations. These scientific merchants might try to sell us portable physics kits, for example, perfect for battling ennui during those long, dull trips to the countryside, or a small pocket-electrical machine that offered a surprisingly strong shock. More dramatically, a trip to the Champ de Mars in the mid-1780s might yield a balloon launch where we, and thousands of other spectators, could pay a small entrance fee, designed to supplement the cost of the balloons, and watch history in the making.[2] Indeed, science in the age of the Enlightenment appeared throughout Paris in a multitude of forms and forums that constituted the public sphere. In addition to the ever-popular query of 'what is Enlightenment?' we might equally pose the question of 'where is Enlightenment?' or, more accurately, 'where is Enlightenment science?' The answer, it seems, is everywhere.

Even if Parisians did not call it the Enlightenment, and even if there was no consensus, then or now, as to the exact nature of the Enlightenment, they knew where to gain access to ideas, books, conversations and demonstrations that purported to

---

1   L.S. Mercier, *Panorama of Paris*, Jeremy D. Popkin (ed.) (University Park: Penn State University Press, 1999), p. 30.

2   For a *cabinet de physique* see the notice for Charles Rabiqueau, *Avant-Coureur*, 15 December 1766, p. 789; for the sale of instruments on the rue de Rohan near the Palais-royal see the notice for Bienvenu, *Journal de Paris*, 7 July 1787, p. 825; for the portable collection and the pocket electrical machine, both sold by Bienvenu, see *Affiches de Province*, 19 February 1784, pp. 105–6; for the balloon launch see the description by Anna Francesca Cradock, *Journal de Madame Cradock: Voyage en France (1783–1786)*, O. Delphin Balleyguier (trans. and ed.) (Paris: Perrin, 896), p. 10. On the balloon designer Montgolfier see Riskin's 'Amusing Physics', Chapter 3 in this volume.

provide the knowledge necessary to participate in an enlightened public sphere. From the Left Bank of Paris, for example, with its colleges, the Sorbonne and other academic establishments, science looked a little different than that which engaged the attention of Parisians on the Boulevard du Temple, where jugglers performed in the streets and entertainment was the order of the day. This chapter examines the geography of experimental physics lecture courses in eighteenth-century Paris in order to analyse the different venues through which people could gain access to scientific information, the level at which that knowledge could be appropriated and, most importantly, the ways in which experimental physics was combined with spectacle to meet the needs of the different audiences. An examination of the locations for the dissemination and appropriation of the Enlightenment within the developing public sphere allows us to trace the changing topography of scientific appropriation and the combination of science and spectacle over the course of the eighteenth century. The level of spectacle attached to experimental physics can be tied to the growth in consumer culture and the development of scientific knowledge as a part of eighteenth-century cultural capital. Popularizers combined spectacle and science, and so created a spectrum of scientific activity that balanced these two notions with respect to the needs and interests of their audiences.

While science could be found almost everywhere in Paris, many of these scientifically oriented sites were, of course, intended for a fairly well to do, or at least very well educated, audience. The Académie royale des sciences and the Jardin du Roy, for example, provided scientific access to a somewhat elite group.[3] As the public sphere grew, so too did opportunities to learn about science through books, the periodical press, and institutions such as salons, freemason lodges, cafés, reading societies, musées such as the Musée de Monsieur and lycées.[4] The focal point for this chapter will be the scientific lecture course and, in particular, courses in experimental physics. Lecture courses offered several advantages for this study. First, while there were a few such courses in preceding centuries, the number and variety of public classes exploded during the eighteenth century. Second, these courses were created by independent popularizers of science who sought to impart a certain level of scientific enlightenment to their audience while simultaneously trying to make a living. Thus, they were very conscious of combining instruction with amusement. Third, mathematical expertise and even literacy were not necessarily factors, since these courses were given orally and were filled with experiments and demonstrations rather than equations. This allowed for a much larger audience than could, for example, read books. Last, the cost of such courses was relatively low and therefore allowed for a broad social and economic spectrum from which the popularizers could draw their audience.

---

3   Chemistry courses at the Jardin du Roy are described in this volume by Lehman 'Between Commerce and Philanthropy: Chemistry Courses in Eighteenth-century Paris', Chapter 7, and by Roberts, 'G.F. Rouelle and the Theatricality of Eighteenth-century Chemistry', Chapter 9.

4   M. Lynn, 'Enlightenment in the Public Sphere: The Musée de Monsieur and Scientific Culture in Late Eighteenth-Century Paris', *Eighteenth-Century Studies*, 32 (1999): 463–76.

The Left Bank

The three main locations for lecture courses in Paris were the Left Bank, the region on and around the Boulevard du Temple, and the area near the Palais-royal. The Left Bank held multiple opportunities for individuals seeking to learn about experimental physics. The audience for the popular science found on the Left Bank came from the educated and the elite. These were people with leisure time and the money to spend on, occasionally, lengthy courses of a relatively sophisticated nature. Both men and women could be found here, although the main clientele were certainly students. Chronologically, the area around the Paris colleges was the first of several sites where popularization activities concentrated.

Experimental physics had been a part of secondary education in Paris since the beginning of the eighteenth century. The efforts of Pierre Polinière, the official demonstrator of experimental physics for many of the Paris colleges at the turn of the century, ensured that the science taught at these institutions reached students through a variety of methods. Students no longer had to endure physics lectures without a visual explication of the phenomena under discussion. Instead, theory and experiment came to be more closely linked together. Polinière, however, never achieved a position as a professor at the colleges; his work was always undertaken outside the official classroom space.

It was not until Louis XV created the post of professor of experimental physics for Jean-Antoine Nollet at the Collège de Navarre in 1753 that individuals who specialized in demonstrations began to enter into the formal educational system. Several popularizers, chief among them Nollet, held jobs in the various colleges and technical schools. Nollet's classes were so popular it was reported that as many as five hundred people would attend each class.[5] Émilie du Châtelet noted that Nollet had 'at his door the carriages of duchesses, peers, and pretty women', adding that with him natural philosophy had come to seek its fortune in Paris.[6] In some colleges, especially the Collège de Navarre and the Collège royal, the classes were open and free to the general public. Professors who held educational positions, such as Mathurin-Jacques Brisson, Jean-Antoine Nollet, and Louis Lefèvre-Gineau, taught courses designed for the general public.[7]

---

5   On Nollet see Riskin, 'Amusing Physics', Chapter 5 in this volume.

6   Châtelet to Francesco Algarotti, 20 [April 1736], in E. du Châtelet, *Les lettres de la marquise du Châtelet*, Theodore Besterman (ed.) (2 vols, Genève: Institut et Musée Voltaire, 1958), vol. 1, p. 112.

7   On Nollet and, more generally, experimental physics and the educational system in Paris, see J. Torlais, 'La physique expérimentale', in R. Taton (ed.), *Enseignement et diffusion des sciences en France au XVIIIe siècle* (Paris: Hermann, 1964), pp. 619–45. L. Pyenson and J.F. Gauvin (eds), *The Art of Teaching Physics. The Eighteenth-century Demonstration Apparatus of Jean-Antoine Nollet* (Sillery, Quebec: Septentrion, 2002).

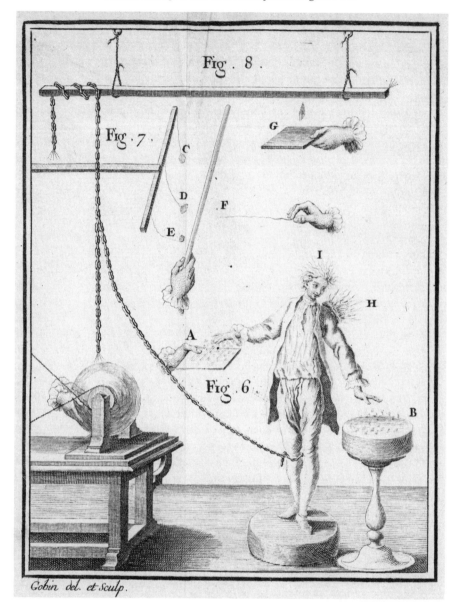

Figure 4.1   Electrical experiments with the possibility of audience participation.
Jean-Antoine Nollet, *Leçons de physique expérimentale* (6 vols, Paris,
1754–1765). Courtesy of the Department of Special Collections,
General Library System, University of Wisconsin-Madison.

Most of the popularization efforts around the Left Bank, however, were due not
to the efforts of the official teachers but to people, like Polinière, who worked as
demonstrators. These individuals performed experiments for the college students

and offered courses on their own time, perhaps with the hope that a more lucrative professorship might become available. Most waited in vain, but a few were rewarded for their patience as well as for their talents. Allard, for example, got a job teaching mathematics at the Ecole royale militaire and Mathurin-Jacques Brisson, who started out as a demonstrator for Nollet, eventually took over his post at the Collège de Navarre. Joseph-Aignan Sigaud de la Fond, however, who also spent many years working for Nollet, failed to acquire any of Nollet's posts. Nonetheless, his series of courses were extremely popular and, when he retired, he passed on the business to his nephew, Rouland, who continued to practise into the period of the French Revolution. These courses were somewhat costly, at around 72 *livres*, and could last as long as three months.

The Boulevard du Temple

While science earned a place within the educational confines of the Left Bank region, other geographic locations also experienced the growth of a conglomeration of scientific enterprises. The main region for such attractions was the Boulevard du Temple, which had long functioned as a centre for popular entertainment. It 'offered spectacles from every genre: besides the comedy theatres, one finds conjurors in their rooms [and] a barker straining himself to announce experiments in physics, card tricks, etc....'.[8] This famous Paris street attracted a socially eclectic crowd that congregated there for a number of different reasons. The Boulevard du Temple, along with the Paris fairs, attracted more than their share of people, thanks to a dense concentration of entertainments. In addition to a number of well-known cafés and shops, this street was home to early wax museums and several theatres that attracted a large and diverse audience. Men and women from all social classes, including the elite, could easily penetrate the more popular milieu of the Boulevard du Temple as well as the Left Bank and the Palais-royal.[9] Everybody could participate in the entertainments found on the Boulevard du Temple and the prices there remained the lowest in Paris.

Some popularizers worked exclusively in the theatres on the Boulevard du Temple. The popularity of these theatres probably aided in attracting an audience for the popular science shows produced there. Unfortunately, little is known about the inner workings of these small theatres. It is unclear, for example, how many people they could seat. It is also unknown exactly what relationship existed between the disseminators and the theatre owners that allowed the theatres to be used for popular science demonstrations between the theatre productions. Perrin, for instance, a 'mechanic, engineer, and physics demonstrator', frequently worked out of the boulevard theatres, usually for several days in a row. In 1787 he performed

---

8   D[oppet, Amédée], *Les numéros parisiens, ouvrage utile et nécessaire aux voyageurs à Paris* (Paris: L'Imprimerie de la Vérité, 1788), p. 86.

9   On social elites mixing with the popular classes, see M. Robert Isherwood, *Farce and Fantasy: Popular Entertainment in Eigtheenth-Century Paris*, (Oxford: Oxford University Press, 1986); and L. Mason, *Singing the French Revolution: Popular Culture and Politics, 1787–1799* (Ithaca: Cornell University Press, 1996).

his 'amusing physics' show out of the Théâtre des délassemens comiques, while in 1789 he used the stage at the Théâtre des associés. His shows leaned heavily towards the spectacular, with a strong emphasis on mechanical automatons and pseudo-magical science demonstrations, in addition to the antics of a very talented spaniel who could read English and French as well as perform physics tricks, to the perennial delight of the ladies.[10] His experiments sound suspiciously like magic tricks or visual conundrums: the 'enchanted tower', the 'incomprehensible inkwell', the 'sympathetic light' and 'the dancing rings'. This latter experiment was a perennial favourite. It called for rings to be donated by the audience; Perrin would then put them into a glass where, through the application of an electrical charge, they would seem to dance about. Perrin designed his experiments in order to maximize both their entertainment and educational value. In other words, he always struggled to ensure that his 'physics games' were also 'very instructive'. In general, these shows relied heavily on entertainment, were relatively inexpensive, and lasted only one day (or, more appropriately, one evening).

The Palais-royal Area

In addition to the Left Bank and the Boulevard du Temple, the Palais-royal also provided access to science and spectacle. Louis-Sébastien Mercier claimed that the Palais-royal was 'the capital of Paris'. Located near the Louvre and the elegant homes and shopping found on such streets as the rue de Saint Honoré, the district around the Palais-royal clearly catered to a social and economic elite. The garden of the Palais-royal was a popular promenade for high society by day and for prostitutes and their clients by night. In spite of its location in a socially and economically elite neighborhood, the inner courtyard of the Palais-royal, sometimes referred to as the Palais marchand, featured a wide variety of shops, cafés and boutiques catering to multiple levels of society. This cultural milieu also included the shops and cabinets of scientific popularizers. Their presence was well established and no description of the Palais-royal went by without mentioning the available physics courses or some of the scientific wares that could be purchased there.[11]

---

10   On boulevard theatre audiences see J. Lough, *Paris Theatre Audiences in the Seventeenth and Eighteenth Centuries* (London: Oxford University Press, 1957), pp. 167–8. On Perrin see *Chronique de Paris*, 1 April 1790, p. 364; Perrin, *Amusemens de physique* (Paris: P. de Lormel, 1787); Perrin, *Amusemens physiques* (Paris: P. de Lormel, 1789); and Perrin, *Prospectus* (Paris: P. de Lormel, 1786). On the culture of the theatre more generally see Jeffrey Ravel, *The Contested Parterre: Public Theatre and French Political Culture, 1680–1791* (Ithaca: Cornell University Press, 1999).

11   For the Palais-royal as the capital of Paris see Mercier, *Panorama of Paris*, p. 202. For general descriptions of the Palais-royal see, for example, *Petit journal du Palais-royal, ou Affiches, annonces et avis divers*, 15 September 1789, pp. 26–8 and 2 October 1789, p. 15; F.M. Mayeur de Saint-Paul, *Tableau du nouveau Palais-royal*, (2 vols, London, 1788), vol. II, pp. 17–21. L.V. Thiéry, *Almanach du voyageur à Paris*, (5 vols, Paris: Hardouin, 1783–1787): For descriptions of the area around the Palais-royal see, for example, the volume for 1786, pp. 324–5, 332–4, 351–2.

Jacques-Alexandre-César Charles was perhaps the most famous popularizer in this area. He started giving lectures in experimental physics in 1780 after losing his job in the office of the controller-general. His lectures, held in his *cabinet de physique* on the Place des Victoires next to the Palais-royal, enjoyed enormous popularity throughout the 1780s and 1790s. Charles convinced his auditors that 'without doubt, nothing is more interesting than the spectacle [of experimental physics]'. During the French Revolution, in addition to his classes, Charles worked for the new government doing inventories of the scientific instrument collections of the émigrés. His own personal collection of instruments was the largest and 'most beautiful *cabinet de physique* in Europe'. Charles's classes attracted amateurs and savants alike: both Franklin and Volta attended his lectures while visiting Paris. He gained even more fame in 1783, when he became the first man to ascend in a hydrogen balloon. Unlike some of his colleagues, and thanks to the work he had performed for the revolutionary government, Charles was able to translate his success as a popularizer into economic security and academic prestige. When the Institut de France rose from the ashes of the Académie royale des sciences, Charles found himself elected one of its first members. Although he never published any of his work, Charles gained fame throughout Europe for his abilities as a demonstrator. His course in physics usually appeared as a chief attraction in contemporary guidebooks. He offered several different classes, including a complete course in experimental physics in 36 lectures and another course in electricity. His chief course, however, contained 60 lectures and covered such topics as mechanics, optics, acoustics, chemistry (usually related to the nature of air and other gases useful for aerostatics) and electricity.[12]

Prospective students could also attend some of the more specialized classes offered by Jacques Bianchi in his *cabinet de physique* on the rue de Saint Honoré. Bianchi, an Italian instrument maker with over 30 years' experience, performed demonstrations in his workshop and offered a series of short courses, usually of four or eight lectures, on topics such as electricity and the inner workings of microscopes.

---

12 Charles did not even begin studying experimental physics until he was 30 years old: For biographical information on Charles, see Jean-Baptiste-Joseph Fourier, 'Eloge historique de M. Charles', *Mémoires de l'Académie royale des sciences* 8 (1829), pp. lxxiii–lxxxviii; Anatole France, *L'Elvire de Lamartine: Notes sur M. et Mme. Charles* (Paris: Champion, 1893); and the anonymous biography in the Fonds Joseph Bertrand at the BI, ms. 2038, ff. 134–52. On his work doing inventories see the Archives nationales (AN), F17-1265, f. 5, and F17-1219. On Charles's instruments collection see Fourier, p. xxvi. For an inventory of Charles's cabinet see AN, C-144, f. 173. On Volta and Franklin see France, *L'Elvire de Lamartine*, p. 19. On his election to the Institut, see Maurice Crosland, *Science Under Control: The French Academy of Sciences, 1795–1914* (Cambridge: Cambridge University Press, 1992), p. 146. For guidebooks, see Jacques-Antoine Dulaure, *Nouvelles descriptions des curiosités de Paris* (2 vols, Paris: Lejay, 1785), vol. I, p. 186; and Thiéry, *Almanach du voyageur à Paris*, vol. II, pp. 606–8. For his courses see, for example, *Journal de Paris*, 25 December 1780, p. 1466 (physics); *Affiches de Paris*, 18 May 1786, p. 1302 (electricity); and M. de la Métherie, 'Précis de quelques expériences électriques, Faites par M. Charles, Professeur de Physique', *Journal de physique*, 30 (1787): 433–6. A brief description of all 60 lectures can be found in 'Cours de Physique. Par Charles, de l'Institut national, an 11, 1802', BI, ms. 2104, pièce 18.

Like Charles, Bianchi had some connections with the more elite savants of his time who, according to Bianchi, visited his shop to consult him regarding various electrical machines. He also garnered praise from the Faculté de médecine, thanks to a new breast pump he had designed. Although he died in 1785, his widow continued to advertise and sell scientific instruments, especially the renowned breast pump, well into the revolutionary period.[13]

François Bienvenu, another popularizer who first appeared during the 1780s, also played a double role by making and selling scientific instruments, in addition to offering classes in experimental physics. His instruments, modelled after those of Nollet, Joseph-Aignan Sigaud de la Fond and Guyot, were sold all over France and included everything necessary for a complete *cabinet de physique*. His courses were clearly designed to show off his instruments. He gave short classes of four to six lessons on such topics as electricity and light. At other times he even gave free demonstrations; one such course examined the nature of gases, probably in order to capitalize on the popularity of ballooning and thereby to draw more people into his shop. Bienvenu also tried to exploit the balloon craze by publishing a short pamphlet outlining several machines he and another savant had contributed to the field of aerostatics.[14]

The courses found near the Palais-royal, in general, tried to achieve a balance between instruction and entertainment while also adding a distinctive commercial element with respect to the sale of instruments, in particular.

Moving from One Bank to the Other

In sum, while science could be found easily almost everywhere in Paris, popularized science in particular had a specific geography that expanded over time and flowed over and through different parts of Paris. Like electricity in the air, popular science moved through the streets and gardens, striking more often in some areas than others. If we overlay the topography of popular science with other cultural elements from

---

13   On Bianchi's early career, see O. Hochadel, 'A Shock to the Public: Itinerant Lecturers and Instrument Makers as Practitioners of Electricity in the German Enlightenment (1740–1800)', in F. Bevilacqua and L. Fregonese (eds), *Nuova Voltiana. Studies on Volta andHis Time*, vol. 5 (Pavia: Hoepli, 2003), pp. 53–68. On electricity, see *Affiches de Paris*, 16 December 1782, p. 2907; on microscopes, see *Journal de Paris*, 19 April 1782, pp. 433–4. For elite savants, see *Journal de Paris*, 26 August 1782, pp. 972–3. On the response of the Faculté de médecine, see, for example, *Bibliothèque physico-économique, instructive et amusante*, 2 (1783), pp. 271–3; and *Journal de Physique*, 27 (1785), pp. 198–203. On the widow Bianchi and her work, see L.V. Thiéry, *Guide des amateurs et des étrangers voyageurs à Paris*, vol. I, pp. 221–3.

14   For demonstrations of gases, see *Affiches de province*, 19 February 1784, pp. 105–6; for his class in electricity, see *Journal de Paris*, 1 May 1786, p. 491; on light, see *Journal de Paris*, 29 August 1787, p. 2052. On Bienvenu see Patrice Bret, 'Un bateleur de la science: "machiniste-physicien" François Bienvenu et la diffusion de Franklin et Lavoisier', *Annales historiques de la Révolution française*, 339 (2004): 95–127; Launoy and Bienvenu, *Instruction sur la nouvelle Machine inventée par MM. Launoy, Naturaliste, & Bienvenu, Machiniste-Physicien* (n.p., n.d.).

the eighteenth century, we can see the connections between popular science and such things as education, entertainment and commerce, that is, between science on the Left Bank, the Boulevard du Temple and in the Palais-royal. People took home a different kind of science, and therefore a different kind of cultural capital, from the Boulevard du Temple than they might from the Palais-royal. The geography of popular science in Paris thus moved and flowed in a variety of ways, and the same popularizer, established in a different spot, engaged in a different kind of work that he could sell for a different price, and that had a different status among his audience.

A good example is that of Nicolas-Philippe Ledru, who began his career as a popularizer on the Boulevard du Temple in the 1750s, where he catered to the 'epidemic curiosity' of Parisians for physics experiments and games. He took his stage name, Comus, from the Roman god of revelry, but not all of his work was exclusively intended to entertain his audience. He also conducted experiments in physics with an eye towards improving the state of knowledge in that subject. In his own words, he hoped to fulfil a dual function and both 'excite the curiosity of the people and extend the progress of physics'. Ledru wasted little time in trying to gain some noble patronage, and by 1769 he had performed some of his experiments for Louis XV. From 1773 to 1776, he gained the patronage of the Duc de Chartres and would often perform electrical experiments and demonstrations for his benefit. Ledru earned a certain amount of respect and admiration from his colleagues at that time, and his experiments were often reported in the *Journal de Physique*. In 1783, Ledru applied for and received a licence from Louis XVI to practise the trade of medical electrician at his new Hospice médico-électrique, located on the Left Bank of Paris. Ledru now dropped his stage name and began working full time, applying his knowledge of electricity to treat patients suffering from ailments such as epilepsy and paralysis, previously thought incurable. That same year, the Paris Faculty of Medicine investigated Ledru's activities and, initially, agreed that medical electricity as practised by Ledru was an effective and useful treatment. By 1784 he had reached the pinnacle of his career and could both use the title of 'King's physicist' and claim the approbation of the Faculty of Medicine for his electrical treatments. It seemed that both the court and elite savants had accepted Ledru into their midst and that he could do no wrong. His least success was dutifully reported in the newspapers; in 1784, for example, the *Journal encyclopédique* claimed that he had cured a white Angora cat of epilepsy.

Unfortunately, Ledru's rise was marred by a vicious attack on his reputation. A rival in the Faculty of Medicine, who practised a similar kind of electric medicine, successfully forced Ledru out of business, or at least out of business in his current location, by claiming he was a charlatan. Ledru survived the accusations and continued to practise during the revolutionary era, despite the tarnishing of his reputation, but he had to change locations again in order to do so. The key here, however, is that Ledru did manage to move from the Boulevard du Temple over to the Left Bank, and thus moved from the entertainment side of popular science towards the elite end of the Republic of Letters. He did this by changing the way he presented his science and shifting the level of spectacle attached to electricity. The balance between science and spectacle within the larger spectrum shifted depending on location, with a greater emphasis on instruction on the Left Bank and a greater focus on entertainment on the Boulevard du Temple. But, no matter where you were, popularizers combined entertainment and knowledge in their public lecture courses.

As the geography of the scientific public sphere changed and developed over time, so too did the nature of the science found within that sphere. Multiple opportunities to gain access to Enlightenment science emerged, some more sophisticated and others more entertaining, that were packaged for the specific audiences found within that particular area. Thus, an examination of the locations in which Parisians obtained science reveals the spectrum of enlightened activities available on the streets of Paris and sheds light on the diversity of Enlightenment science in its many forms. In particular, the variegated nature of Enlightenment science, when observed as a function of geography, suggests that where you were in Paris could affect your view of the Enlightenment itself.[15]

Disseminators of popular science depended on an audience in order to make a living. Thus, they were very cognizant of the wants and needs of their audience and, in order to ensure their livelihood, clearly targeted their courses to specific groups. In this way, the public influenced the form and the content of the information presented to them. The geography of popular science outlined here reveals the ways in which popularizers combined science with spectacle in order to address the interests of their consumers.

---

15 A similar point of view, that where you were influenced the Enlightenment, has been articulated for the Enlightenment on a national level; see Roy Porter and Mikulas Teich (eds), *The Enlightenment in National Context* (Cambridge: Cambridge University Press, 1981).

Chapter 5

Domestic Spectacles: Electrical Instruments between Business and Conversation

Paola Bertucci

From Schools to Public Squares and Salons

On 18 March 1755, Benjamin Franklin told Dr L. of Charles-Town, in South Carolina, the story of Mr Domien, 'a native of Transylvania, of Tartar descent, but a priest of the Greek Church':

> [He] travelled through Germany, France, and Holland, to England. […] He came to Maryland; thence he went to New-England, returned by land to Philadelphia; and from thence travelled through Maryland, Virginia, and North-Caroline to you. He thought it might be of service to him in his travels to know something of Electricity. I taught him the use of the tube; how to charge the Leyden phial, and some other experiments. He wrote to me from Charles-Town, that he had lived eight hundred miles upon Electricity, it had been meat, drink and cloathing to him. His last letter to me was, I think, from Jamaica, desiring me to send the tubes you mention, to meet him at Havanah, from whence he expected to get a passage to La Vera Cruz; designed travelling over land through Mexico to Acapulco; thence to get a passage to Manilla, and so through China, India, Persia and Turkey, home to his own country; proposing to support himself chiefly by Electricity. A strange project![1]

Strange as it may have seemed to Franklin, Domien's project was not extraordinary in Europe. From Dublin to Rome, through London, Leipzig and Paris, itinerant demonstrators entertained curious crowds with marvellous electrical shows: in public squares, lecture theatres or coffee houses their dramatic displays of the latest experimental novelties were tailored to a heterogeneous range of paying audiences. It was thanks to a number of such itinerant demonstrators that the electrical machine came to be widely known in Italy.

In the years of the War of the Austrian Succession (1740s), Franco-Spanish and Austrian armies flocked to the Italian peninsula. Away from the battlefields, numerous soldiers and army physicians also introduced crowds to the marvels of electricity by performing spectacular experiments in the public squares of Italy. It was from these venues, the sites of jugglers and mountebanks too, that the electrical machine found its way into the world of educated elites south of the Alps. In 1745

---

1   B. Franklin, *Experiments and Observations on Electricity* (London, 1769), p. 320.

the Saxon physician Christian Xavier Wabst, in attendance at the Austrian army, began to offer electrical performances to paying audiences in Venice. One year later, there was also Francisco Bossaert who, 'after serving for a long time the Spanish marine, travelled the world, and with a small machine displayed many electrical experiments'.[2] In 1747 Bossaert moved from Venice to various other Italian towns, entertaining local academics and aristocrats alike with the marvels produced by the electrical machine.

The presence of other demonstrators, mainly from the German countries, south of the Alps can be traced in private correspondences between local electrical amateurs or in passing references in publications on electricity that appeared copiously in Italy in the second half of the 1740s. In 1747 the Jesuit Giambattista Faure reported that a 'Saxon professor' offered public demonstrations in Rome, both at the university and in the salons of local aristocrats. After attending the performances, Faure resolved to replicate them in the house of a local patron.[3] Faure's case was not an isolated one. In the same year 1747, the performances of a Saxon (probably the same who performed in Rome) sparked interest in the electrical machine and its marvels in Naples. In the Italian peninsula enthusiasm for spectacular electrical experiments quickly spread from one aristocratic salon to another.

The electrical machine was simple to make, and its price such as not to 'upset the financial management of a family', which caused the science of electricity to move from the 'schools of honourable men to public squares and to the salons of gentlemen and princes'.[4] In social contexts in which careers depended heavily on relationships of patronage, performing for a local nobleman could mark the beginning of an institutional career. In 1748 Carlo Alfonso Guadagni, a public lecturer in Florence, obtained the chair of experimental philosophy at the University of Pisa, thanks to an aristocratic patron in whose palace he used to display the marvels of the air pump and the electrical machine. In the span of a few years electricity became so popular in the peninsula as to excite the disdainful comments of another Jesuit living in Parma, Jacopo Belgrado:

> Electrical phenomena have become so common and vulgar nowadays, that even the roughest and vilest people boast of having observed them, and claim their rights at reasoning about them, almost placing themselves at the same level as the sharpest philosophers.[5]

If the public consumption of electrical science provoked the disdain of elitist Jesuits, the transfer of natural philosophical knowledge to wider audiences was a significant process of the Enlightenment. As has been pointed out, the audience–performer relationship informed eighteenth-century natural philosophy and the spectacularization of electrical experiments was one of its distinctive features.[6]

---

2   G.F. Pivati, *Della Elettricità Medica* (Lucca, 1747), p. xii.

3   G. Faure, Congetture Fisiche Intorno alle Cagioni de' Fenomeni Osservati in Roma nella Macchina Elettrica (Roma: Bernabò e Lazzarini, 1747), p. x.

4   J. Belgrado, *I fenomeni elettrici con i corollari da lor dedotti* (Parma, 1749), p. 1.

5   Belgrado, *I fenomeni elettrici*, pp. 1–2.

6   S. Schaffer, 'Natural philosophy and public spectacle in the eighteenth century', *History of science*, 21 (1983): 1–43; L. Stewart, *The Rise of Public Science. Rhetoric, Technology and*

Leading electricians made public spectacles the means through which to bestow credibility upon their theories. Among them, the Abbé Nollet was probably the most successful and imaginative performer. His experiments with electric shocks given to hundreds of soldiers holding hands became famous throughout the republic of letters and were variously imitated. Nollet did not hide his belief that a consenting audience secured fame and philosophical authority. He regarded his public as 'a tribunal in which I shall never be condemned, all the times that the majority of votes prevails; for, what I claim here, I demonstrated during my public Lectures before over six hundred people'.[7]

Electrical performers sought to astonish their audiences with spectacular displays of the electric fire on the other side of the Channel also. While Benjamin Rackstrow, Benjamin Martin, James Ferguson and other itinerant demonstrators entertained paying crowds with their public lectures on experimental philosophy, William Watson – the leading electrician of the Royal Society – was no less imaginative.[8] In the attempt to measure electricity's speed, he made the electric fire cross the Thames, in the presence of the President and other Fellows of the Royal Society. The experiment was so spectacular as to attract the attention of many people 'who many times broke the connecting wire and otherwise greatly incommoded them'.[9] In the 1770s, when the controversy over the shape of lightning rods broke out, one of the electricians involved, Benjamin Wilson, performed dramatic experiments in support of his views at the Pantheon in London, which became well known to the contemporary reading public.[10]

Real drama and literary fiction were inextricably linked to the new science. Electricians related new electrical phenomena with characteristic emphasis. The Leipzig professor John Henry Winkler, after reading of the effects produced by

---

Natural Philosophy in Newtonian Britain, 1660–1750 (Cambridge : Cambridge University Press, 1992); and Chapter 1 in this volume. A. Morton and J.A. Wess, *Public and Private Science. The King George III Collection* (Oxford: Oxford University Press, 1993).

7 J.A. Nollet, *Recherches sur les causes particulières des phénomènes électriques* (Paris, 1749), p. 14. On Nollet, see L. Pyenson and J.A. Gauvin (eds.), *The Art of Teaching Physics. The Eighteenth-Century Demonstration Apparatus of Jean-Antoine Nollet* (Sillery, Québec: Les éditions du Septentrion, 2002). See also Riskin 'Amusing Physics', Chapter 3 in this volume. On Nollet's journey to Italy, see P. Bertucci, 'Sparking Controversy: Jean-Antoine Nollet and Medical Electricity South of the Alps', *Nuncius*, 20 (2005): 153–87; P. Bertucci, 'Back from Wonderland: Jean-Antoine Nollet's Italian Tour', in L. Evans and A. Marr (eds), *Curiosity and Wonder from the Renaissance to the Enlightenment* (Aldershot: Ashgate, 2006).

8 On the role of experimental philosophy and electricity in particular, see Larry Stewart, Chapter 1 in this volume.

9 W. Watson, 'A Collection of the Electrical Experiments Communicated to the Royal Society', *Philosophical Transactions*, 45 (1748): 49–92, p. 53. On Martin and Ferguson: J. Millburn, *Benjamin Martin: Author, Instrument-maker and Country Showman* (Leyden, 1976); J. Millburn, *Wheelwright of the Heavens: The Life and Work of James Ferguson, FRS* (London, 1988).

10 On which see T.A. Mitchell, 'The Politics of Experiments in the Eighteenth Century: the Politics of Audience and the Manipulation of Consensus in the Debate over Lightning Rods', *Eighteenth-Century Studies*, 31 (1998): 307–31.

discharging a Leyden jar on a bird, decided not to repeat the experiment, since the animal suffered 'a great pain thereby' and he thought 'it wrong to give such pain to living creatures'. Instead, he tried the shock on himself: the discharge of the Leyden jar put his blood 'into great agitation' and made him feel convulsions all over his body, as if he had 'an ardent fever'. Notwithstanding the headache that the shock gave him, and in spite of the repeated bleeding in his nose, he also involved his wife in such experiment. The woman, 'who had only received the electric flash twice', was 'so weak after it, that she could hardly walk. A week after, she received only once the electrical flash; a few minutes after it she bled at the nose.'[11]

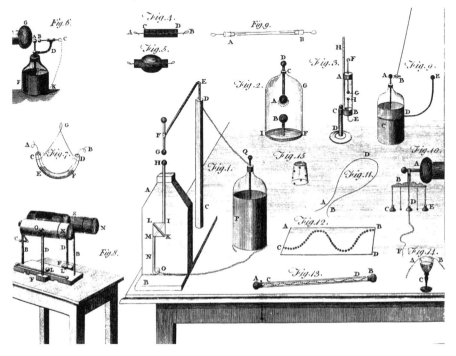

Figure 5.1   Table showing portable electrical instruments: fig. 1 is a thunder-house, fig. 10 electric bells, fig. 12 a magic board, fig. 13 a luminous tube. Tiberius Cavallo, *A treatise on electricity*, 1795. Courtesy of the Bakken Library and Museum for Electricity in Life.

Electricity was spectacular even when it killed. In 1753 Georg Richmann, professor at St Petersburg, died struck by lightning while he was experimenting on atmospherical electricity. His sudden death, engraved by the artist he had wanted there so as to immortalize the astonishing effects of natural electricity, became an icon of the dangers deriving from dealing incautiously with the electric fire. However, while magazine readers would learn that atmospherical electricity could

---

11   J.H. Winkler, 'An Extract of a Letter ... concerning the Effects of Electricity upon Himself and his Wife', *Philosophical Transactions*, 44 (1746): 211–12.

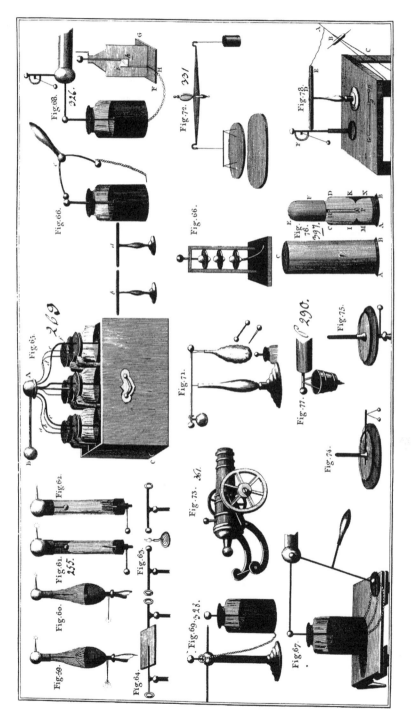

Figure 5.2   Table showing portable electrical instruments: fig. 59 and 60 represent an aurora flask, fig. 73 is an electric cannon. George Adams, *An essay on electricity*, London, 4th edn, 1792. Courtesy of the Bakken Library and Museum for Electricity in Life.

be extremely dangerous, electrical performers would show them how to play safely with the electric fire. Thanks to a number of electrical toys, the spectacle of electricity could easily – and safely – be replicated in their salons. During their demonstrations, lecturers would entertain and educate audiences by means of electric carillons, luminous tubes, apparatuses to produce 'electric hail', sparking candle lighters, electrical planetariums, magic boards and, later in the century, even the chemico-electrical pistol invented by Alessandro Volta (Figures 5.1 and 5.2).

A Piece for Learned Conversations

The spectacularity of electrical experiments, in association with the spread of public science, engendered a growing demand for domestic shows that made the fortunes of instrument makers and public lecturers. While electricians disputed as to whether conductors should be blunt or pointed, instrument makers and electrical performers alike lined their pockets by selling the controversy in miniature. They marketed little thunder-houses that showed the usefulness of metallic conductors to protect buildings from lightning. Their customers could buy both pointed and blunt conductors, affix them to the roofs of their little thunder-houses, and decide for themselves which was more efficacious. Designed in many different shapes so as to comply with diverse demands – from the simplest models made of a wooden façade only, to the most elegant with paper figurines inside – they were ever present in the collections of electrical amateurs.

As the century progressed and new extraordinary natural phenomena such as lightning, thunder, earthquakes, aurora borealis and volcanic eruptions came to be incorporated in electrical systems, instrument makers marketed new electrical toys that illustrated the role of the electric fire in the economy of nature. Turned into one of the many electrical wonders, even the aurora borealis could be recreated in smaller scale thanks to the 'aurora flask', an electrical instrument designed by John Canton. With the flask and an electrical machine, amateurs could see for themselves how the electric fire caused the marvellous spectacle of the Northern Lights. Books such as Ferguson's *An Introduction to Electricity* offered directions on how to perform the 'finest of all electrical experiments' at home.[12] Guadagni promptly included the aurora experiment in the 'familiar course' that he held in Florence in the house of his patron.[13]

The expanding market for cultural products created the conditions for the domestication of electrical experimental philosophy. Bouncing from one magazine to another, the most recent electrical novelties became part of the general knowledge expected of educated gentlemen and, in a few cases, ladies. Electrical science represented a productive intersection of business and conversation: while electrical practitioners designed new instruments to entertain and instruct, 'the rumour of their [electric forces] prodigious effects penetrated into the most learned conversations,

---

12   J. Ferguson, *An introduction to electricity* (London, 1770), p. 64.
13   C.A. Guadagni, *Prospetto di un corso familiare di Fisica Esperimentale* (Pisa, 1770).

moved the curiosity of assemblies and excited the wonder of princely courts'. In the Italian states the new branch of experimental philosophy was especially appreciated because it suited 'the spirit of conversation ... and people of any faculty, institute and profession, are desirous of and seek to being admitted to the rare marvels that can be learnt by this means'.[14] The new subject appealed in particular to the upper classes, who were keen on entertainment and cultural novelties. They welcomed skilled performers, especially if they brought philosophical curiosities from abroad.

On 6 April 1747 Francesco Bossaert was in Turin, where he performed experiments by 'rubbing a glass globe in the Royal Apartment, in the presence of both His Majesty and Her Most Serene Majesty'.[15] In the private settings of castles, villas and palazzi, the electrical machine became a conversation piece and a means of making new acquaintances: 'the houses of those who delight in such studies are very frequently visited'.[16] Following the great interest aroused by the spread of the electrical machine, in 1746 an anonymous author published in Venice the first Italian book on electricity: *Dell'elettricismo, o sia delle forze elettriche dei corpi* (*On electricity, or on the electric forces of bodies*). The book is commonly attributed to a local physician, Eusebio Sguario, but contemporary gossip indicates Wabst as the real author. In fact, Sguario and Wabst were good friends, and I would suggest that the book was the result of their combined efforts.[17] In any case, the text became extremely successful and soon afterwards a large number of booklets on the same subject were published in other Italian towns. Such publications – celebrative or didactic poems, short treatises or, more often, popular texts – cast light on the otherwise hidden context of 'domestic science', revealing in particular the presence of women and their active involvement in experimental philosophy.

Recent studies have highlighted the role of women in the Italian scientific scene during the Enlightenment. Laura Bassi, Maria Gaetana Agnesi, Anna Morandi – to mention the most famous ones – managed to make their own way into traditionally men-only institutions. But even when they did not aim at a public career, women were but indifferent to the world of modern natural philosophy. On the contrary, they fed their interest in the subject, becoming enthusiastic consumers of new cultural products. Their involvement in science was clearly visible to their contemporaries.[18]

---

14 [E. Sguario], *Dell'Elettricismo, o sia delle Forze Elettriche de' Corpi* (Venezia, 1746), p. 37.

15 Torino, Biblioteca Reale, *Orioles, Cav., Giornale di quanto avvenne alla corte in Torino, dal 1714 al 1748*, f. 98. Storia Patria 932.

16 [Sguario], *Dell'Elettricismo*, p. 37.

17 P. Bertucci, *Viaggio nel paese delle meraviglie. Scienza e curiosità nell'Italia del Settecento*, Torino: Bollati Boringhieri, 2007, chapter 6.

18 M. Cavazza, 'Between Modesty and Spectacle: Women and Science in Eighteenth-Century Italy', in Paula Findlen and Catherine M. Sama (eds), *Italy's Eighteenth Century. Gender and Culture in the Age of Grand Tour* (Stanford, CA: Stanford University Press, 2008); M. Cavazza, 'Dottrici e lettrici dell'Università di Bologna nel Settecento', *Annali di storia delle università italiane*, 1 (1997): 109–26; P. Findlen, 'Science as a Career in Enlightenment Italy: the Strategies of Laura Bassi (1711–1778)', *Isis*, 84 (1993): 441–69; P. Findlen, 'Translating the New Science: Women and the Circulation of Knowledge in Enlightenment Italy', *Configurations*, 2 (1995): 167–206; P. Findlen, 'A Forgotten Newtonian:

One effective example is offered by the lectures that Prospero Mariotti, professor of theoretical medicine and botany in Perugia, gave to a group of local aristocratic ladies. The lectures took place in the salon of Fancesco Neri, Professor of Mathematics at the same university, who owned a collection of physics instruments. Mariotti employed his colleague's instruments for his course and, starting in 1746, when the electrical machine arrived in Perugia, he began to lecture also on electricity. His *Lettera scritta ad una Dama Sopra la cagione de' Fenomeni della Macchina Elettrica* (*Letter to a Lady on the Cause of the Phenomena of the Electrical Machine*), published in 1748 in Perugia, casts light on the cultural interests and activities in a remote province of the republic of letters and it testifies to the rapid circulation of the electrical machine south of the Alps. It also portrays a group of women who interacted actively with the lecturer, questioning the theories that he presented to them. Mariotti's *Lettera* was addressed to one of the talented ladies who attended his lectures.

The financial opportunities that could derive from the publication of small booklets on fashionable subjects were obvious to publishers. They realized that the new science attracted the attention of learned readers and eagerly sought for authors who could write on the marvels of electricity. Readers in the provinces could thus partake of capitals' ferments by fancying themselves in sumptuous salons and, in the shoes of 'ladies and gentlemen of quality', engage in electrifying seduction games.

Sparks and Seduction

Exhibited in private collections or in the cabinets of academies and universities, in the lecture theatres of itinerant demonstrators or in public squares, represented in popular books, journals, dictionaries and instrument makers' trade cards, the electrical machine became an inspiring muse, often associated with love and seduction. A painting by Louis-Léopold Boilly well exemplifies this association. Boilly, whose erotic scenes were particularly appreciated by wealthy patrons in France, was himself seduced by electrical instrumentation. His *The Electric Spark* (1792) represents two lovers in an alchemist's workshop; the young man holds the young lady by the arm as she approaches Cupido's arrow with her finger. The observer notices that, being connected to an electrical machine, the arrow will issue an electric spark.

Similar association of the electric spark with the flame of love, or of electric attraction with sexual attraction was often employed in erotic poems. They were usually composed by local poets on the occasion of the wedding of high-ranking people. In 1748 in Bologna three illustrious protagonists of the town's cultural life published *Amore Filosofo* (*Love Philosopher*), a collection of three poems written for the wedding of the Marquis Francesco Albergati with the Countess Teresa Orsi.[19]

Women and Science in Italian Provinces', in W. Clark, J. Golinski and S. Schaffer (eds), *The Sciences in Enlightened Europe* (Chicago and London: University of Chicago Press, 1999), pp. 313–49; M. Mazzotti, 'Maria Gaetana Agnesi: Mathematics and the Making of the Catholic Enlightenment', *Isis*, 92 (2001): 657–83; R. Messbarger, 'Waxing Poetic: Anna Morandi Manzolini's Anatomical Sculptures', *Configurations*, 9 (2001): 65–97.

19   *Amore Filosofo. In occasione delle nozze solenni de' nobilissimi signori Marchese Francesco Albergati e Contessa Teresa Orsi* (Bologna: Dalla Volpe, 1748).

Francesco Maria Zanotti, who was the Secretary of the Bologna Institute of Sciences, his brother Giampietro, and the physician to Pope Benedict XIV, Giuseppe Pozzi, all celebrated the event with recourse to electrical metaphors. They described Eros as a young god who, after his first glance at the electrical machine, hung up his bow and arrows and began to electrify young people's hearts. Once electrified by Love, the bride and the groom were irresistibly attracted to each other. The content of the poems is summarized in the pamphlet's frontispiece, which is itself a fascinating instance of the replacement by electrical equipment of the traditional symbolism associated with courting and love. Eros is represented there while he rubs the glass cylinder of an electrical machine with his hand. His bow and arrows are left aside, and at first glance he seems to be playing a musical instrument (Figure 5.3). The same frontispiece was employed for *La forza elettrica dell'amore* (*The electric force of love*), another celebratory poem published in Bologna by Luigi Maria Sambuceti on the occasion of the wedding of Count Filippo Marsigli with the noblewoman Elena Mariscotti.[20]

Figure 5.3   Frontispiece of *Amore Filosofo*, Bologna, 1748 (detail). © Biblioteca universitaria Bologna.

---

20 L. Sambuceti, *La forza elettrica dell'amore, componimento poetico* (Bologna, 1763).

Some of the most popular electrical experiments simulated mundane interactions between ladies and gentlemen, providing them with erotic metaphors or allusions. Aided by the darkness in which they took place, electric soirées created a flirtatious atmosphere. During the 'electric kiss', for example, gentlemen were invited to approach a lady's lips with their own, soon to be prickled by a sharp spark issuing from her mouth. Electric symbolism was generously employed to provoke malicious smiles in the eyes of voracious readers. The rubbing of bodies that excited the electric fire lent itself particularly well to such purposes.

> What makes our first felicity,
> But this pure electricity,
> Divested of all fiction:
> Motion makes heat, and heat makes love,
> Creatures below, and things above,
> Are all produc'd by friction.[21]

So did the globe of the electrical machine.

> Each charm, by turns, reveal'd, must fuel prove,
> To feed the gentle, lambent flame of love,
> But most the beauties of the *Bosom* please,
> Nor any female charm can vie with these!
> The tempting seat of all that's sweet and fair,
> For Nature's Electricity is there![22]

Consumption of 'electric' literature could be a pleasure in itself, but it could also be the first step towards new forms of learning. Fictional situations describing a man leading a woman down the path towards natural philosophical knowledge – famously introduced by Fontenelle and proposed again by Algarotti – could became an inspiration for real-life relationships modelled upon that literary fiction.[23] This was the case of the first Italian text on electricity.

An Electrifying Tale

Well aware that 'dealing with tedious subjects' was for any author 'a very serious crime' and that 'philosophical matters ... bore more than all the others', the anonymous author (probably the physician Eusebio Sguario) chose to introduce his readers to the marvels of electricity by means of a 'gallant and philosophical tale'.[24] He knew that,

---

21　A. Strong, *The Electrical Eel: or, Gymnotus Electricus. Inscribed to the Honourable Members of the R***l S*****y, by Adam Strong, Naturalist. The third edition, with considerable Additions* (London, 1777).

22　[Anonymous], *The Semi-Globes, or Electrical Orbs. A Poem* (London, 1787), p. 4.

23　Paula Findlen, 'Becoming a Scientist. Gender and Knowledge in Eighteenth-Century Italy', *Science in Context*, 16 (2003): 59–87.

24　[Eusebio Sguario], *Dell'Elettricismo, o sia delle Forze Elettriche de' Corpi* (Venezia, 1746), p. vii. I believe that Sguario was the author of the 'novella filosofia e galante' that introduces the treatise, which he wrote in association with Christian Xavier Wabst.

if properly presented, even philosophy could 'pass from deserts and gloomy caverns, to the hands of witty people and in the amusing conversations of the century'.[25] Treading in the footsteps of Algarotti and Fontenelle, he prefaced the treatise with a fictional tale in which he vividly portrayed a verisimilar situation in which two travellers who arrived in a small town of the Venetian mainland were admitted to the conversation of a local learned countess. Although a work of fiction, the tale offers an interesting view of the social context in which electricity was first cultivated in Italy. It also offers a glimpse of female participation in the world of experimental philosophy. Setting the scene in a villa in the mainland of the Venetian Republic, the author lifts the curtain on the domestic setting in which such participation most often took place. The female protagonist of the tale is the wife of an old count, a woman who is 'well versed in philosophical studies, to which she had dedicated herself many years ago'.[26] Unlike Algarotti's marchioness, this countess is not to be guided by a man along an enlightening path towards knowledge, but it is she who will lead the whole assembly.[27] She is well read in natural philosophy, endowed with intelligence and wit, and her conversation demonstrates that 'women too, when they cultivate their ingenuity, can succeed just as well, or maybe better, than man'.[28]

Travelling amateurs in natural philosophy are involved in the play, such as the Count of B., 'having travelled through all European Courts', who is as inclined towards the art of war as he is towards the sciences and used the latter 'in order to look more desirable and delightful in Conversations', or the Marquis de la F., who has learned experimental philosophy from the members of the Académie des sciences during his stay in Paris.[29]

The countess is not shy in showing off her culture. After the usual duties of *bienséance*, and after noticing her guests' philosophical interests, she initiates the conversation with a long digression on the 'glories of electricity'. Philosophical and mundane themes intersect at various points in the gallant tale, especially when the Count of B. relates to the company the exciting electrical soirée he has attended in Leipzig. After asking the ladies to stand on insulating resin cakes, the demonstrator exclaims: 'ban any sad thought, this place is enemy to melancholy!' He then begins a 'wonderful show' of sparks bursting in the dark, electrified swords igniting spirits placed in small cups, lightweight pieces of paper floating in the air towards the ladies' hands and other spectacular experiments that culminate in the thrilling explosion of the globe of the electrical machine.[30]

---

25 Sguario, *Dell'Elettricismo*, p. x.

26 Sguario, *Dell'Elettricismo*, p. 23

27 On Algarotti's *Newtonianism for Ladies*, see Massimo Mazzotti, 'Newton for Ladies: Gentility, Gender and Radical Culture', *British Journal for the History of Science*, 37 (2004): 119–46.

28 Sguario, *Dell'Elettricismo*, p. 23.

29 Sguario, *Dell'Elettricismo*, p. 4.

30 Sguario, *Dell'Elettricismo*, p. 46.

The Circulation of Electrical Knowledge

The change of setting from the countess' salon to one in Leipzig reveals the lack of similar events in the Venetian Republic previous to 1746. Yet, during that year the Italian peninsula was flooded by a wave of electrical excitement. Men and women of letters exchanged information about electrical events and gossiped about the reactions that they provoked. In the aftermath of the publication of *Dell'elettricismo*, electrical soirées were often staged in the salons of the aristocracy. The secretary of the Duc of Modena in Venice reported to his correspondent Ludovico Muratori on the electrical soirée that entertained 'our five *serenissimi* princes with their retinue of ladies and gentlemen'; he praised the courage of the young princes who intrepidly underwent electrification, and scoffed at the princesses' fear of the noxious effects of electricity. He even related the attempts to perform an experiment (eventually was not realized) during which the little prince's urine would be electrified so as to shine in the dark as a luminous fountain.[31]

While *Dell'elettricismo* popularized electrical experiments among the reading public, Bossaert and other demonstrators exhibited the marvels of electricity in various Italian cities, attracting the attention of local professionals and amateurs. In 1746 Wabst was in Venice, performing for 40 *soldi*, while Bossaert was in Padua, performing for the professor of experimental philosophy, the Marquis Giovanni Poleni. The professor, who was responsible for the 'theatre of experimental philosophy' of the university, learned from the demonstrator how to perform electrical experiments, which he subsequently performed on aristocrats visiting his theatre in Padua. He recommended Bossaert to his friend the Veronese antiquarian Scipione Maffei, praising his gentlemanly manners. Maffei invited the Fleming to his house and hosted him for some time; he was so impressed as to write letters of recommendation for him when he eventually decided to leave for Turin via Brescia.[32] Bossaert's trajectory through the Italian peninsula and his performances in salons, academies and universities show that there was no one-way circulation of electrical knowledge from academic to domestic settings. On the contrary, in the Italian states academic interest in electricity appears to have been sparked by the performances of itinerant demonstrators.

Only one year after Bossaert's visit to Maffei, there were eight electrical machines in Verona. Maffei declared that electricity had become 'the main curiosity around here': a group of 'curious' people often performed electrical experiments in their own houses.[33] The fictional situation described by the 'gallant tale' came close to reality in various contexts. Still in Verona, the Count Gazola and his wife, the Countess Guarienti, were particularly active in staging experiments for their own pleasure. 'Bewitched by electricity', they placed an electrical machine in their salon

---

31   See, for example, the correspondence between Pietro Gherardi and Ludovico Muratori, in Guido Pugliese (ed.), *Edizione nazionale del carteggio di L.A. Muratori*, 20 vols, vol. 20: *Carteggio con Pietro E. Gherardi* (Firenze: Olschki, 1982).

32   See Scipione Maffei, *Epistolario, 1700–1755*, ed. Celestino Garibotte, 2 vols, Milan: A. Giuffrè, 1955, vol. 1, pp. 1170, 1176, 1178.

33   Ibid., vol. 1, p. 1178 (Maffei to Muratori, 10 April 1747).

and experimented with the ignition of spirits, with sparking kisses and various other entertaining experiments. Yet their enthusiasm for electricity was not confined to entertainment. Their aspiration was to contribute to the new science: they joined Maffei in his attempts to measure the speed of electricity and tried to find some sort of mathematical law linking the mechanical power that was necessary to operate the electrical machine with the intensity of electric fire that it produced. In those days electrical activity in Verona must have been really hectic: 'I would never stop, if I wanted to tell you all that has been done in my house on this account,' Maffei confessed to his London correspondent Richard Mead.[34]

In the span of a few years electricity became fashionable in numerous Italian towns. To the dismay of elitist philosophers such as the Jesuit Belgrado, electrical demonstrations did not remain confined to cultural institutions but spread to public squares and private salons. The focus on the domestic settings in which electrical natural philosophy came to be first cultivated, in Italy and in other countries, questions any rigid distinction between performers and spectators. Often, the display of the electric fire engendered in the audience the desire of active participation in the new experimental philosophy. The range of electrical toys and portable instruments that instrument makers marketed in the second half of the eighteenth century testifies to the widespread interest in this branch of natural philosophy. Together with other historical documents that I have presented here, they also indicate that the salon was a key site for both consumption and production of electrical experimental philosophy.

---

34 Scipione Maffei, *Della Formazione de' Fulmini* (Verona, 1747), p. 152.

Chapter 6

The Sale of Shocks and Sparks: Itinerant Electricians in the German Enlightenment

Oliver Hochadel

Making a Living from Electricity

In his *History and Present State of Electricity*, published in 1767, Joseph Priestley wrote of the invention of the Leyden jar in 1745:

> It was this astonishing experiment that gave eclat to electricity. From this time it became the subject of general conversation. Everybody was eager to see, and ... to *feel* the experiment; and in the same year in which it was discovered, numbers of persons, in almost every country in Europe, got a livelihood by going about and showing it.[1]

Who were these scientific salesmen who made a living from their electrical demonstrations? Priestley was probably right in claiming that they were to be found all over Europe (Figure 6.1). Yet with the exception of England,[2] little is known about itinerant electricians. Here I will focus on the German-speaking territories and on an electrician named Martin Berschitz, who was at least for a couple of years the most famous of them. When he performed at his best, around the early 1780s, he was even mentioned in an entry on electricity in an encyclopaedia of the time: 'Some of these itinerant electricians proved to be very successful. A certain Martin Berschitz, for example, shows the most striking, extraordinary and powerful experiments for money.'[3]

---

1   J. Priestley, *The History and Present State of Electricity* (London: Dodsley, 1767), p. 84. On Priestley's lectures see J. Golinski 'Joseph Priestley and the chemical sublime in British public science', Chapter 8 in this volume.

2   On other British public lecturers, see John Millburn, *Benjamin Martin, Author, Instrument-Maker, and 'Country-Showman'* (Leyden: Noordhoff, 1976). See also the two articles by S. Schaffer, 'Natural Philosophy and Public Spectacle in the Eighteenth Century', *History of Science*, 21 (1983): 1–43, and 'The Consuming Flame: Electrical Showmen and Tory Mystics in the World of Goods', in J. Brewer and R. Porter (eds), *Consumption and the World of Goods* (London: Routledge, 1993), p. 488–526.

3   H.M.G. Köster and J.F. Roos (eds), *Deutsche Encyclopädie oder Allgemeines Real-Wörterbuch aller Künste und Wissenschaften*, vol. 8 (Frankfurt: Varrentrapp und Wenner, 1783), p. 215. All translations are my own.

Ekcktrisiren für 1 Schilling.

Figure 6.1   The showman offering electrification for one shilling is presumably the
Swiss itinerant lecturer Claudius Boitoux, performing in Hamburg in
December 1755 (sketch by Cornelius Suhr, ca. 1808). © Hamburgische
Elektrizitätswerke.

If one were to look for references to Berschitz in a library nowadays, one would have a hard time tracking him down at all. Virtually the only time his name appears in print in the 20th century is in the edition of the letters of the German physicist Georg Christoph Lichtenberg. And because Lichtenberg misspelled his name, it is also misspelled in the index, where Berschitz is listed under Berschütz or Bergschütz.[4]

No letters from or to him, no publications, no birth certificate, no death record have been found. Sources other than Lichtenberg's letters on the itinerant life of Martin Berschitz are hard to find, beyond some municipal records scattered in archives in several countries and dealing with Berschitz's requests for a permit to stage his show, as well as newspaper notices and broadsheets to advertise his lectures. If we put all the scattered pieces together, we are still far away from a complete biography.

Berschitz was born in Vienna some time before 1750 and probably died there some time after 1800. He started off as an assistant to Joseph Franz, a Jesuit natural philosopher and a kind of court physicist who staged public experiments with electricity for the Austrian Emperor as early as the 1740s.[5] Berschitz's first recorded show took place in Berlin in 1771, his last in Nördlingen in Swabia in 1798.

Unlike England or France, Germany did not have an administrative capital, it was not even yet a state. The German Enlightenment is often described as polycentric, with many medium-sized cities such as Göttingen, Halle or Königsberg. There was no capital for public science either, which may explain why there seem to have been more itinerant lecturers in Germany than, say, in France.[6] While the metropolis of Paris seems to have provided a more or less sufficient income for a good number of electrical demonstrators, their German colleagues had to travel around to make a living.

Berschitz's period of travel spanned almost three decades, and nearly forty places can be traced where he put on his show. He ventured as far as Bratislava in the southeast, Berne and Solothurn in the south-west, Lille and Louvain in the west, Bremen and possibly Hamburg in the north. By and large, he remained within the German-speaking territories, and most of his performances took place in southern Germany. He visited towns such as Augsburg and Munich several times.[7] Yet the records are patchy and it is very likely that there were a few Vienna-based years in between.

What exactly did Martin Berschitz show? His broadsheet named more than a dozen experiments, including the demonstration of positive and negative electricity according to the theory of Benjamin Franklin, the melting of metals and the demonstration of the use of a lightning rod with the help of a thunder-house. Berschitz also described at length his experiments with 'inflammable air' and – if the opportunity arose – the detonation of gunpowder under water. In December 1781

---

4   G.C. Lichtenberg, *Briefwechsel*, U. Joost and A. Schöne (eds), vol. 2 (München: C.H. Beck, 1985).

5   Lichtenberg, *Briefwechsel*, vol. 2, p. 448; for Franz's public demonstrations see *Wiener Diarium*, 43 (1746).

6   On public lectures and scientific spectacles in the capitals see in this volume Chapter 1 by Larry Stewart; Chapter 2 by Liliane Hilaire-Pérez, for London; and Chapter 4 by Michael Lynn and Chapter 7 by Christine Lehman, for Paris.

7   The precise references are in O. Hochadel, *Öffentliche Wissenschaft. Elektrizität in der deutschen Aufklärung* (Göttingen: Wallstein, 2003).

he staged one of his electrical explosion shows in Cassel in central Germany. He caused much sensation with his electro-magnetic experiments by showing entirely new experiments with different kinds of inflammable air. He also had the opportunity to conduct experiments in the presence of the ruling landgrave of Hesse-Cassel and other persons of high rank. Among those experiments was one to ignite powder under water, some 50 feet away from the machine, so as to blow up the water under a small ship which went up into the air and came back down in pieces. A specially built powder magazine was set on fire near the water with the help of electricity to show the speed of lightning. The powder magazine went up in smoke, crackling and pounding. There were more of such unexpected experiments, for which his highness expressed his merciful pleasure. The landgrave ordered the entire machine, with the best experiments, to be bought from Berschitz and put in his cabinet.[8]

The only material remnant I have been able to find is a Leyden jar in a museum in Cassel. 'MARTIN BERSCHITZ MECHANIC D'WIEN' is written across it. And there is some reason to believe that the electrical machine in the same museum is the one the landgrave purchased in 1781.[9] Having read this spectacular report, we understand why Berschitz earned himself a paragraph in the encyclopaedia, quoted above, where it says that he 'shows the most striking, extraordinary and powerful experiments'. His underwater explosions did not resemble the cute, small-scale parlour demonstrations with electric spiders and igniting of brandy that had made electricity so popular in mid century.

Berschitz staged his shows at very different venues. To conduct demonstrations in front of a landgrave was, of course, every electrician's dream. Not only was a landgrave a wealthy customer, but an aristocratic audience ennobled the show and yielded valuable social prestige. Mostly, though, Berschitz had to content himself with back rooms in inns, with rented theatre venues or a stand at a fair. Occasionally, he also performed for monks in a monastery. These kinds of venue restricted the scale of his demonstrations, though. For his explosions he needed open-air venues. He usually settled in a place for a couple of weeks, trying to attract spectators and to sell instruments, sometimes collaborating with local instrument makers. Once the market was exhausted or relations with the locals had turned sour, he moved on to the next place. For example, in October 1782 the magistrate of Münster in western Germany ordered his instruments to be confiscated because he had not paid the rent for the theatre where he had performed. In 1800 Berschitz announced in a Viennese paper that his travelling years had come to an end and that he only intended to serve his home town from now on. The retiring itinerant continued to offer his electrical services, that is, selling instruments and providing electrotherapy.[10]

How representative was Berschitz as an itinerant lecturer? And how many were there in the German-speaking territories? In the second half of the eighteenth century there were maybe two or three dozen itinerant lecturers who showed electrical experiments at one time or another. Yet hardly any of these electricians restricted themselves to electrical experiments. Depending on the demands of the public and

---

8   *Augsburger Staats- und gelehrte Zeitung*, 16 January 1782.
9   Museum für Astronomie und Technikgeschichte, Kassel.
10 *Wiener Zeitung*, 19 July 1800.

on the integration of new instruments into their demonstrations, they showed all kinds of optical, mechanical or chemical tricks. Berschitz, for example, also showed experiments with magnets, as well as astronomical representations (probably some kind of orrery). Berschitz's experiments may have been very spectacular but, all in all, his career and the problems he had to face did not differ very much from those of other itinerant lecturers: the economic ups and downs, the need for constant self-advertising, quarrels with his 'colleagues', troubles with the authorities and condescending comments from the academic natural philosophers.

Following this very sketchy biographical outline, we will now try to reconstruct Berschitz's relatively well-documented encounter with one of the leading German natural philosophers of the time. How well did high and low science mix?

When Berschitz met Lichtenberg

Berschitz probably came to Göttingen, where he visited Georg Christoph Lichtenberg (1742–1799), in March 1782. This encounter brought together two people who could hardly have been more different. A professor of physics whose reputation was steadily growing, and the semi-educated artisan whose status in natural philosophy and society was precarious; the shy savant who would have loved to travel more and the itinerant lecturer who had been on the road for years; Lichtenberg, the sharp-witted satirist, and Berschitz with his pretentious air, eliciting the mocking of the former. And not least, Lichtenberg, nowadays better known for his literary achievements than his physics, is one of the best-edited German writers of the eighteenth century. Hence, in reconstructing this encounter, the asymmetry in the sources has to be kept in mind: we have only the letters of Lichtenberg and his correspondents, and not a single word from Berschitz himself, since his letters to Lichtenberg were not preserved.

At the start, Lichtenberg tried to be of help and recommended Berschitz's performance to his students in his own lecture. Berschitz's show at the 'Kaufhaus' eventually attracted 74 spectators. Lichtenberg gave Berschitz a 'nice electrical tube' and 'other trifles' as a present. He granted Berschitz that he was a manually skilled experimenter and acknowledged that he did some 'pretty splendid experiments' and that his 'meltings are also very nice, yet he made a bit too much noise about it'. Eventually, Lichtenberg wrote him a letter of recommendation, saying 'that even connoisseurs would see some of his experiments with pleasure'.[11]

Lichtenberg was partly annoyed, partly amused by Berschitz's pompous behaviour. He wrote to J.A.H. Reimarus in Hamburg: 'He is the greatest *ignoramus* and the most gushing windbag, one could think of. His explanations in Austrian peasant language are truly entertaining.' Lichtenberg also described Berschitz's appearance quite vividly:

> It is not rare that he starts off his sentences with nota benig [nota bene] and speaks of Professor Francolini. He spreads bronze tempered with oil onto a copper plate on which the Emperor and the Prussian king are engraved. Then he pours plaster over it, hits it with

---

11 Lichtenberg, *Briefwechsel*, vol. 2, p. 303, last quote p. 317.

an electric spark and tells the people that the lightning has melted [the engraving]. He has more of those swindles yet he did not dare to show them to me.[12]

Lichtenberg called Berschitz an 'Electrophorus', which refers to an electrical instrument but literally means 'carrying electricity'.[13] Very witty indeed, because an itinerant lecturer such as Berschitz did indeed carry electricity around, to Hanover, for example, where he headed after his departure from Göttingen. The effect of his stay in Hanover was described sarcastically by Franz Ferdinand Wolff in a letter to Lichtenberg of 17 May 1782: 'On his departure Bergschütz has left enchanted people behind him: at all corners and places one can see glasses being turned untiringly by all kinds of people. The aim of these sweaty labours is to produce sparks incessantly and to thunder with the bang air.'[14]

Wolff indicates that all this glass turning led to nothing, it was only about sparks and explosions. This was the first of Wolff's many letters to Lichtenberg – in fact, the beginning of a wonderful friendship. It is telling that already in the second paragraph of his letter, Wolff compares himself to Berschitz and states 'that all his experiments were performed by me long before, as Bergschütz has to admit himself'. Wolff continues that he did not write to Lichtenberg 'because of this or that amusing experiment', but to enter into a serious exchange 'with a superior in natural philosophy'. In his response, Lichtenberg confirmed in his first sentence that Wolff 'does not belong to those people in Hanover, in whom Mr Berschütz had to awaken a liking of physics'.[15] The scientific salesman served as a welcome criterion by which to demarcate and define one's own status.

The following months seemed to confirm Lichtenberg in his assessment of Berschitz as a dubious character: 'Daily I hear something that proves what a loathsome windbag this Berschitz is.' Lichtenberg had heard that Berschitz had fooled somebody out of his money. He was also annoyed that Berschitz apparently made an unseemly use of his letter of recommendation by 'trying to diminish' him with the addressees while playing up his own merits. After Berschitz fell into disgrace with Lichtenberg, Lichtenberg felt obliged to warn his correspondents, J.A.H. Reimarus and G.A. Ebell.

And Berschitz felt Lichtenberg's influence. While in Hanover, he also tried to sell his lightning rods to the 'Kriegs Cantzley', the administration of the military. Models were made of Berschitz's scheme and sent to Lichtenberg, with a request for expert advice. Lichtenberg insisted that he did not want to thwart Berschitz but that he could not approve of his design. Yet not for purely scientific reasons, it seems, because Lichtenberg continued: 'If this man's rods, which he owes to an itinerant Italian, had been erected there [in Hanover], one would have invited the ridicule of all connoisseurs travelling through. This would also have affected nearby Göttingen.'[16]

---

12   Lichtenberg, *Briefwechsel*, vol. 2, pp. 317f; 'Francolini' is, of course, Benjamin Franklin.

13   Lichtenberg called Berschitz 'Electrophorus' several times: Lichtenberg, *Briefwechse*, vol. 2, pp. 317, 338, 448.

14   'Bang air' was a mixture of oxygen and hydrogen; see below.

15   Lichtenberg, *Briefwechsel*, vol. 2, pp. 331, 334.

16   Lichtenberg, *Briefwechsel*, vol. 2, pp. 317, 303 (quote).

Berschitz, probably entirely unaware that Lichtenberg was torpedoing his business, kept sending letters to Göttingen asking for specific information. Lichtenberg had shown Berschitz his experiments with 'dephlogisticated air'. These explosions 'had astonished him so much, that his lower jaw sagged'.[17] Again, we have to remind ourselves that we are only getting Lichtenberg's perspective on the events.

'Dephlogisticated air' (oxygen) mixed in a certain ratio with inflammable air (hydrogen) turns into 'bang air'. Lichtenberg knew how to produce all kinds of effects with it, for example, the noisy bursting of soap bubbles.[18] At first he did not mind at all instructing Berschitz, 'who had simply no idea how to produce dephlogisticated air'. 'Yet he [Berschitz] must have completely forgotten it when he came to Hanover, because he tortured me by nearly every post to describe the procedure to him.' Lichtenberg was perfectly clear about Berschitz's motivation: 'He knew well that his audience would have been much larger had he had this air. That's why he was so eager, he even bribed me with presents.'[19]

Berschitz surely wanted to expand his repertoire of explosive demonstrations. As late as October 1782 he begged Lichtenberg in a 'very miserable letter' from Münster to inform him about the 'experiment with the mainspring'.[20] In a bell jar filled with dephlogisticated air, a mainspring is suspended from a piece of wire. The dephlogisticated air is ignited by tinder or an electric spark. Wire and mainspring melt and produce a very bright glow: 'All the people who have seen this experiment at my place, even the greatest connoisseurs, were absolutely delighted; when the mainspring starts to burn, it becomes so bright that I can read the *Göttingischen gelehrten Anzeigen* [a learned journal] at a distance of eight feet.'[21]

Lichtenberg did not hesitate to explain to his new friend Wolff several ways to produce dephlogisticated air.[22] Yet Berschitz begged in vain. One might describe him in a derogatory way as a parasite of natural philosophy, as somebody who tried to capitalize on other people's inventions or discoveries. Yet for an itinerant electrician it was a perfectly rational way to act. Berschitz's 'research' consisted in scanning recent developments in natural philosophy, singling out those that could be put to spectacular use. For him, natural philosophy provided practical knowledge, it was 'applied science' in a very concrete sense.

Experimental knowledge was worth money, it gave an edge in a competitive market. In order to be able to compete with his colleagues the itinerant lecturer had to update his repertoire regularly. Lichtenberg knew this all too well. In the postscript to his *Mixed Ideas on the Aerostatical Machines*, he mentioned his experiments with small air balloons:[23] 'This experiment turned out nicely. It also struck people who had got used to the other phenomenon as something new. Therefore I recommend

---

17 Lichtenberg, *Briefwechsel*, vol. 2, pp. 344, 350.

18 Lichtenberg's experiments with dephlogisticated air can be contrasted with Priestley's experiments, see Jan Golinski, Chapter 8 in this volume.

19 Lichtenberg, *Briefwechsel*, vol. 2, p. 344.

20 Lichtenberg, *Briefwechsel*, vol. 2, p. 348.

21 Lichtenberg, *Briefwechsel*, vol. 2, p. 350.

22 Lichtenberg, *Briefwechsel*, vol. 2, pp. 344–8.

23 Spectacles with balloons are described in this volume by Jessica Riskin, 'Amusing Physics', Chapter 3.

this experiment to all itinerant lecturers of natural philosophy.'[24] Lichtenberg's mockery gets to the core of the itinerant business: the 'market orientation' of their demonstrations. Experiments did get 'used up' and the itinerant lecturers always had to brag about their 'new' experiments, even if these new experiments were merely variations on others.

Experimental Physics as Business

Larry Stewart wrote of 'Newtonian Britain' that the 'experimentalists were essentially entrepreneurs cashing in on the fashions of philosophy'. It was not any different in continental Europe. A.G. Kästner, later in his career a colleague of Lichtenberg in Göttingen, wrote in 1747: 'The lust for the marvellous is so natural, that many use it to direct people according to their own aims'. Kästner included 'the teacher of nature' who 'procures himself listeners for his lectures'. The more spectacular the presentation, the larger the audience. And the more cash the itinerant lecturer takes. This also held more or less true for the professor of physics. Being paid only a modest basic salary, professors at many universities depended on the attendance fees from their students for so-called 'private lectures'.[25] A professor in Göttingen needed about 80 to 100 students per semester, each paying 5 *taler*, for a decent income. 'A physical experiment that bangs is worth more than a silent one' – Lichtenberg's bon mot may also be understood very literally.[26]

Experimental physics was an expensive business. Its success depended not least on the quality and the number of instruments at hand. Lichtenberg was well aware of this. When Kästner told him that he could lecture on physics, Lichtenberg immediately concerned himself with the expansion of his cabinet. He had hoped to purchase parts of the collection of instruments of J.C.P. Erxleben, his late predecessor, and was ready to spend 150 to 160 *taler*, nearly half his annual salary. Yet Erxleben's widow sold the entire collection to somebody else and Lichtenberg found himself in a difficult position. He pinned his hopes on Georg Drechsler, an instrument maker from Hanover. For one of his instruments, in which he was 'willing to invest more',

---

24   G.C. Lichtenberg, *Schriften und Briefe*, W. Promies (ed.), vol. 1 (München: Hanser, 1967), p. 75.

25   In the eighteenth century, universities in the German Empire and beyond differed a lot, for example with respect to the funding of their cabinet of physics; at some universities there was a fund for the purchase and repair of the instruments; cf. G. Wiesenfeldt, *Leerer Raum in Minervas Haus. Experimentelle Naturlehre an der Universität Leiden, 1675–1715*, (Amsterdam/Diepholz: Koninklijke Nederlandse Akademie van Wetenschappen/GNT-Verlag, 2002), ch. 6.

26   L. Stewart, *The Rise of Public Science. Rhetoric, Technology and Natural Philosophy in Newtonian Britain, 1660–1750* (Cambridge: Cambridge University Press, 1992), p. 128; *Hamburgisches Magazin*, 1 (1747), 1–10, p. 1; sums are given by U. Joost, 'Georg Christoph Lichtenberg: Aus Vorlesungen', in E.P. Wieckenberg (ed.), *Einladung ins 18. Jahrhundert* (München: C.H. Beck, 1988), pp. 129–48, p. 130; last quote: Lichtenberg, *Schriften und Briefe*, vol. 1, p. 624.

Lichtenberg asked J.A. Schernhagen, one of his superiors, for a loan. 'As soon as I am paid for some private lectures, I will pay it back with thanks.'[27]

The connection between investment and return is made explicit here. In this respect, the professor of physics was as much an entrepreneur as the itinerant lecturer. Within the University of Göttingen, Lichtenberg competed for some time with Johann Beckmann, until the latter discontinued his lectures in natural philosophy in 1786. Lichtenberg announced triumphantly that he had 'broken his bank', of course 'unintentionally'.[28]

Berschitz, too, had to invest in his instruments and hold his ground against competitors. The parallels between professor and itinerant go even further. Lichtenberg asked himself how to win his audiences over:

> The reasonable ones study the sciences because of their utility. Yet the more elegant part of the world only starts to study if one proves to them that natural philosophy can be fun too or something to play with. That is how the Récréations mathématiques ... came into being; that is why the greatest natural philosopher has to take a middle road in his lecture between the entertaining and the serious.[29]

One might call this Lichtenberg's didactic of the 'middle road', which he also tried to apply in his teaching: 'In lectures on experimental physics one has to play a little; the sleepy one will be woken up and the waking one will see the playful demonstrations as opportunities to see the matter from a new perspective.'[30] In other words, 'playful demonstrations' were not to be damned outright. They were considered useful in promoting reflection by the students.

Now let us briefly exchange perspectives and move from the podium to the benches and ask: What expectations did an audience have of a lecture on experimental physics? It was 'an expectation that communicates a primacy of entertainment. If need be, the professor has to comply with the verdict on complicated explanations or even mathematical formulas.' Or, as John Heilbron put it more succinctly, 'The successful professor of experimental physics had to be a showman.'[31]

In 1782, the year of Berschitz's visit, Lichtenberg complained in a letter: 'For my physics 104 [students] have registered. Yet they skip lectures until there is lightening and thunder.' With an air of resignation he admitted: '[In natural philosophy] one can only teach the simplest things. It is unbelievable how ignorant the studying youth is

---

27 Lichtenberg, *Briefwechsel*, Joost U. and Schöne A. (eds.), vol. 1 (München: C.H. Beck, 1983), pp. 794, 829, 834, 849f, 851; quotes: pp. 853, 852. See also R. Stichweh, *Zur Entstehung des modernen Systems wissenschaftlicher Disziplinen. Physik in Deutschland 1740–1890* (Frankfurt a.M.: Suhrkamp, 1984), p. 328, on the experimental physicist 'as entrepreneur'.

28 Lichtenberg, *Briefwechsel*, Joost U. and Schöne A. (eds.), vol. 3 (München: C.H. Beck, 1990), p. 198.

29 Lichtenberg, *Schriften und Briefe*, Promies, W. (ed.), vol. 3 (München: Hanser, 1971), p. 315.

30 Lichtenberg, *Briefwechsel*, vol. 2, p. 344.

31 R. Stichweh, *Zur Entstehung*, p. 341; J.L. Heilbron, *Electricity in the 17th and 18th Century: A Study of Early Modern Physics* (Berkeley: University of California Press, 1979), p. 140.

on entering university. If I calculate or do geometry for only ten minutes, a quarter of the audience gently falls asleep.'[32] Lichtenberg often stressed the importance of mathematics for physics. Yet in his own lectures he by and large renounced mathematized physics.[33] He had no illusions with regard to the motivation of his students, who wanted to become lawyers, clerks or ministers. Hence he did not hesitate to perform all kinds of 'playful demonstrations' in his own lectures: electrical chimes sounded, spirits were ignited, cotton set on fire and a pistol charged with 'bang air' shot. Lichtenberg ended his lectures on electricity with luminous effects created in a vacuum.[34]

If we push this comparison further, we find that, with respect to practical abilities, Berschitz was superior. Lichtenberg was a skilled experimenter but he bought his instruments. In his lectures he had an assistant who helped him with the experiments and kept the instruments in good condition. By contrast, Berschitz was an instrument maker himself. Both were fascinated by the news of the Montgolfier brothers' balloon ascending into the sky in June 1783, but they reacted in very different ways. As early as September 1783, Berschitz tried to launch an air balloon in Lille. The attempt failed and those financing the balloon were very annoyed.[35] In April 1784 he announced another launch in Aachen, but it is not clear whether this attempt ever took place.[36] Lichtenberg did not even try. He was offered the enormous sum of 1,000 *taler* to cover the expenses but backed down, referring to his bad health. Instead, he contented himself with having a pig's bladder ascend to the ceiling of his study.[37] Lichtenberg was just as fascinated with underwater explosions as were his contemporaries. Yet all he did was to ignite turpentine oil in the pond behind his house.[38]

Itinerant Electricians and the 'Progress' of Natural Philosophy

Itinerant lecturers and local (non-travelling) instrument makers provided instruments for all kinds of private and public collections as well as for all sorts of institutions of learning, ranging from universities to secondary schools. They also supplied the instructions on how to use the instruments, either in print or through personal communication. And nearly all of them propagated the introduction of lightning rods and offered to put them up. Berschitz put up lightning rods in Augsburg, Berne, Ulm, Kempten and other places.

32　Lichtenberg, *Briefewechsel*, vol. 2, pp. 351, 431.

33　For Lichtenberg's emphasis on mathematics, see G.C. Lichtenberg, *Physikalische und mathematische Schriften*, L.C. Lichtenberg and F. Kries (eds), vol. 9 (Göttingen: Dieterich, 1806), p. 142.

34　G. Gamauf, *Erinnerungen aus Lichtenbergs Vorlesungen über Erxlebens Anfangsgründe der Naturlehre*, vol. 3 (Wien/Triest: Geistinger, 1812), pp. 225–30, 351.

35　Archives municipales Lille, A 6 703, Police des spectacles (registre no. 65, fol.13) and C 703 O 10. My thanks to Marie Thébaud-Sorger for this reference.

36　*Stadt-Aachener Zeitung*, 24 April 1784.

37　Lichtenberg, *Briefwechsel*, vol. 2, pp. 754, 759, 798, 810.

38　Lichtenberg, , *Briefwechsel*, vol. 1, pp. 852f.

So itinerant lecturers and instrument makers met a considerable demand for instruments and related 'services' in a new market. The emergence of an 'entertainment industry' relied on itinerant lecturers and instrument makers because they produced the hardware and demonstrated phenomena to a broad public. Scientific commodities formed a part of the emerging consumer society in the eighteenth century.[39]

The emergence of a new market also brought about competition between the different 'providers'. The competition was particularly stiff in electricity, because the novelty of certain show pieces wore off fast, and so the demonstrators had to think of more exciting and crowd-winning experiments. In their rhetoric they never tire of emphasizing that they will show new tricks, never seen before. Competition was also fierce with respect to the introduction of lightning rods. At least twice Berschitz tried to convince the local authorities – in Augsburg and in Berne – that the existing lightning rods were dangerous and that they should be replaced with ones of his own design.[40]

The scientific salesmen often rebuilt the electrical machines of better-known instrument makers and tried to 'improve' them, that is, to make them more powerful (longer sparks), portable, nicer to look at or simply cheaper. So the competition between instrument makers increased the variety and availability of electrical instruments. Yet itinerant lecturers and instrument makers not only made the distribution of electrical machines possible. As quoted above, Wolff, Lichtenberg's correspondent in Hanover, reported that Berschitz spread an enthusiasm for electricity among the inhabitants of the town. The igniting spark for many amateur scientists, among them Benjamin Franklin, to do research in electricity actually came from the electrical machine of an itinerant lecturer or a local instrument maker.

Thus, the audience of itinerant lecturers and instrument makers reached far beyond, let us say, that of the professor of experimental physics. The reading public learned about electricity by reading the countless reports of electrical demonstrations and medical electricity in the journals of the time, but electricity was something that needed to be seen or even felt directly. Yet electrical shows were not open to everyone; because they were not free of charge, one had to have the means to purchase a ticket.

To say that itinerant lecturers only performed eye-catching tricks, while the institutional scientists focused exclusively on 'research' would be to misconstrue the character of eighteenth-century scientific practice. Natural philosophy and, in particular, electricity were fashionable, not because they were useful but because they were entertaining. The visual and 'performative' character of natural philosophy was not peripheral but central to its 'success', that is, the widespread public attention. Thus, a strict dichotomy between the 'playful' electricians and the 'serious' natural philosophers would be misleading. The practice of electricity in academies and universities was often no less performative than that of itinerant lecturers.

---

39 Schaffer, 'Natural Philosophy and Public Spectacle'.

40 O. Hochadel, '"Hier haben die Wetterableiter unter den Augsburger Gelehrten eine kleine Revolution gemacht." Die Debatte um die Einführung der Blitzableiter in Augsburg (1783–1791)', *Zeitschrift des Historischen Vereins für Schwaben*, 92 (1992): 139–64.

Yet a professor of physics did not want to be compared to a scientific salesman. Thus, itinerant lecturers and instrument makers also fulfilled another function, rather unwillingly. They served as a useful contrast for the institutionally established natural philosophers. The concept of the natural philosopher was still in flux. He tried to prove his utility to society but had not too much to show for it in terms of applicable inventions or discoveries. He had to work hard on his public image.

For Lichtenberg, Berschitz was a fraud, a pompous charlatan and a welcome target for his mockery. He disapproved of Berschitz's lightning rods when called on by the authorities. For him, Berschitz's demonstrations had nothing in common with the knowledge-yielding, sometimes arduous practice of serious natural philosophers. A contrast was provided by the figure of Alessandro Volta, Lichtenberg wrote in 1782:

> According to [the natural philosopher J.A. Deluc] Volta is an admirable man, distinguishing himself considerably from the common electricians. The experiments are not as stunning for the crowd, if compared with the ones Mr Volta first made himself a name with but they are very important for theory.[41]

This reminds us that Volta first became known for the invention of the electric pistol, an instrument considered rather as a toy by most of his contemporaries.[42]

The encyclopaedia entry quoted at the beginning of this chapter conceded that Berschitz's experiments were very impressive but stressed at the same time that they were 'known to all natural philosophers', that is, Berschitz had no claim to any discovery or invention of his own. And the anonymous author did not omit to point out that he showed the experiments 'for money',[43] something unworthy of a true philosopher, who is only interested in increasing our knowledge of the natural world and not in material gain. An itinerant lecturer was everything a German professor did not want to be – quite the opposite, in fact. So when Kästner really wanted to insult S.J. Hollmann – both were professors of mathematics and physics in Göttingen – he claimed that his colleague was no better than a charlatan 'showing' experimental physics at a fair.[44]

Itinerant lecturers and instrument makers formed part of a very rich and complex culture of scientific practices in the eighteenth century. Their contribution to the 'progress' of electricity is difficult to measure and cannot be stated in terms of the number of inventions made or concepts developed. Yet they played a crucial role in the 'electrical movement' of the Enlightenment and the flourishing of natural philosophy in general, reaching a large public, generating widespread interest in the subject matter and providing a practical grounding through their instruments and services.

---

41 Lichtenberg, *Briefwechsel*, vol. 2, p. 418.

42 Cf., for example J. Ingenhousz, *Anfangsgründe der Elektricität* (Wien: Wappler, 1781), p. 115.

43 *Deutsche Encyclopädie* (1783), p. 215.

44 A.G. Kästner, *Vermischte Schriften*, part 2, new and enlarged edn (Altenburg: Richter, 1783), p. 363.

Although natural philosophy transformed itself into science and established itself in universities and research institutions, the appeal of spectacle never vanished in science teaching. The need to celebrate human control over the forces of nature seems to be a historical constant. In February 1900 the German industrialist Walter Rathenau showed a spellbound audience, which included Emperor Wilhelm II, the astonishing powers of electrical engineering. In April 2004 the Austrian physicist Anton Zeilinger, nicknamed 'Mr Beam', demonstrated the first bank transfer that relied on quantum mechanics or, more precisely, on quantum cryptography – to the astonishment of the Viennese mayor and the media. The use of two miraculously entangled twin photons – one staying with the sender, the other sent to the receiver – is supposed to make the transaction 100 per cent safe,.[45]

---

45   B. Joerges, *Technik. Körper der Gesellschaft. Arbeiten zur Techniksoziologie* (Frankfurt a.M.: Suhrkamp, 1996), pp. 217–28; www.newscientist.com/channel/fundamentals/ quantum-world/dn4914 (accessed 14 August 2005).

Chapter 7

Between Commerce and Philanthropy: Chemistry Courses in Eighteenth-century Paris

Christine Lehman

Along with optics and electricity, courses in chemistry and the accompanying practical demonstrations constituted an important means for the dissemination of science in French society during the Enlightenment. However, due to their close association with the professional training of apothecaries and doctors, demonstrations in chemistry differed significantly from demonstrations in the other sciences. The *Gazette de médecine* from 1761 provides us with a whole panorama of such courses.[1]

Here, I want to look at three types of course: at the Jardin des apothicaires, at the Jardin du Roy, and private courses. My aim is to sketch the style of presentation and the accompanying experiments, the social status of the teachers, and the nature of the public that attended, in order better to understand the goals of these enterprises. I will then outline the evolution of these courses during the last quarter of the eighteenth century.

Public Courses at the *Jardins*

Chemistry courses were offered at the Jardin des apothicaires (the Apothecaries' Hall), starting around 1700, as part of the training of future apothecaries provided by the Guild of Merchant Apothecaries and Spicers (la Compagnie des marchands apothicaires-épiciers).

> [E]very year, one of the apothecaries from the aforementioned guild will offer a free, public chemistry course for the instruction of those who practice medicine and pharmacy...[2]

The very existence of these courses calls to mind the enduring alliance between chemistry and pharmacy, centred on the production of both medicines and other laboratory products. The Jardin des apothicaires, founded in the middle

---

1   *Gazette de médecine*, 1761, pp. 199–200.

2   Archives of the *Faculté de pharmacie de Paris*, register 37 folio 58, quoted in G. Planchon, *L'enseignement des sciences physico-chimiques au Jardin des apothicaires et à l'Ecole de pharmacie de Paris* (Paris: Flammarion, 1897), p. 12. A fund was established 'pour subvenir aux frais que l'on peut faire pour la demonstration du cour de chymie quelle (la Compagnie) desire qu'on fasse tous les ans', folio 59.

of the sixteenth century by Nicolas Houël, was a philanthropic institution whose functioning and finance were entirely supported by the Guild of Apothecaries. It was intended to instruct orphan children 'in piety, to serve and to honour God, in letters and subsequently in the Art of the apothecary'.

[199]

Il s'en fait un chaque année au Jardin du Roi, par MM. Bourdelin, Profeffeur, & Rouelle, Démonftrateur, l'un Médecin, l'autre Apothicaire, tous les deux de l'Académie des Sciences.

M. Poiffonnier, Médecin, & Profeffeur Royal, joint des Expériences à fes Leçons de Chymie, au Collège Royal de France, place de Cambray.

M. Bellot, Médecin, & M. la Planche, Apothicaire, commenceront Mercredi prochain, trois Juin, le Cours annuel de Pharmacie Galénique & Chymique, aux Ecoles de Médecine, rue de la Bucherie.

MM. Couzié, de Moret, Julliot, la Planche, Bataille, Santerre, Laborie, Azema & Trevez Apothicaires, font alternativement un Cours d'Expériences Chymiques, au Jardin des Apothicaires, rue de l'Arbalère.

M. Rouelle, qui a plus contribué que Perfonne à répandre en France le goût de la Chymie, & que la plûpart de nos Chymiftes fe font un honneur de regarder comme leur Maître, fait, tous les ans, des Cours particuliers de Chymie & de Pharmacie, dans fon Laboratoire, rue Jacob.

M. la Planche en fait également de l'une & de l'autre efpèce, dans fon Laboratoire, rue de la Monnoye; fourniffant ainfi, avec un zèle inexprimable, trois carrières à la fois. C'eft le triple Gerion échauffé par le *Phlogiftique*.

[200]

Enfin M. Macquer, Médecin, célèbre par des Elémens de Chymie Théorique & Pratique, écrits avec une précifion & une netteté dont on avoit peine à croire que cette Science fût fufceptible; & M. Baumé, Apothicaire, qui femble avoir un fonds inépuifable de nouvelles Expériences à offrir, prefque coup fur coup, à la curiofité publique, font de concert de femblables Cours dans leur Laboratoire, rue Saint Denis, vis-à-vis Saint Leu.

Notre Feuille ne fuffiroit pas pour faire connoître en détail, tous ceux qui brûlent du Charbon à Paris, dans la vue d'éclaircir telle ou telle vérité Chymique; & un *In-folio* fuffiroit à peine pour nommer fimplement ceux qui en brûlent, fans fçavoir pourquoi.

De l'Imprimerie de J. A. GRANGÉ, rue de la Parcheminerie.

Le Bureau d'Adreffe eft à M. MIGNOT, Commis au Recouvrement de la Gazette de Médecine, rue du petit Bourbon, vis-à-vis du Louvre, entre le quai de l'Ecole, & le paffage de Saint Germain de l'Auxerrois.

Figure 7.1   *Gazette de Médecine*, 1761. Courtesy of the Bibliothèque Interuniversitaire de Médecine, Paris.

Chemistry courses were announced by means of some 500 to 1,000 posters pasted up around Paris. They took place regularly between 1702 and 1723, and again starting in 1753, before being ended in 1768 by order of the Faculty of Medicine, which was unhappy with the idea of apothecaries pretending to the status of professors. The advertisement for these courses presented the names of nine demonstrators, each of whom taught a lecture in turn. The experiments and course content were decided collectively, without the possibility of any one individual imposing his will. During the first period (1702-1723) the course was taught annually by a single teacher. No one person held the teaching position permanently, as the professorship was limited to two years.

The courses were held in the laboratory of the Jardin des apothicaires, which had been constructed in 1700. The amphitheatre was used exclusively for the teaching of chemical operations and preparations, and was an integral part of the laboratory. An 'Inventory of the House and Garden known by the name of the Collège de Pharmacie' was drawn up in 1788 and offers a very detailed description of the building:

On the left we find a laboratory in which a large, tiered seating arrangement has been constructed of oak, composed of nine tiers, with two benches on the floor. The tiers are surrounded by a barrier.

On the right of the fireplace there is a counter on which one can place the objects for the demonstrations, as well as the ovens and tools for the same end ... At the back of the laboratory there is a mantle over the fireplace constructed along the whole of its length ... Under the aforementioned fireplace there are limestone supports for the ovens ... In the aforementioned laboratory there are fifty of the most ordinary chairs.[3]

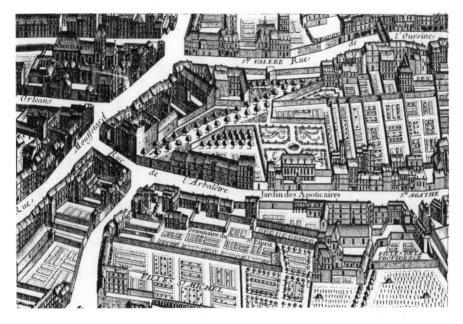

Figure 7.2   *Le Jardin des apothicaires* from a map by Louis Bretez, commonly known as the *plan Turgot*, 1739 [public domain

The domain of the demonstrator – between the hearth and the the demonstration bench – was distinct from that of the public, separated and protected by a barrier. The tiered seating allowed everyone to follow the demonstrations, but the mention of 'fifty of the most ordinary chairs' is most surprising, particularly as the seats seem to be included in the laboratory equipment, along with the fireplace, the ovens, the glassware and the porcelain. This suggests that the laboratory was conceived of as a meeting place involving the seated spectators. Outside the official courses, the public were free to witness the pharmaceutical preparations being carried out in the laboratory. One of the Guild's deliberations of 1763 reminds us of the possibility of using the laboratory 'to work at all sorts of preparations, both chemical and Galenic,

---

3   Archives of the *Faculté de pharmacie de Paris*, register 43, pages 19–20. 'Etat de la Maison et Jardin appelé "Collège de Pharmacie" par M. Essart Me Maçon demeurant rue St Etienne près St Etienne du Mont; à la réquisition de Mrs Bataille et Solomé prévôts et du Sr Santotte Ecrivain déchiffreur'.

that will be carried out there with all possible care and precision under the eyes and the by the hands of the Master apothecaries'. Thus, everything was organised at the Jardin des apothicaires so that the experiments would be carried out under the gaze of spectators, and with the exclusively pedagogical aim of transmitting an art by means of instruction through gestures and manipulations.

While professional training was important, and the public for these courses was principally composed of apprentice apothecaries. Because the Paris Faculty of Medicine did not offer its own chemistry courses, apothecary students were joined by doctors and medical students. But we should also note the mention of 'a multitude of amateurs and of students from all states, both national and foreign who have come here to learn', which may explain why the laboratory needed to be enlarged in 1760. While the heterogeneity of their public audience was characteristic of all chemistry courses around the middle of the eighteenth century, the courses at the Jardin des apothicaires lay outside the circuit of polite society, belonging to a system of apprenticeship enabling entry into a guild, rather than to the culture of curiosity.

In contrast to the courses at the Jardin des apothicaires, those offered at the Jardin du Roy (the Royal Botanical Gardens) were a royal institution. Essentially dedicated to the collection of medicinal plants, the Jardin du Roy initially limited its teaching to botany. Nevertheless, chemistry succeeded in grafting itself on to this original teaching mission and came to represent an ever more significant proportion of the instruction. Two positions, one as professor and the other as demonstrator, were created to teach the composition of medicinal plants. The description of the professor's responsibilities changed several times, but always towards a growing preponderance of chemistry.[4]

Nearly all the chair holders, as well as their successors, were members of the Paris Academy of Sciences, and all except Simon Boulduc were doctors, while all the demonstrators (except for Davisson) were pharmacists. The case of Boulduc, who first held the professor's chair (as a successor to Fagon) and later was moved to the demonstrator's chair, suggests that there was no clear hierarchy between the two functions. Moreover, since Boulduc also taught at the Jardin des apothicaires in 1707 we can assume that there was no competition between the two Jardins. The best known of the demonstrators, Guillaume-François Rouelle (1703–1770), was a member of the Academy of Sciences, while the last on the list, Antoine-Louis Brongniart, had already been appointed demonstrator at the new Collège de pharmacie, founded in 1777, when he joined the Jardin du Roy two years later.

Prior to the renovations undertaken by Georges Louis Leclerc, Comte de Buffon in 1787, the chemistry courses at the Jardin du Roy were held in an amphitheatre that Antoine-Laurent de Jussieu described in the following terms: 'This amphitheatre, which could hold 600 students, was located in the building that lay between the large entrance to the Jardin and the terrace of the great hillock.' André Thouin added the information that 'it was too small by half to contain the members of the audience'.[5]

4   J.P. Contant, *L'enseignement de la chimie au jardin royal des plantes de Paris* (Cahors: A. Coueslant, 1952).

5   Bibliothèque centrale du Muséum national d'histoire naturelle Ms 1934, 3rd notice, p. 6 note(s). The sixth notice, p. 17 states : 'L'amphithéâtre ancien situé entre la cour et une

Here, then, was a 600-place amphitheatre, and it was only half the required size! Thus, there must have been at least one thousand people attending courses at the Jardin du Roy, an impressively large public.

The plan for the Jardin drawn up by Buffon's architect, Edme Verniquet,[6] in 1783 enables us to locate both the chemistry laboratory (L) and the amphitheatre (H). It is surprising to see that the theoretical and practical parts of the teaching were offered in separate places. Did the students move from amphitheatre to laboratory in order to watch the practical operations, or was the material carried into the amphitheatre? The question remains open.

The amphitheatre was multipurpose, being used for the anatomy course in the winter. With the arrival of spring, however, the rising temperature meant that the cadavers became difficult to preserve, and so anatomy gave way to the botany and chemistry courses for the duration of the summer months, as advertised in the *Gazette de médecine* of 1761.[7]

The position of Rouelle as demonstrator is unique in the history of the Jardin du Roy, as he was appointed with the title 'demonstrator of chemistry at the Jardin des plantes with the title of professor of chemistry'. His teaching was not coordinated with that of the professor, Louis-Claude Bourdelin. Thus, he needed to present both the chemical processes and chemical theory simultaneously. The notes taken by Rouelle's students suggest that most of his presentations consisted in experimental preparations, but they were nevertheless shot through with theory. It was Rouelle who spread the doctrine of the German chemist Stahl to France, although as more than a simple interpreter or disciple.[8] The course lasted for three years and treated the three kingdoms of nature, although with an emphasis on the mineral kingdom. The testimonies of his contemporaries provide a colourful image of an untidy, warm, enthusiastic, loud professor who knew how to communicate his passion for chemistry to his audience.[9] Several anecdotes related by Friedrich Melchior Grimm convey the eccentric side of his personality, as well as the difficulty involved in 'doing' and 'talking' at the same time.[10]

Rouelle had two assistants, his brother Hilaire-Marin and his nephew. Their role was not only to prepare the experiments but also to avoid any accidents, as is suggested by Grimm's famous account of an explosion. The experiment involved igniting an essential oil with spirit of nitre. On this particular day, Rouelle was on

---

rue très passagère étoit trop resseré pour le nombre des élèves qui venait assister aux divers cours et les leçons étoient interrompues par le bruit des voitures. Il étoit dans le bâtiment qui existe entre la porte d'entrée et la terrasse de la grande butte.'

6   Bibliothèque centrale du Muséum national d'histoire naturelle, Plan Verniquet 1783, p. 1112.

7   'Cours de Chymie au Jardin du Roy', *Gazette de médecine*, 1761, vol. 1, p. 352.

8   R. Rappaport, 'Rouelle, Stahl: The Phlogistic Revolution in France', *Chymia*, 7 (1961): 73–102.

9   On the theatrical nature of Rouelle's lectures see Lissa Roberts, Chapter 9 in this volume.

10   P.A. Cap, *Guillaume-François Rouelle, Biographie chimique* (Paris: De Fain et Thumot, 1842), pp. 17, 23–24.

his own and left the experiment alone for a moment to finish his explanation. While he turned in the direction of the audience,

> suddenly, the ignition experiment exploded and broke the lid with a crack, giving off a bright light and filling the amphitheatre with thick and suffocating smoke. The terrified public immediately started to flee and fanned out through the garden in fear, while the operator, stunned and motionless, had escaped with only the loss of his wig and shirt-cuffs.'[11]

These courses enjoyed considerable success. According to Denis Diderot, they attracted 'a quarter of the city' from every class of society, including 'the children of nobles who wanted to learn'. Rouelle not only trained most of the chemists in the eighteenth century – Joseph Macquer (c. 1740), Gabriel-François Venel (1746), Antoine-Louis Brongniart, Jean-Baptiste Bucquet, Balthazar-Georges Sage (c. 1758), Antoine-Laurent Lavoisier (1762–63), to mention but the best known – but also the *philosophes* of the Enlightenment, Jean-Jacques Rousseau (1744–45), Denis Diderot (1753–56), Etienne-François Turgot, Chrétien-Guillaume de Lamoignon de Malesherbes, as well as various other members of polite society.

Thus, the courses offered at the Jardin du Roy responded both to a demand for training and to a demand for culture. They helped to make chemistry a fashionable science in the eyes of the public and one cultivated by the *philosophes*. Furthermore, the success of these public demonstrations helped to raise the status of experimental practice. Both Venel in his article on chemistry in Diderot's *Encyclopedia* and Diderot himself in his *Interprétation de la nature* praised the 'experimental manual workers' and the heroism of the chemist-as-artist.[12] But these were by no means spectacular experiments. Indeed, the chemist's heroism lay in his effort, in his labouris, 'the passion of a madman' that such experiments demanded. The spectacular, the explosions, were quite exceptional.

Private, Fee-paying Courses

Alongside these public courses, which were free, there also existed a long tradition of private, fee-paying courses that continued throughout the eighteenth century. Among the best known were those taught by the two Geoffroy brothers, both master apothecaries and members of the Academy of Sciences, with Etienne-François, the elder brother who was also a physician, famous for his 'Affinity Table'. They taught the course in their pharmacy in the rue Bourtibourg, while Rouelle taught in the rue Jacob from 1746, Macquer and Baumé in the rue St Denis starting in 1757, and de La Planche in rue de la Monnaie.

These courses, known as *cours particuliers*, were advertised in medical journals or by means of posters, and the advertisements sometimes required that students sign up for the course in advance. These courses always took place in the personal

---

11 Cap, *Guillaume-François Rouelle*, pp. 17, 23–4.

12 D. Diderot, *Discours sur l'interprétation de la nature*, 1753, re-edition (Paris: Garnier, 1964).

laboratory of an apothecary. What kind of transaction could occur in this private space – at one and the same time a place for the preparation of medicines and of commerce, considerating the fact that it was an annex of the pharmacy itself?

The teaching mainly dealt with pharmaceutical preparations, principally chemical medicines, meaning that experiments could not be avoided. Thus, the courses were practical rather than spectacular, with the aim of instructing the students in laboratory technique. The public came to the demonstrations to learn how to *do* things; by *seeing* and *hearing*, they were supposed to learn the gestures and delicate manipulations required for the craft. Thus, the teaching on offer was located in a no-man's-land between the methods of apprenticeship whereby artisans acquire their know-how, their 'habitus' and their manual skills through practising the art, and the bookish knowledge that one acquires by reading a treatise. Indeed, many of the courses were accompanied by treatises, and sometimes buying such a treatise was one of the preconditions of attending the course.

The courses took place on the apothecaries' territory – in the laboratory adjoining the pharmacy – and the teacher was sometimes an apothecary himself, although during the eighteenth century the apothecaries who taught these courses often collaborated with physicians. Thus, in Paris, the doctor Pierre-Joseph Macquer taught with the apothecary Antoine Baumé, and in Montpellier, Gabriel-François Venel, who was a physician, paired up with Jacques Montet. In the 1780s, an apothecary called Laurent-Charles de La Planche started a new course in partnership with Bucquet, a medical doctor. Why did these teaching duos become the norm? It seems that the collaborations were initiated by the physicians, who were usually members of academies of science. The fact was that physicians needed the apothecaries because of the statutes that governed their own guild. Medical doctors were required to teach in full costume and their lessons could not be other than '*scriptis et auribus*', written or oral, and they were explicitly prohibited from carrying out any manual operations. Indeed, Vicq d'Azyr points out how they were bogged down in their pomp:

> For a number of centuries physics has been nothing but a tissue of systems, a patchwork of authorities drawn from the ancients, which the doctors, fenced around with magisterial pomp, teach to their disciples. When the progress of knowledge forced them out of their schools to interrogate nature in the laboratory, they thought that, to retain their dignity, they needed to appear in their robes: these outfits mean they are reduced to the situation where it is impossible to do anything other than talk.[13]

As far as the apothecaries were concerned, the statutes of their guild forbade anyone who was not a qualified apothecary from presenting a demonstration. This prohibition applied particularly to medical doctors. Hence, the complex relationship between doctors and apothecaries, which oscillated between complementary cooperation and direct competition. In general, the apothecaries occupied a subordinate position, with physicians' organizations policing the preparation of drugs and inspecting the

---

13   F. Vicq d'Azyr, 'Eloge de M. Macquer', *Histoire de la Société royale de médecine*, 1782–1783 (Paris: Théophile Barrois, 1787), p. 74. Here he evokes the courses at the Jardin du Roy, but this applies equally to private courses.

pharmacies. Nevertheless, the doctors depended on the apothecaries to perform the experiments, because they themselves were not supposed to get their hands dirty.

These dual roles affected the relationship between theory and practice.

> Custom dictates that theory should be kept apart from demonstration and that these two aspects, which are mixed together in order to render teaching attractive, should be dealt with by two men, one of whom only talks, while the other acts and talks simultaneously.[14]

In principle, the role of experiments was simply to make the theory that the professor was presenting accessible to the audience's senses of sight, smell and touch. Nevertheless, it is clear that apothecaries did not avoid theory. They operated in both fields, combining word and gesture, and eventually dominating the stage, relegating the physician to the role of 'narrator'. De La Planche, for example, who taught his own private course as well as teaching at the Jardin des apothicaires and the Faculty of Medicine, would start with theory.[15] Then, while teaching the vegetable kingdom, he would present technical operations, maceration, infusion, decoction, etc. Wherever possible, he would put the emphasis on applications, such as the 'art of the bulk treatment of ores'. He also proposed 'curious chemical experiments' on metals, and promised to develop experiments on the theme of 'the discoveries made by some of the most famous chemists in Europe'. His advertisement offered a veritable technical training, but he subtly integrated theory, even including it in his title *A Course of experimental chemistry, following the principles of Becher, Stahl and Boerhaave*.

According to Baumé, his courses included more than two thousand experiments, during the course of which he would analyse the three kingdoms, a common element in the advertisements by Jacques-François Demachy, Rouelle and de La Planche. Thus, everything suggests that the combination of theory and experiment, even in the most technical aspects of the course, served as advertising slogans. Rouelle, for example, who announced his private course under the title of 'chemical experiments', lured potential clients by announcing the products he would extract or synthesize. From plants, he would extract 'essential oils, essential salts, fixed salts'. He would not only present the combinations of vegetable matter, but also, and above all, propose practical applications; the preparation of varnish or of coloured precipitates that could be used in dyes and paint. The last part of Rouelle's course was to deal with 'the substances that are taken from the bowels of the earth' and would be the object of 'unusual experiments' on bitumen, nitre, marine salts and the acids. He would show 'the phosphorous from England known only by a few persons up to now and which is the product of the most violent fire'. The effects of all the mixtures would produce 'changes in colour, detonations and the production of flames'!

But for all this, Rouelle did not neglect the matter of useful recipes: to promptly determine the metal content in an ore, to perform an assay with precision, to separate metals from one another, to use metal salts to make coloured glass. Rouelle promised

---

14   Vicq d'Azyr, 'Eloge de M. Macquer', p. 74. A footnote mentions that the custom of a professor and a demonstrator jointly teaching courses was still current in several universities in Germany and Italy.

15   Announcement of de La Planche's course, *Gazette de Médecine*, 1762, pp. 342–3.

both the spectacular and the useful. The conclusion of his advertisement clearly expressed this intention:

> With these experiments we will limit ourselves to making the advantages that physics and medicine have drawn from works of chemistry known. Further, we will make every effort to give examples of the utility of these same operations in several arts, and even their utility in everyday domestic uses.[16]

Who were the public for these private courses? We have no data about the courses in Paris. But, from data on similar courses held in the provinces, it seems that there were several dozens of people: in 1764, Venel claimed to have 42 students, in Nancy in 1777–79 there were 18. As private demonstrators had to equip a laboratory and buy the raw materials for their experiments, the courses were very expensive. It cost 96 *livres* to follow Macquer and Baumé's course (half price for those who had already taken a private chemistry course). The course offered by Venel and Montet in Montpellier cost half that amount. This was the price that students of medicine and pharmacy were expected to pay for receiving a professional training. However, these students were not alone: amateurs were ready to pay this price just to satisfy their curiosity.

Changes in the 1770s

During the 1770s, the chemical education of medical doctors and of pharmacists was taken in hand by, respectively, the Faculty of Medicine and the College of Pharmacy. Parallel to these institutional changes, chemistry itself underwent dramatic changes due to the study of gases. Pneumatic chemistry was a competitive domain, which at the same time reinforced the traditional links between medicine and chemistry. 'Aeriform fluids' captured the attention of medical doctors concerned with respiration and the salubrity of atmospheric air, and who worked hard to promote the therapeutic uses of the newly discovered gases. At the same time, pneumatic chemistry attracted chemists because it was the field where new theoretical hypotheses were developed that would lead to the 'chemical revolution'.[17]

What happened, then, to the long tradition of chemistry courses? Although courses for medical students were institutionalized as aspects of the medical curriculum, chemistry courses in general retained their large and heterogeneous public. In fact, the audience for chemistry grew in parallel with the territory covered by that science, which by the end of the eighteenth century included not only mineralogy but also the new sciences of electricity and pneumatic chemistry.

Advertisements no longer appeared exclusively in journals dedicated to medicine and pharmacy, as had been the case twenty years earlier, but were now to be found in the daily papers. The auditorium of the College of Pharmacy was crowded, from

---

16 Announcement of Rouelle's course *en sa maison*, rue Jacob, and starting on 17 November 1766, Bibliothèque nationale de France, digital document S 6436.

17 See B. Bensaude-Vincent and I. Stengers, *A History of Chemistry* (Cambridge, MA: Harvard University Press, 1996), pp. 75–82.

1778 to 1788, with an average of 100 people, ranging from a minimum of 57 in 1780 to a maximum of 228 in 1787. Part of the audience received a certificate validating their attendance at the course. Registered students made up a quarter to one half of the whole audience, depending on the year. Sometimes the register records the social standing (*qualité*) of the students. Half of them were pharmacy students, thus maintaining the tradition in pharmaceutical chemistry. Fewer than 10 per cent were medical students, and this proportion decreased over the decade as the number of courses offered in medical faculties increased.[18] By contrast, surgery students represented one-third of the audience for chemistry courses in the 1770s and 1780s.

Un cours de l'École royale des Mines au XVIIIᵉ siècle, dans la grande salle du Musée.
(Gravure de Née. — Musée de la Monnaie.)

Figure 7.3   Mazerolles (1907), *L'hôtel des monnaies*, Paris: Renouard, H. Laurens, p. 82. Courtesy of the Bibliothèque de l'Institut de France.

The contents of the public courses that were published during this decade share another striking feature, with a noticeable increase in mineral chemistry and docimasy, both of these being added to the pharmacy-oriented chemistry that had prevailed during the previous decades. This marked rise in interest in mineralogy may be linked with the undertaking of the *Atlas minéralogique de la France*, edited by Etienne Guettard, one of Rouelle's former students. Although there is no evidence for this connection, the Ancien régime witnessed a revival of interest in mining. This prompted the creation of the Royal School of Mines in Paris in 1784,

---

18   However, in the registers of attendance there is a medical doctor who presented himself as an *amateur de chimie* as well as two or three midwives per year.

where Balthazar-Georges Sage offered free courses in mineralogy and docimasy. This course, which was both free and widely publicized, began on 2 December 1778. It was a hybrid enterprise, since it took place in a school but was open to a wider public. An advertisement appeared in the daily paper *Le Journal de Paris* announcing that the course would be held on Monday, Wednesday and Friday of each week and mentioning that 'although this course is free, those who would like to attend should enrol for it'. Moreover, 'they will have to be introduced to the professor before attending his lectures'.[19] This course enjoyed considerable success, as is demonstrated by François-Denis Née's print in the work dedicated to *l'Hôtel des monnaies* (the Royal Mint, Figure 7.3).[20]

Since an official training in chemistry was now available for pharmacists and medical doctors in their own schools, one might think that this would have signalled the end of the private, fee-paying courses offered by pharmacists, but this was not at all the case. Public and private courses still flourished in Paris, although they seem to have developed in two diverging directions.

On the one hand, some courses increasingly favoured dramatic spectacle. The new star was the electrical fluid, which permitted Brongniart both to perform and to treat the sick using his magnetic fluid in the style of Frantz-Anton Mesmer's cures.

The effectiveness of the electric fluid in treating several diseases, and especially in paralyses and deafness, etc. proven by a large number of experiments has persuaded M. Brongniart to receive patients at his home. The administration of this fluid will always be overseen and conducted by a physician of the Paris Faculty who has worked a great deal with this form of cure, and who will follow up the patients with much precision and care. Those who would like to be electricized may engage their own regular doctor to follow them.[21]

The new gases gave rise to a range of impressive experiments, often astonishing and sometimes very smelly. Thus, Brongniart proposed a second part of his course where he would deal with 'air':

The different elastic emanations known under the general name of air, will be analysed in the greatest detail. Fixed air or mephitic acid, the knowledge of which brought about such a great revolution in physics and chemistry will be treated most accurately. We will demonstrate the new apparatus required easily to perform the interesting experiments enabled by these special fluids.[22]

---

19 *Le Journal de Paris*, no. 322, 18 November 1778.

20 F. Mazerolle, *L'hôtel des monnaies* (Paris: Renouard, H. Laurens, 1907), p. 82. Sage's course had such a wide reputation that the painter Gabriel de Saint Aubin executed three ink drawings of the courses in 1779. See E. Darcier, *Gabriel de Saint Aubin peintre (1724–1780)* (Paris: Bruxelles, 1929), plate 14.

21 *Journal de Paris*, (Paris: de Quillau), no. 111, 21 April 1778.

22 *Journal de Paris*, no. 37, 6 February 1778. Not everyone agreed with the publicity or more generally the noise around the 'airs' intended to attract the public. Mitouard, chemistry professor at the Collège de pharmacie, announced that 'Les expériences sur les différentes espèces d'air étant inséparables de la Chymie, il ne croit pas devoir en faire une mention particulière', *Journal de Paris*, no. 314, 10 November 1778.

For all this, the spectacular did not displace utility; the analysis of mineral waters remained a theme throughout, and mineralogy mounted its own notable ascent in the last quarter of the eighteenth century. Thus, one can observe a revival of interest in the exploitation of subterranean resources, and a number of landowners either searched for or started to exploit mineral reserves. In his study of the elements, which covered both water and the earths, Brongniart proposed some other practical applications:

> The analysis of different mineral waters can help country landowners throw light on the salubrity of the waters they find on their land. We will show them by what means – as uncomplicated as they are easy – they can know the quality of these waters, and how to render them into such a state that they can serve different everyday uses. Finally, we will see ... the special analysis of different earths; the art of making glass, mirrors, and that of making pottery from simple earthenware to the finest porcelain. The arts of the plasterer, the lime burner, and the brick maker will be carefully presented in detail.[23]

Thus, by the end of the eighteenth century, chemistry courses had become less and less specialized. They were no longer addressed to targeted audiences of pharmacists or medical doctors. Rather, they were aimed at an elite who supposedly wanted to be aware of what was happening around them in order 'not to feel like strangers in the middle of their property'.

On the other hand, there was another development in chemistry courses, far removed from chemistry as entertainment. These courses aimed at the 'refoundation' of the discipline on new ground. The generation of chemists of the 1770s and 1780s – Bucquet, Darcet and Fourcroy, to name but three – had a deep concern with educational issues. Like the Abbé Etienne Bonnot de Condillac, they did not separate education from the refoundation of knowledge itself.[24] Thus, the approach from the simple to the complex, moving from the known to the unknown, became a guide for teaching as well as for refounding chemistry. This conjunction is already well documented in various studies of textbooks and the reform of chemical language in 1787.[25] The study of chemistry courses adds a new dimension to this ambitious project, this time with the emphasis on experiments. Take, for example, Bucquet's and Lavoisier's collaboration in the 1770s. In 1777, Bucquet, who was offering a private course in rue Jacob at the time, gave a few lectures at Lavoisier's official residence at the Arsenal. While the circumstances that prompted this collaboration remain obscure, the results are all too evident: 26 memoirs co-signed by Bucquet and Lavoisier were presented before the Paris Academy of Science.[26] The public

---

23   Announcement of Brongniart's course, *Journal de Paris*, no. 37, 6 February 1778.

24   W. R. Albury, 'The Logic of Condillac and the Structure of French Chemical and Biological Theory (1780-1800)', PhD dissertation, Johns Hopkins University, 1972.

25   M. Beretta, *The Enlightenment of Matter: The Definition of Chemistry from Agricola to Lavoisier* (USA: Science History, 1997). B. Bensaude-Vincent, A. Garcia-Belmar, and J.-R. Bertomeu, *L'émergence d'une science des manuels. Les livres de chimie en France (1789– 1852)* (Paris: éditions archives contemporaines, 2003).

26   C. Perrin, 'The Lavoisier-Bucquet collaboration: A Conjecture', *Ambix*, 36 (1989): 5–13.

experiments performed by Bucquet and Lavoisier with the help of a technician provided opportunities for testing a number of hypotheses that Lavoisier wished to investigate, as he was already experiencing strong doubts concerning the phlogiston theory. From these public experiments emerged their project of 'repeating all the fundamental experiments of chemistry', including the oldest and the most difficult ones, in order to base chemistry on more solid foundations. This project, which would lead them to write a textbook, was ended by Bucquet's premature death in 1780. It was, however, resumed by Lavoisier alone in 1789, when he wrote his *Traité élémentaire de chimie*. He could then dispense with the fastidious task of repeating all the experiments, thanks to Condillac's analytical logic, which was assumed to be the logic of nature itself. Nevertheless, so long as the project of refounding chemistry was based on experiments, it had to be achieved through experimental demonstrations, whether performed in public or in private courses, to defray the high cost associated with performing all these experiments. Thanks to this subtle combination of education and entertainment, the public was able to contribute to the reconstruction of chemistry in the roles both of sponsor of and witness to these experiments.[27]

Spectacular experiments were raised to a new status during the 1780s, even within the academic community. In the context of a controversy, a spectacular *mise en scène* of particular chemical reactions could be used as a stage for mounting some proof aimed at convincing or 'converting' other chemists. Such was the case with the famous public experiment of the analysis and synthesis of water performed by Antoine Laurent de Lavoisier in February 1785. Lavoisier's decomposition and recomposition of water is still celebrated as a mythical experiment, a symbol of modern chemistry understood as a quantitative and experimental science based on the method of the balance sheet – nothing is created and nothing is destroyed. Indeed, Lavoisier is still credited with inventing this maxim, although it had been used by many generations of chemists before him. This lasting effect is due to the power of spectacular experiments such as that performed by him in 1785.

Conclusion

Overall, the different chemistry courses offered to the public in eighteenth-century France reflect a number of distinctive features of chemistry itself. First, public and private teaching operated side by side for the whole of the century, often with the same demonstrators teaching in both contexts. The fact that the same chemists gave private courses in addition to their free, public ones suggests that there was sufficient public demand to sustain these additional courses.

The majority of the public for these courses was interested in receiving a professional training, and we need to remember that, at the time, chemistry only existed as a service science, an auxiliary to medicine and pharmacy. Nevertheless,

---

27 M. Daumas and D.I. Duveen, 'Lavoisier's relatively unknown large scale experiment of decomposition and synthesis of water. February 27–28, 1785', *Chymia*, 5 (1959): 111–29. J. Golinski, 'Precision Instruments and the Demonstrative Order of Proof in Lavoisier's Chemistry', *Osiris,* 9 (1994): 30–47.

even if the main orientation in the cases presented above was towards practical pedagogy, it is important to recognize the mixed, heterogeneous public for the courses. Chemistry attracted its share of *philosophes* as well as those who were simply inquisitive, and was fully integrated into Enlightenment culture as a science that could usefully contribute to the public good. Despite being the favourite hobby for many amateurs, chemistry could not be considered simply as entertainment, as the subject matter remained very extensive, and much dedicated work was required to master the field.

With the introduction of the study of gases in the 1770s, a number of chemical demonstrations became more and more spectacular, rivalling those performed in the physics cabinets. However, other chemistry courses went in a different direction, serving ambitious projects for the reconstruction of the discipline.

Finally, public demonstrations of chemical experiments, a long-standing tradition in France, provide a good example of the changing functions of this kind of public presentation in science. They were initially meant to provide professional training for pharmacists and medical doctors, but they came to attract a broader audience of amateur scientists and philosophers. Experimental demonstrations in chemistry were first and foremost a spectacle, intended to be seen, heard and smelt, although this spectacle has never been presented as being simply for amusement, and was always meant to be instructive and yet appealing at the same time. The meaning of the word 'demonstration' was, however, in the process of changing: less and less intended to denote a visual show and more and more to signal a mode of argumentation, especially in the project of the refounding of the discipline. The demonstration was addressed less and less to the spectators' eyes and increasingly to their minds or their faculties of judgement.

Chapter 8

Joseph Priestley and the Chemical Sublime in British Public Science

Jan Golinski

Much of the scientific practice of the eighteenth century was 'public science': it was aimed at a general audience and performed in the social spaces characteristic of the Enlightenment public sphere. In an age when learned academies declined to segregate professionals from amateurs, or natural philosophy from literature, experimental demonstrations often straddled specialist research and popular entertainment. This situation poses particular challenges for historians of Enlightenment science. Although we know the identities of many scientific practitioners, and something about the composition of their audiences, what their activities meant to those who witnessed them remains elusive. We might surmise that some of those who attended public lectures and demonstrations wanted them to yield technical information, while others sought theological edification; some might have derived from them a sense of participation in enlightened culture, while others simply relished their entertainment value. To go beyond this to specify the precise meanings imputed to particular displays by particular audiences requires a sensitive reading of the textual evidence and some degree of speculation.[1]

In this chapter, I shall focus on chemistry in Britain in the 1770s and 1780s, a period in which the discipline assumed a more prominent place in public science than it had previously enjoyed. At this time, many writers and lecturers were focusing on newly discovered gases – those now known as carbon dioxide, hydrogen, oxygen, nitric oxide, and a few others. Joseph Priestley, the dissenting minister from Yorkshire who first produced many of these gases, worked hard to make them part of public scientific displays. He employed a material technology that allowed them to be readily reproduced in experimental demonstrations, and his writings described them and spelled out their meanings. The key to these meanings, I shall argue, was the term 'sublime', a term loaded for Priestley with theological, aesthetic and political significance. By using the term in connection with public science, especially with the new gases, Priestley asserted that scientific discoveries

---

1   On Enlightenment public science in general, see Simon Schaffer, 'Natural philosophy and public spectacle in the eighteenth century', *History of Science*, 21 (1983): 1–43; Larry Stewart, *The Rise of Public Science: Rhetoric, Technology, and Natural Philosophy in Newtonian Britain, 1660–1750* (Cambridge: Cambridge University Press, 1992); Jan Golinski, *Science as Public Culture: Chemistry and Enlightenment in Britain, 1760–1820* (Cambridge: Cambridge University Press, 1992); Geoffrey Sutton, *Science for a Polite Society: Gender, Culture, and the Demonstration of Enlightenment* (Boulder, CO: Westview Press, 1995).

properly appealed to the emotions of the public. He also suggested the historical importance of the new gases in the context of a prospect of enlightenment that was also designated 'sublime'. Grasping this, we can see why Priestley's pneumatic chemistry became increasingly controversial as political divisions deepened toward the end of the eighteenth century. In the context of fierce debate about the benefits of general enlightenment and its potential destabilizing effects on society, the meanings of public science established by Priestley and others came under suspicion from political conservatives. The episode was of critical importance in sealing the fate of public science as it had been known in eighteenth-century Britain. From this crisis emerged a different configuration of scientific institutions, a new enterprise of popularization, and an altered significance for the aesthetics of the sublime.

Passionless Chemists

Scientific demonstrations had first entered the public domain in Britain in the opening decades of the eighteenth century. Lecturers including William Whiston, Humphry Ditton, John Harris and J.T. Desaguliers took Newtonian concepts of astronomy and mechanics to audiences in coffee-shops, inns and assembly rooms, initially mainly in London. They devised apparatus to demonstrate basic mechanical and astronomical ideas and mapped out the syllabus for public lectures on experimental natural philosophy. By the 1740s, the movement was spreading beyond the capital, led by the brilliant entrepreneur Benjamin Martin, who took his apparatus on the road to captivate audiences in provincial towns such as Bath, Birmingham, Chester and Shrewsbury. Martin incorporated into his syllabus the phenomena of electricity, dubbed by journalists the 'science à la mode' of the decade.[2] Improved apparatus such as frictional generators and, later, the Leyden jar allowed lecturers to show their audiences the astonishing effects of conduction and attraction, sparks and shocks. Electricity strengthened the appeal of scientific demonstrations to the senses – the fount of all knowledge according to empiricist philosophy – and also elicited audiences' emotions. Wonder was regarded as the first step toward philosophical understanding; it was recognized as a legitimate means of evoking the interest of the public in natural philosophy. Electricity seemed to operate physiologically in ways that bypassed the rational intellect; it connected the forces of nature with the refined 'sensibility' that was prized as an attribute of polite and enlightened people. Communication of the electrical fluid from person to person in the context of experimental displays served as a kind of concrete metaphor of the process of enlightenment itself, giving participants a physical sense of the diffusion of knowledge through social interaction.[3]

---

2   John R. Millburn, *Benjamin Martin: Author, Instrument-maker and 'Country Showman'* (Leiden: Noordhoff, 1976).

3   On sensibility and electricity, see Jessica Riskin, *Science in the Age of Sensibility: The Sentimental Empiricists of the French Enlightenment* (Chicago: University of Chicago Press, 2002). On wonder, see Lorraine Daston and Katharine Park, *Wonders and the Order of Nature, 1150–1750* (New York: Zone Books, 1998), pp. 329–63; Mary Baine Campbell,

Chemistry lagged well behind natural philosophy in recruiting an audience in the public sphere. For several decades, chemical lecturers – even those operating outside educational institutions – looked for customers to those who had a vocational interest in pharmacy and other chemical arts. George Wilson advertised his chemistry courses in London in the 1690s for 'Doctors of Physick, Apothecaries, Chirurgeons, and others, Studious of Physick, or curious in Chymical Operations'. He charged three guineas for a course – a substantial sum, indicating that the audience was drawn from those seeking professional training rather than general enlightenment.[4] In the 1730s, the lectures of Peter Shaw marked a step toward enlisting a wider audience for the discipline, though he continued to rely partly on a medical clientele. Shaw began his lecturing career in London but moved in 1733 to the Yorkshire resort town of Scarborough, where he reduced the fee for his course from five guineas to two. He found a genteel audience and aristocratic patrons among the fashionable crowds at the seaside resort, which was also renowned for its medicinal spa. The lectures covered various chemical operations and practical arts, including pharmacy, wine making and mining; they concluded with spectacular demonstrations of the properties of phosphorus. Shaw's success with Scarborough's polite society was significant, but it had little lasting impact. Shaw himself turned his social connections to account by moving into practice as a physician. Chemical lecturers who followed his lead in England during the succeeding three or four decades continued to align themselves closely with the interests of the medical community.[5]

In the Scottish universities, chemistry became prominent in the curriculum in the middle decades of the century. Edinburgh University professors William Cullen and Joseph Black were still mostly teaching medical students, but they also assumed a significant public profile. They needed to cultivate aristocratic patrons, and their drawing power with students was important for the city's prosperity. Cullen worked to demonstrate the applications of chemistry to agriculture, bleaching, mineralogy and other arts, to prove its 'philosophical' credentials and make it 'the study of a gentleman'.[6] His pupil and successor, Black, became famous for the demonstrations accompanying his lectures. After Black's death, the editor of his manuscript notes was to find them 'full of references to processes going forwards, or which have been gone thro' in the Class, and pointing to things on the table'.[7] The journalist and educational reformer Henry Brougham reminisced about the 'perfect philosophical calmness' that Black displayed in making his classroom demonstrations:

Wonder and Science: Imagining Worlds in Early Modern Europe (Ithaca: Cornell University Press, 1999).

4   F.W. Gibbs, 'George Wilson (1631–1711)', *Endeavour*, 12 (1953): 182–5, quotation on p. 183.

5   F.W. Gibbs, 'Peter Shaw and the revival of chemistry', *Annals of Science*, 7 (1951): 211–37; Jan Golinski, 'Peter Shaw: chemistry and communication in Augustan England', *Ambix*, 30 (1983): 19–29.

6   Golinski, *Science as Public Culture*, pp. 11–49.

7   John Robison, quoted in Eric Robinson and Douglas McKie (eds), *Partners in Science: Letters of James Watt and Joseph Black* (London: Constable, 1970), p. 343.

I have seen him pour boiling water or boiling acid from a vessel that had no spout into a tube, holding it at such a distance as made the stream's diameter small, and so vertical that not a drop was spilt.... The long table on which the different processes had been carried on was as clean at the end of the lecture as it had been before the apparatus was planted upon it. Not a drop of liquid, not a grain of dust remained.[8]

Brougham's recollection captured something fundamental about Black's philosophical persona. The Scottish chemist's passionless calm was frequently remarked upon as an aspect of his character. Brougham also recorded that, at the moment of his death, Black slipped from life so gently that a bowl of milk held on his lap was undisturbed.[9] In these stories, Black's ability to avoid spilling liquids seemed to represent his stoical imperturbability, his capacity to remain emotionally undisturbed even in the face of death. More generally, the emotionless demeanour and methodical neatness evident in Black's lecture demonstrations reflected the ideals of Scottish chemistry as a whole. Theoretical speculation and 'projecting' (seeking private profit through commercial schemes) were both curbed by the canon of modesty to which chemists were expected to adhere. Brougham said of Black that his opinions 'on every subject were marked by calmness and sagacity, wholly free from both passion and prejudice'.[10] To be emotionally undisturbed was to be epistemologically unprejudiced. A calm and modest demeanour allowed for the collection of facts that could then be methodically arranged in chemical lectures. In order for chemistry to become fully public, it had to be pursued in the correct philosophical spirit. For the Scottish chemists, the keynote of that spirit was the restraint of the passions to let facts be apprehended unclouded by prejudice. Hence, in lectures, students' senses were enlisted to listen and observe (and sometimes also to touch, smell and taste), but their passions were held firmly in check lest they disturb the smooth assimilation of factual knowledge.

Enthusiasm for the Wonders of Nature

In the 1770s, Joseph Priestley's discoveries of previously unknown gases launched chemistry into a new trajectory in the realm of public science. Priestley taught at various dissenting academies in England, and he inspired a whole generation of public lecturers to reproduce the phenomena he revealed. Through personal contacts and detailed descriptions in his writings, he demonstrated the apparatus needed to replicate his findings. The equipment was avowedly simple, composed partly of readily available household objects (candles and a fire-grate for heat, a wooden basin), and partly of specially made but cheap accessories (glass and ceramic tubes and vessels). The simplicity of the apparatus allowed it to be widely reproduced, so that the gases could be experienced by many people.

---

8   Henry Brougham, *Lives of the Philosophers of the Time of George III* (Edinburgh: Adam and Charles Black, 1872), pp. 19–20.

9   Brougham, *Lives of Philosophers*, p. 24.

10   Brougham, *Lives of Philosophers*, p. 22.

Priestley claimed that the process was essentially one in which nature revealed itself. The role of the human discoverer was incidental and unworthy of particular attention. As he put it, 'discoveries have been made so much by accident, that it is more the powers of nature, than of human genius, that excite our wonder with respect to them'.[11] The epistemological modesty of this stance was founded – as in the Scottish case – on fundamental empiricist principles. It was assumed that the philosopher's mind passively received the input of the senses to form knowledge of the natural world. But, in contrast to the Scottish chemists, Priestley enlisted the senses of his audiences in a way that did not exclude engagement of their passions. In fact, he quite deliberately set out to excite their wonder. The language with which he surrounded his discoveries appealed to what recent scholars have called 'the culture of sensibility', the cultural climate in which certain feelings and sensitivities were valued as attributes of refinement.[12] Priestley worked to convey to his readers the sensory experiences of chemical phenomena, and he also enlisted their emotions, including wonder, awe and surprise. This way of appealing to his audience's sensibility – an aesthetic and at the same time a social strategy for communicating the results of his work – is what I am calling 'the chemical sublime'.

Priestley's interest in the rhetorical impact of experimental demonstrations, their history and their role in general public enlightenment, was originally developed in the 1760s in connection with the phenomena of electricity. In the preface to his *History and Present State of Electricity* (1767), he wrote that the pleasure of studying the science resembles 'that of the sublime, which is one of the most exquisite of all those that affect the human imagination'.[13] A reviewer of the volume noted that the author's description of the Leyden jar was written 'under the influence of the surprise and terror excited by a *new* and *unexpected* feeling, of a most peculiar kind'.[14] When he turned to pneumatic chemistry in the 1770s, Priestley continued to be interested in evoking these feelings. Experimental demonstrations of new gases were interpreted as 'sublime' in two senses: first, the displays were revealing powers of nature that elicited emotions of wonder and surprise in human spectators. And second, the revelation of these powers at this time was part of the process of enlightenment under the superintendence of divine providence. For Priestley, this historical process was itself a sublime prospect: it showed how experimental science contributed to the diffusion of knowledge and the advance of human freedom.

The most influential discussion of the sublime in English during this period was Edmund Burke's *Philosophical Enquiry into the Origin of our Ideas of the Sublime and the Beautiful* (1757). For Burke, astonishment was central to the experience, 'and astonishment is that state of the soul, in which all its motions are suspended,

---

11   Joseph Priestley, *The History and Present State of Electricity* (London: J. Dodsley et al., 1767), p. xiii.

12   G.J. Barker-Benfield, *The Culture of Sensibility: Sex and Society in Eighteenth-Century Britain* (Chicago: University of Chicago Press, 1992). Riskin, *Science in the Age of Sensibility*.

13   Priestley, *History of Electricity*, p. ii.

14   *Monthly Review*, 1st ser., 37 (1767), p. 101.

with some degree of horror'.[15] Anything terrifying was therefore sublime for Burke: dangerous animals, the ocean, darkness or vast spaces. More generally, anything that displayed the powers of nature could produce the requisite state of astonishment. Earthquakes, thunder, even the light of the sun, were therefore sources of the sublime.

Priestley presumably knew of Burke's treatment of the sublime, although he didn't directly mention it in his own discussion of the topic in his *Course of Lectures on Oratory and Criticism* (1762). He distanced himself from Burke by detaching the sublime from the feeling of fear or apprehension of pain. For Priestley, the sublime was a wholly positive experience, caused by sentiments that 'relate to great objects, suppose extensive views of things, require a great effort of mind to conceive them, and produce great effects'. Even silence, if it fixes the attention and stills the mind, may partake of the sublime. Priestley noted that authors who invoke the sublime are more likely to be admired and remembered than those who merely aim to please, since they represent nature 'in the grandest and noblest point of light'. The sciences of astronomy and his own field of natural philosophy, in particular, 'exhibit the noblest fields of the sublime that the mind of man was ever introduced to'.[16]

These aesthetic notions guided Priestley's presentation of his discoveries in his writings on pneumatic chemistry. In his *Experiments and Observations on Different Kinds of Air* (1774–77), he meticulously catalogued the sensory qualities of the different gases he had found – their colours and odours, their capacity to support or extinguish combustion, the colours of electrical sparks discharged in them. He followed his precursors in the tradition of chemical pedagogy by training his audience to use their senses or instrumental surrogates for them. He used mice systematically to test the suitability of gases for respiration, finding them more reliable than the human sense of smell for this purpose. Readers' sympathies were engaged by sombre accounts of mice passing out or dying in unbreathable atmospheres. Most prominent among the emotions stirred by Priestley's narrative was surprise. He wrote that, when teaching experimental philosophy to students, 'curiosity and surprise [*sic*] ... should be excited as soon as possible'.[17] Incidents such as the discovery of 'dephlogisticated air' (later named oxygen) were described as especially surprising. The 'nitrous air test', devised by Priestley as a means of assessing how good a sample of air was for respiration, was said to be particularly astonishing, since it resulted in diminution of the volume of gas as a portion of it dissolved in water. Priestley noted, 'I hardly know any experiment that is more adapted to amaze and surprise than this.'[18] At one point he interjected, 'I wish my reader be not quite tired with the frequent repetition of the word surprise, and others of similar import; but I must go on in that style a

---

15   Edmund Burke, *A Philosophical Enquiry into the Origin of our Ideas of the Sublime and the Beautiful*, ed. James T. Boulton (Notre Dame: University of Notre Dame Press, 1987), p. 57.

16   Joseph Priestley, *A Course of Lectures on Oratory and General Criticism* (London: J. Johnson, 1762), pp. 154, 162, 157.

17   Joseph Priestley, *Experiments and Observations relating to Various Branches of Natural Philosophy*, 3 vols (London: J. Johnson, 1779–86) vol. 1, p. x.

18   Joseph Priestley, *Experiments and Observations on Different Kinds of Air*, 2nd edn, 3 vols (London: J. Johnson, 1775–77) vol. 1, p.111.

little longer.'[19] Going on in this style was Priestley's way of showing his readers that he was just as astonished as they were by what he had found. The wonder he shared with his audience at the sublime powers of nature was a mark of his candour as an experimenter and a writer.

Striking this note in the preface to the second volume of *Experiments and Observations*, Priestley connected the unprejudiced candour of the experimenter to the second dimension of the chemical sublime: its relation to the historical process of enlightenment. He designated himself an

> instrument in the hands of divine providence, which makes use of human industry to strike out and diffuse that knowledge of the system of nature, which seems, for some great purpose that we cannot as yet fully comprehend, to have been reserved for this age of the world.[20]

For Priestley, the revelations of new gases were providentially intended to spread the light of natural knowledge, advancing the process of enlightenment that he regarded as the fulfilment of biblical prophecies. He also saw as 'sublime and glorious' the prospect of an indefinite continuation of scientific research, endlessly pushing back the boundary of darkness and ignorance.[21] In the first volume of the work, he had already quoted a passage from Alexander Pope's *Essay on Criticism* about climbing in the Alps, where, as each peak is surmounted, further vistas appear for contemplation and further peaks to be conquered. In the same way, the history of experimental science offered a sublime spectacle, one more worthy of awe than the messy and contingent history of human society. This was because it manifested a steady, providentially guaranteed progress toward general enlightenment – a process not usually evident in the chaos of civic history. Sciences like pneumatic chemistry and electricity, 'in which we see a gradual rise and progress in things, always exhibit a pleasing spectacle to the human mind ... [which] bears a considerable resemblance to that of the sublime'.[22] The method of historical narrative, which Priestley carried over from his surveys of optics and electricity to the accounts of his own chemical discoveries, engaged his readers in the pleasure of this sublime spectacle.

For Priestley, then, the revelations of pneumatic chemistry were signs of the 'very particular providence' directing human actions toward 'other changes in the state of the world, of much more consequence to the improvement and happiness of it'.[23] The situation demanded a sustained effort of public education to make the new knowledge as widely available as possible. Accordingly, Priestley personally encouraged the introduction of pneumatic chemistry into the repertoire of scientific lecturers who were recruiting public audiences in various parts of England. They included Adam Walker, John Warltire, John Arden, Benjamin Donn, John Banks and Henry Moyes. Most of these men had been lecturing from the established natural philosophy syllabus, but they quickly saw the value of incorporating Priestley's chemical discoveries. In

---

19 Priestley, *Experiments ... of Air*, vol. 2, p. 42.
20 Priestley, *Experiments ... of Air*, vol. 2, p. ix.
21 Priestley, *Experiments ... of Natural Philosophy*, vol. 2, p. ix.
22 Priestley, *History of Electricity*, p. i.
23 Priestley, *Experiments ... of Air*, vol. 1, pp. xiii–xiv.

most cases, they visited Priestley to learn at first hand how to handle pneumatic apparatus, and then replicated his experiments in their performances.[24] Arden shared Priestley's view about the importance of sensory experience in learning the sciences; he displayed apparatus for 'medicating and inspiring air' and showed the nitrous air test in his courses in Yorkshire and later at Bath. Warltire, who assisted Priestley in the first experiments on 'dephlogisticated air', performed pneumatic demonstrations in lectures at Bath, Bristol and Birmingham in the late 1770s. Donn's apparatus was said to be 'not as gaudy as some, or so pompous as others; being in general, simple in the construction'.[25] He expanded his syllabus to incorporate Priestley's discoveries at the end of the 1770s. Moyes, who was blind, already had a syllabus focused on 'philosophical chemistry'; working with an assistant to perform the experiments, he included the new pneumatic discoveries in the early 1780s.

The most famous public lecturer whom Priestley inspired was Adam Walker. He became an itinerant teacher of astronomy and physics in the mid-1760s, travelling through northern England, Scotland and Ireland. From 1773, he was including Priestley's chemical discoveries in lectures in York. Five years later he visited Priestley in London and was given pneumatic apparatus to use in his displays. For the remainder of his career, until his death in 1821, he worked mostly in London, teaching astronomy, natural philosophy and chemistry.[26] Walker seems to have shared Priestley's views about the providential character of scientific discoveries and the role of education in public enlightenment. He lauded the rational knowledge of God, which came from the study of nature, while castigating superstition and political tyranny. He praised his audiences for their sensibility and politeness, while promising not to ask their assent to any proposition that had not been proven by experiments. He disclaimed 'the enchantments of the theatre ... the thunder of eloquence, [and] the sublime of inspiration', as contrary to the moral purpose of scientific education.[27] The role of the lecturer, he insisted, was simply to open the book of nature before his audience – nature itself was the sublime force that would work its moral effect with minimum rhetorical mediation. As the *European Magazine* noted, in a review of Walker's career in 1792, 'The simple but animated manner in which these sublime ideas are explained, is one of our Author's first merits.'[28]

---

24 Golinski, *Science as Public Culture*, pp. 93–105.

25 Benjamin Donn, *An Enlarged Syllabus for a Course of Lectures in Experimental Philosophy*, 2nd edn, (Bristol: for the author, 1780), p. 2.

26 *European Magazine and London Review*, 21 (1792): 411–413.

27 Adam Walker, *A System of Familiar Philosophy*, London: for the author, 1799, p. x. See also Walker, *Analysis of a Course of Lectures on Natural and Experimental Philosophy*, (4th edn [London]: for the author, [1780?]), pp. 23–31; Walker, *Analysis of a Course of Lectures in Natural and Experimental Philosophy* (14th edn, London: J. Barfield, 1807), pp. iii–vi.

28 *European Magazine and London Review*, 21 (1792), p. 412.

The Wonders of Science

The scientific lecturers who took up his discoveries put Priestley's chemical sublime into practice in public enlightenment. They evoked the sensibility of their audiences with displays of striking and surprising phenomena, telling them that the discoveries of new gases were integral to material progress and moral improvement. They emphasized the powers of nature rather than the spectacular scale or expense of their apparatus, since they claimed simply to be allowing nature to reveal itself. Pneumatic chemistry nonetheless became intensely controversial in the last decade of the eighteenth century, as the connection between natural powers and the emotional responses of public audiences came under scrutiny. In the reactionary climate of the 1790s, as the British government cracked down on political dissent in the face of the French Revolution, Priestley and his associates were accused of exploiting popular credulity and unleashing social unrest. The spectre of 'enthusiasm', familiarly attributed to fringe religious movements since the seventeenth century, was invoked again.

Priestley knew that he was courting the label of 'enthusiast' with his appeal to wonder and surprise and his confidence that pneumatic discoveries were intended for some specific providential purpose. In the *Experiments and Observations*, he professed himself 'perfectly easy under the imputation'.[29] But, after his house in Birmingham was ransacked by a loyalist mob in 1791, and he was driven into exile in the United States, he was forced to acknowledge the dangers of collective unreason and violence. In the eyes of his critics, Priestley had reaped the rewards of his own indulgence of enthusiasm – the predictable consequences of inciting popular passions. Burke and other conservative writers attacked the socially subversive tendencies of public education and the institutions of intellectual debate. They metaphorically identified the revolutionary fervour they feared would spread from France with Priestley's gases and phlogiston. An incautious statement by Priestley about corrupt governments having reason to fear the influence of the air pump and the electrical machine was frequently turned against him. In caricature, he was accused of 'priestcraft', routinely reviled by enlightened *philosophes* and Protestant Englishmen alike – an accusation that, with cruel irony, identified the Unitarian dissenter with Catholicism.[30]

From the crucible of the 1790s, new forms of public science emerged in Britain. The sublime, as an underlying aesthetic of chemical display, was appropriated by Humphry Davy in the following decade, albeit significantly reconfigured. In the early 1800s, Davy showed spectacular experiments on electrochemistry to audiences at the Royal Institution in London. In 1802, he asserted that chemistry 'must be always more or less connected with the love of the beautiful and the sublime; ... [being] eminently calculated to gratify and keep alive the more powerful passions and ambitions of the soul'.[31] Unlike Priestley, however, Davy assumed those

---

29 Priestley, *Experiments ... of Air*, vol. 1, p. xiii.

30 Golinski, *Science as Public Culture*, pp. 176–87.

31 Humphry Davy, *The Collected Works of Sir Humphry Davy*, ed. John Davy, 9 vols, (London: Smith, Elder, 1839–40) vol. 2, p. 325.

powerful passions to himself, displaying the emotional intensity of a scientific 'genius' to his appreciative public. He built a reputation as a brilliant lecturer to fashionable metropolitan audiences by (in the words of one observer) presenting 'most strongly to the popular observation the attributes of genius'.[32] Rather than inviting his audience to share in the wonders of scientific inquiry, Davy focused attention on his own persona. The result was to detach the chemical sublime from its subversive political associations.

Davy showed how the wonders of chemical science could be deployed in a controlled setting without stirring fears of social unrest. He set the terms for the nineteenth-century enterprise of popularization, which enlisted passive support for elite scientific institutions but did not seek to recruit participants for public science. For Priestley and his associates, on the other hand, experimental display had been tied to a democratic ideal of progressive enlightenment. Priestley believed that the dissemination of knowledge required universal participation, which in turn required emotions to be stirred and channelled. As an aesthetic of enlightened public science, the chemical sublime had this specific social and political meaning, which tends to be obscured by its subsequent association by Davy with the category of Romantic genius.

It is hard, however, to avoid hindsight altogether. Looking back to the formation of the chemical sublime in the 1770s, one can discern inherent instabilities that subsequent political disputes were to accentuate. An emblem of these is a painting by Joseph Wright, an artist working in the Midlands city of Derby, closely associated with the leading figures of the local scientific elite and the Lunar Society in nearby Birmingham (Figure 8.1).

In 1771, as Priestley was beginning his work on pneumatic chemistry in Leeds, Wright produced his depiction of an alchemist's discovery of phosphorus.[33] The work nicely captures the ambiguities of the chemical sublime, especially the uncertainty as to whether astonishing discoveries are a spur to enlightenment or a path back into superstition. The alchemist, searching for the philosopher's stone, is taken by surprise (as Priestley frequently was) by an unexpected revelation. Phosphorus is a natural marvel, surely worthy of wonder, but the alchemist's response is to fall to his knees. The full title of the painting tells us that he is praying 'for a Successful Conclusion of his Operation, as was the Custom of the Ancient Chymical Astrologers', leaving doubt as to whether his devotion is a rational one or an expression of antique mysticism. Can the accidental discovery of a sublime phenomenon like phosphorus really be a token of the progress of scientific knowledge? The painting has generally been read as an illustration of the emergence of science out of superstition, but (as Janet Vertesi has drawn out in a recent analysis) it is really much more ambiguous than that.[34] In Wright's better-known depictions of experiments with the orrery and the air

---

32   Harriet Martineau, *The History of England during the Thirty Years' Peace, 1816–1846*, 2 vols (London: Charles Knight, 1849–50) vol. 1, p. 594. See also: Golinski, *Science as Public Culture*, pp. 188–203.

33   Judy Egerton (ed.), *Wright of Derby*, London: Tate Gallery, 1990, pp. 84–6.

34   Janet Vertesi, 'Light and Enlightenment in Joseph Wright of Derby's *The Alchymist*', unpublished M. Phil. dissertation, (Department of History and Philosophy of Science,

pump, the origins of light are clearly also the sources of intellectual enlightenment. But here the situation is not so clear. There are three sources of illumination: the phosphorus itself in the vessel and the jet of gas issuing from it, the moon in the sky outside the window, and the flame lighting the faces of the boys in the background. Whence, then, is the light of knowledge to emerge? And the actions of the witnesses are also disturbing. Does the alchemist's attitude of prayer mean that worship is the appropriate response to what could be a divine revelation? Does the painting show how science conquers superstition, or rather how superstitious wonder continues to hold sway over the practitioners of the chemical sciences? In raising but not answering these questions, Wright's work brilliantly captures the uncertainties of the chemical sublime – the experiences of wonder and enthusiasm that Priestley confidently believed he could control but which proved to be impossible to confine within the parameters of the Enlightenment public sphere.

University of Cambridge, 2002).

Figure 8.1   *The Alchymist, in Search of the Philosopher's Stone, Discovers Phosphorus and Prays for a Successful Conclusion of his Operation, as was the Custom of the Ancient Chymical Astrologers*, by Joseph Wright of Derby (1771). Courtesy of the Derby Museums and Art Gallery.

Chapter 9

Chemistry on Stage: G.F. Rouelle and the Theatricality of Eighteenth-century Chemistry

Lissa Roberts

Spectacles exist in tandem with spectators, both etymologically and in fact. In the eighteenth century, as many have argued, their relation entailed the growth of an increasingly bourgeois public sphere – an arena whose contours depended on attempts to manage an authoritative distance between the dictates of elite sophistication and vulgarly popular judgement. Eighteenth-century Parisian spectatorship, in its public incarnation, experienced the formation of a morally tinged public opinion and the disciplining of sensible experience. Each struggled against elite culture's institutional fiat and popular culture's Rabelaisian undertow. As such, spectatorship was manifested in new forms of art and music criticism, new architectural spaces in which to house public spectacles, 'bourgeois drama' and public demonstrations of nature's truths. All of these were contested sites whose combined propriety and popularity depended on maintaining just the right cultural tension between high and low.[1]

My purpose in this chapter is to use this view of eighteenth-century spectatorship as an entrance into the question why the public chemistry course taught by Guillaume François Rouelle at the Jardin du Roy between 1742–1768 was so incredibly popular.[2] Though rarely studied, Rouelle is generally regarded as one of the most important chemists of eighteenth-century France prior to the chemical revolution. Assessments of the man and his work vary, and have done so since the establishment of his public career. He is highly regarded by Gabriel-François Venel, the author

1   J. Habermas, *The Structural Transformation of the Public Sphere: an Inquiry into a Category of Bourgeois Society*, trans. T. Burger and F. Lawrence (Cambridge, MA: MIT Press, 1989). J. Johnson, 'Musical Experience and the formation of a French musical public', *Journal of Modern History*, 64 (1992): 191–226. T. Crow, *Painters and public life in eighteenth-century Paris* (New York: Yale University Press, 1985), M. Fried, *Absorption and Theatricality: Painting and Beholder in the Age of Diderot* (Berkeley, University of California Press, 1980). J. Rave, 'Seating the public: spheres and loathing in the Paris theatres, 1777–1788', *French Historical Studies*, 18 (1993): 173–210.

2   On the context of Rouelle's demonstrations at the Jardin du Roy see C. Lehman, 'Between Commerce and Philanthropy: Chemistry Courses in Eighteenth-century Paris', Chapter 7 in this volume.

of the article 'chymie' of the *Encyclopédie.*[3] For others, he has been characterized as a chemist of little originality, but is recognized for having introduced Stahlian chemistry to France. For others still, Rouelle's importance rests in his pedagogical function as teacher to an entire generation of French chemists, including Lavoisier.[4] But an internal examination neither of his theoretical commitments nor of his discipline-building efforts can answer the question posed here. Alternatively, to respond that his course was popular because science was more generally fashionable in the eighteenth century is only to beg the question. For we have also to understand why some of the most popular shows along the Boulevard du Temple (the centre of Parisian entertainment) and at the Parisian fairs – performed right next to bawdy pantomimes, puppet shows and midget acrobats – were demonstrations of 'nature's most extraordinary wonders'.[5]

Perhaps rather than using the popularity of science as a black-boxed explanation for Rouelle's success, we can invert the equation and investigate the popularity of Rouelle's course as a means of exploring the general attraction of public science during the French Enlightenment. Simultaneously, we might elucidate the continuity between the culture of science and the broader field of Parisian culture during the eighteenth century. Finally, we might explore whether such a 'cultural history' approach can take us beyond a description of the milieu in which science was practised, to allow for a culturally specific analysis of scientific content.

A Free Space of Learning

When Rouelle came to the Jardin du Roy in 1742, chemistry had already been taught there for 96 years, long enough for many to forget how rigorously the Faculty of Medicine had attempted to block the course's establishment at the outset.[6] Like so many elite institutions of corporate France, the Faculty claimed an offically sanctioned monopoly, in this case of medical education and all that attended that

---

3   G.F. Venel, 'Chymie', in Denis Diderot (ed.), *Encyclopédie, ou Dictionnaire raisonné des sciences, des arts et des métiers* (vol. 3, Paris, 1753), pp. 408–447.

4   C. Secrétan, 'Un aspect de la chimie pré-lavoisienne, le cours de G.F. Rouelle', *Mémoires de la société vaudoise des sciences naturelles*, 50 (1943): 220–444 ; R. Rappaport, 'G.F. Rouelle, his *Cours de Chimie* and their significance for eighteenth-century chemistry', unpublished master's thesis, Cornell University (1958); R. Rappaport, 'G.F. Rouelle: An eighteenth-century chemist and teacher', *Chymia* 6 (1960): 68–101; R. Rappaport, 'Rouelle and Stahl – the phlogistic revolution in France' *Chymia* 7 (1961): 73–102. More recently, Mi Gyong Kim has updated Rappaport's approach, claiming that Rouelle's advocacy of Stahlian chemistry helped to create a simultaneously cognitive and social space in which chemistry might publicly be recognized as a science (M.G. Kim, *Affinity, that Elusive Dream* (Cambridge, MA: MIT Press, 2003)). In this chapter I examine instead the cultural space within which questions of knowledge – that is, what Rouelle taught – and popularity were intimately related.

5   R. Isherwood, *Farce and Fantasy: Popular Entertainment in Eighteenth-century Paris*, (Oxford: Oxford University Press, 1986).

6   On chemistry teaching at the Jardin du Roy see J.P. Contant, *L'enseignement de la chimie au jardin royal des plantes de Paris* (Cahors: A. Coueslant, 1952).

discipline. To maintain the Faculty's elite status and unique position, distinctions were formalized so that no one would be able to confuse its mission with that of the Jardin du Roy. Courses at the Jardin were open to the general public. They were taught in French rather than Latin, required no registration or tuition fee and led to no degree or certificate.

Whatever the motivations behind drawing these particular distinctions, they freed Jardin instructors from the constraints of traditional university culture and enabled them to present their subject in a potentially novel way. Further, this official bifurcation between the elite institutions of science – the universities and academies on the one hand and public courses such as those taught at the Jardin du Roy on the other – led to very different histories. While universities and academies were suppressed during the first years of the French Revolution, the Jardin saw new life as the Muséum d'histoire naturelle, and became a public showcase.[7]

This brief history of institutional rank pulling is far from unique in seventeenth- and eighteenth-century France and we can draw at least a partial parallel with what was taking place in the contemporary domain of French theatre. Claiming a royally sanctioned monopoly on theatre production, the Comédie française, the Opéra comique, and the Comédie italienne did what they could to prevent encroachment on their dramatic territory by any number of popular theatre troupes and public spectacles. In forcing the regulation of popular entertainment in Paris, the official theatres unwittingly abetted their social inferiors' innovative approaches and consequent appeal. Elitism proved a mortal disability for royally privileged theatre during the French Revolution, and entertainers were finally freed from the shackles of Ancien régime corporatism, though it must be added that new social and political pressures rushed in to take their place.[8]

The parallel I have drawn is certainly not total, nor is it sufficient, on its own, to enable a claim of cultural continuity between public science and popular entertainment. Unlike boulevard theatres, for example, the Jardin du Roy was a royal institution, subject to the regime of government oversight and patronage. Further, this regime was reconstituted within the Jardin's administration, most notably under the suzerainty of Buffon. Nonetheless, it was indeed the case that the Jardin served as a public meeting place, with all the social and cultural dynamic that entailed, and that the courses offered there were (at least partially) reactively shaped by the Parisian universities' corporatist claims of priority. In any event, though we need to say much more before the fruitfulness of drawing this (partial) parallel is evident, it does serve to usher us into the cultural context in which both chemistry and theatre developed: corporate French society, replete as it was with its hierarchical structures and relations.

---

7   E. Spary, *Utopia's Garden: French Natural History from Old Regime to Revolution* (Chicago: The University of Chicago Press, 2000).

8   Isherwood, *Farce and Fantasy*; M. Root-Bernstein, *Boulevard Theatre and Revolution in Eighteenth-century Paris* (Ann Arbor: UMI Research Press, 1981); F. Brown, *Theatre and Revolution: The Culture of the French Stage* (New York: Viking Press, 1980).

Natural Pantomime and Bourgeois Drama in Nature's Theatre

The variegations of Parisian culture in the eighteenth century were as geographically specific as they were institutionally bound. Thus, in housing Rouelle's lectures, the Jardin du Roy lent them an element of its 'personality', not so different from the atmosphere of the Parisian fairs in the sense of being a gathering centre for people from virtually every rank of society seeking entertainment. This can be seen from the official attempts to regulate the behaviour of visitors at the Jardin as well as from the text of placards that publicly advertised the courses taught there.

Under Buffon's leadership, beginning in 1739, the Jardin du Roy became an increasingly fashionable meeting place. Open every Tuesday and Thursday, it drew between 1,200 and 1,500 visitors a week. Since its very beginning, though, it had proven a popular place for public gathering and spectacles. Louis XIV himself attended the public autopsy, held at the Jardin's 600 seat amphitheatre, of an elephant that died at the Versailles ménagerie. While decorum was probably maintained in the hall during the Sun King's presence, rowdy behaviour was a common problem during most anatomy lessons, as it was throughout the Jardin. Just as was the case with unruly audiences at the popular theatres of Paris, visitors to the Jardin had to be policed. Formal regulations were published as early as 1640, admonishing visitors to arrive in a timely manner for lectures and not to loiter afterwards; to enter the Jardin peaceably and in proper attire – no long cloaks allowed; to stay on the paths intended for pedestrians; to mind the lecturer and ask no questions while lectures were in session. In case these regulations were not sufficiently well known, their thrust was underlined by the text of placards that were posted to advertise forthcoming courses. The announcement of Rouelle's chemistry course, for example, appeared on the Jardin's gate (and probably in various other locations throughout the city) with its contents spelled out in Latin. At the bottom of the placard, however, in bold text and in French, one read that the wearing of swords and canes was strictly forbidden. Such a prominent warning would certainly not have been necessary had the atmosphere at the Jardin not been at least a bit carnivalesque.[9]

And what was it like to attend Rouelle's lectures in particular? I want to pursue this question by examining eyewitness accounts of Rouelle's performance and lecture notes that describe him and his course, intermingling this material with a brief look at popular theatre and dramatic theory from the same period. In this way, I hope not only to link the performative aspects of Rouelle's course to contemporary popular entertainment, but also to show a link between their contents, thus revealing both to be part of one larger culture.

Contemporary descriptions of Rouelle range from depicting him as a veritable buffoon, to the hero of some great moral drama. But whatever his character, it is clear that his lectures were always lively and predictably unpredictable in their content. The promise of entertainment figured prominently even in the prospectus that advertised the course. It stated that the course was divided according to the three

---

9   R. Taton (ed.), *Enseignement et diffusion des sciences en France au XVIIIe siècle* (Paris: Hermann, 1964), pp. 300–16; M. Daumas, *Lavoisier* (Paris: Gallimard, 1949), pp. 33–4.

reigns of nature and that each section would be illuminated by demonstrations of nature's 'most singular wonders', be it the glow of phosphorus, the production of spectacular flames and glorious changes of colour, or the fermentation of spiritous liqueurs. Further, from the widespread circulation of lecture notes, students knew that lectures were just as likely to focus on subjects such as ancient Egyptian techniques of embalming or the composition of aphrodisiacs as they were on chemistry's more prosaic processes.[10]

Two Diverging Witnesses

Upon Rouelle's death, the Académie des sciences eulogized him as a naturally sweet and gentle man who came to life when discussing chemistry. Should anyone contradict him in the least, Rouelle's blood would begin to boil and he would respond with vehemence. But even when not being challenged, he tended to speak with such enthusiasm about his subject that his gestures often took on the character of an almost convulsive tic. Indeed, Rouelle was famous for both his apparently unselfconscious demeanour and his periodic outbreaks of vituperation, aimed against other scientists for their ignorance and purported plagiarism of Rouelle's work or against the latest political scandal.[11]

Students came to know on what day a particular natural philosopher was going to be attacked and flocked to the lecture when the target was particularly prominent. But every lecture was 'show time', given Rouelle's absorption in the material at hand. He would pace furiously across the stage, tufts of his red hair escaping from beneath an increasingly embattled wig. As the lecture continued and Rouelle became ever more involved, he would begin removing layers of clothing in an almost ritual striptease; first his jacket, then his waistcoat, next his cravat and wig.[12]

While Rouelle's official position at the Jardin du Roy was that of 'Demonstrator of Chemistry under the title of Chemistry Professor', he was actually known as a fairly maladroit experimenter who relied on his none-too-reliable brother and nephew to perform the demonstrations that illustrated his lectures. When they could not be found, which was often enough, apparently, Rouelle performed the demonstrations himself, with potentially explosive results. Diderot recounted one occasion when he witnessed Rouelle handling phosphorus. 'A devouring fire enveloped his hands from every direction,' Diderot recounted, 'penetrating and consuming them before

10 For details on the content of Rouelle's courses that support the argument being made here, see L. Roberts, 'The death of the sensuous chemist: the "new" chemistry and the transformation of sensuous technology' *History and Philosophy of Science*, 26 (1995): 503–29.

11 J.P. Grandjean de Fouchy, 'Eloge de Rouelle', *Histoires et mémoires de l'Académie royale des sciences* (Paris, (1770/1773) pp. 137–49.

12 Such stories can be found in various sources. See, for example, Daumas, *Lavoisier*, pp. 25–7.

he even noticed that something had gone wrong.'[13] On another occasion, Diderot continued, Rouelle was demonstrating a distillation process:

> 'Messieurs,' he addressed us, 'one must proceed here with the greatest of caution; one bit of charcoal too much would shatter the container and threaten to smother us.' Precisely as he spoke, the fire began to accumulate, the enormous glass container burst with a huge explosion; smoke filled the room and students soon found themselves outside in the garden, unable to return until their coughs and terror dissipated.[14]

We can read such reminiscences in two mutually supportive ways. First, I would argue that authors such as Diderot cast their memories in the mould of contemporary character types that one might encounter on the stage. That is, given the impossibility (and undesirablity) of exhaustively recording every aspect of Rouelle's life and the literary necessity of giving form to what one writes, these authors relied on stock character traits such as honesty, clumsiness, absent-minded genius and moral goodness to paint their descriptions and evoke the desired reaction from their audiences. Whatever the complex actuality of Rouelle's public and private life, he was portrayed for posterity in a theatrical way – as a character one might find, for better or for worse, portrayed in a contemporary theatre piece.

Second, one of the things that stands out in such descriptions is the way in which Rouelle remained so dominantly visible throughout his public performances. Exemplary public demonstrators ranging from Robert Hooke to Michael Faraday have been praised by historians for their ability to become 'transparent' – to make it seem as though it was nature's handiwork rather than their own that was on display. Rouelle's popularity and effectiveness, contrariwise, seem to have been wrapped up in the fact that he was rarely depicted receding into the background while performing in 'Nature's theatre'.[15] A continued focus on *his* sense experiences was crucial to the lessons he wished to convey.

According to the testimony of Friedrich Melchior Grimm, whose *Correspondance litteraire* served as a gossipy newsletter for the smart set of European royalty and nobility, Rouelle was not only maladroit, but uncouth and uncultured as well. His genius somehow managed to surmount the confusion of his lecture style and his inability to write or speak with clarity and coherence, but his brutish behaviour and sharp tongue left him with a number of enemies. Grimm painted Rouelle as the quintessential country bumpkin, a walking caricature that any gentleman might view should he deign to visit the popular stage – worlds away from the high drama

13   D. Diderot, 'Notices sur le peintre Michel Vanloo et le chimiste Rouelle', in J. Assézat and M. Tourneux (eds), *Oeuvres complètes*, vol. IV (Paris, 1875) pp. 405–10, on p. 408.

14   Diderot, 'Notices'; see also F.M. Grimm, *Correspondance littéraire, philosophie et critique par Grimm, Diderot, Raynal, Maeister, etc.*, ed. M. Tourneux (Paris: 1877–1882), vol. 9, p. 108.

15   I use the term 'nature's theatre' to distinguish descriptions of Rouelle's public demonstrations from Michael Faraday's goal of demonstrative transparence by which he hoped to transport his audiences to 'Nature's school'. See D. Gooding, '"In Nature's School": Faraday as an Experimentalist', in D. Gooding and F. James (eds), *Faraday Rediscovered* (Macmillan/American Institute of Physics, 1985) pp. 104–35.

of official French theatre and equally far removed from the refined eloquence that polite society seemed to cherish. From this culturally elite standpoint, Rouelle held a certain vulgar appeal. Unschooled in the ways of polite society, he charmed precisely because he was the 'savant sauvage'.[16]

But this elitist perspective was countered by the testimony of others who praised Rouelle as they simultaneously championed the development of a new sort of drama and by scientific colleagues who also took part in the adventure of education at the Jardin du Roy. What these supporters of Rouelle had in common, besides their veneration for him, was their interest in replacing the stolid form of their predecessors' art. In dramatic terms this meant developing a genre of theatre that spoke naturally and to the heart. In terms of science pedagogy, it meant developing a lecture style whose approach was rooted in sensible demonstration. Either way, the goal was twofold: first, to steer a productive course that avoided equally the stultifying dominance of elite culture and the unreflective sensations of popular enthusiasm and second, to educate sense and sentiment so that the audience might be drawn closer to a knowledge of self and the world.

Along these lines, Louis Sébastien Mercier, author of the multivolume *Tableau de Paris* and perhaps the most knowledgeable reporter of Parisian life at the time, claimed that Rouelle and Diderot were the two most eloquent men he had ever met.

> When Rouelle spoke, he inspired, he overwhelmed; he made me love an art about which I had not the least notion; Rouelle enlightened me, converted me; it is he who made me a supporter of that science [chemistry] which should regenererate all the arts, one after the other ... without Rouelle, I would not have known how to look above the apothecary's mortar.'[17]

Félix Vicq d'Azyr, who taught comparative anatomy at the Jardin, agreed, commenting that Rouelle's

> eloquence was not that of language: he presented his ideas as nature offers its productions, in a disorder that always pleases and with an abundance that never fatigues. He was indifferent to nothing: he spoke with interest and warmth about the least processes, and he was sure to keep his audience's attention, because he was able to move them.[18]

If we accept Mercier and Vicq d'Azyr's testimonies, we can see why Grimm and his aristocratic readers might have thought Rouelle an inarticulate rustic. Rouelle's was an eloquence not based on polished turns of phrase, or encapsulated in a set of philosophic first principles. It was a natural language that movingly joined the sensibilities of his audience to the qualities of the sensible world.

The highly gestural language used by Rouelle was very much in vogue among both artists and reform-minded *philosophes* in the second half of the eighteenth century. Physically introduced into French culture's performative repertoire by popular theatre troupes who sought creative ways to escape the strictures placed on

---

16   Grimm, *Correspondance*, pp. 106–9.

17   L.S. Mercier, *Tableau de Paris* (Amsterdam, 1782–1788), vol. 11, pp. 178–9.

18   Quoted in Contant, *L'enseignement de la chimie*, p. 107.

them by the elite institutions of French drama, the rich possibilities of pantomime were celebrated by authors such as Condillac and Diderot as enabling one to convey complex ideas and feelings that escaped the descriptive abilities of philosophical speech. Not only might pantomime and hieroglyphs (pantomime's written or pictorial counterpart) help reveal the historic purity of language, which many believed to be in need of reform. Their expressive wealth might also hold the key to reform in the pictorial, literary and dramatic arts. They were also seen by some to have quite practical application, such as in the creation of sign language for the deaf. It was in this context that Rouelle's natural pantomime – his ability to engage with nature on stage through the disciplined agency of his senses and thereby reveal its deepest secrets – set him above the great philosophical orators of his day.[19]

Rouelle, Champion of Sense and Sensibility

According to the lecture notes taken by students such as Diderot and the botanist Antoine Laurent de Jussieu, Rouelle saw it as his primary purpose to educate his students' senses.[20] But it was not his goal simply to train a generation of chemical craftsmen. Educating the senses related more fundamentally to Rouelle's view of chemical knowledge and how to attain it. As borne out on almost every lecture note page, Rouelle was convinced that knowledgeable determination in chemistry rested directly on the evidence of sense. Knowledge about the world was to be found through the corporally disciplined analysis of smells, tastes, textures and colorus, not in mathematical or rational abstractions. If his audience took away an appreciation for phlogiston's explanatory power, as historians have emphasized, it is even more true that Rouelle entreated his audience to examine and measure the world through the carefully calibrated use of their senses. It is no coincidence that claims of phlogiston's active presence were so intimately tied to the evidence of sense, be it colour, texture or smell.

Rouelle began his course by explaining that the chemist's task was not to establish superficially general laws, but to analyse nature's peculiarities and generate

---

19   Diderot frequently discussed pantomime as a 'natural language of action' in his aesthetic writings and writings on the theatre. See, for example, D. Diderot, *Lettre sur les sourds et les muets*, ed. J. Assézat and M. Tourneux, *Oeuvres complètes* (Paris: 1875), vol. 1, pp. 343–428; D. Diderot, *Entretiens sur le fils naturel*, ed. Assézat and Tourneux, *Oeuvres complètes* (Paris: 1875) vol. 7, pp. 3–168 ; 'Second entretien' pp. 102–33. On the introduction and use of pantomime in Parisian popular theatre, see Isherwood, *Farce and Fantasy*. For a more general discussion of pantomime in the French Enlightenment, see S. Rosenfeld *A Revolution in Language: the Problem of Signs in Late Eighteenth-Century France* (Palo Alto, CA: Stanford University Press, 2001).

20   D. Diderot, *Introduction à la chymie; manuscrit inédit de Diderot, publié avec notice sur les cours de Rouelle et tarif des produits chimiques en 1758*, par M.C. Henry (Paris: E. Dentu, 1887). A.L. Jussieu, *Cours de Chymie, recueilli des leçons de M. Rouelle Apothicaire, Demonstrateur en Chymie au Jardin du Roi, de l'Acadèmie Royale des Sciences de Paris* (Paris: Bibliothèque du Muséum d'histoire naturelle, 1767) Ms. 1202.

individual facts.[21] Working chemists, however, also had to produce marketable results, requiring them to attend to the signs of repeatability – what characteristics indicated that the same result could be produced again and again? If nature was a realm of the delightfully unique, then its analysis also revealed patterns that could be turned to productive exploitation. Training the senses was crucial to both these purposes; it advanced both the popularity and productivity of chemistry.

The image that one gets from reading either the Academy's eulogy or Diderot's memorial homage is that Rouelle was more than just a brilliant chemistry teacher. They paint his entire life as a tribute to virtue. From Rouelle's own student days in Paris, when he existed on bread and water so that he might afford books, to his appointment at the Jardin du Roy based solely on merit (quite an achievement in patron-ridden, *ancien régime* France) and his tender-hearted service to the poor in his capacity as Inspector General of the pharmacy at the Hôtel-Dieu, Rouelle's very life was a lesson in bourgeois decency. As the Academy's eulogy put it: 'Rouelle's reputation for knowledge and probity were on a par with each other. He was so well known for both that others sent their students to him, knowing he would place the way to form science and virtue equally before their eyes.'[22]

This draws us back to a parallel with contemporary theatre. For the newly emerging bourgeois drama, developed in part by Diderot, sought equally to reveal the true nature of things through a sort of sentimental education. Popular entertainment was traditionally a bawdy affair awash with scatological references and sexual innuendo. Increasingly, in the second half of the eighteenth century, reforming authors sought to replace this bawdiness with sentimental lessons aimed at moral restraint. The body was to be brought under control, both in terms of the intended effect on the audience and in terms of what the actor must do to convey moral lessons in the most natural and moving way possible.

In the *Paradoxe sur le comédien*, Diderot zeroed in on the artifice required to render an actor's performance emotionally effective. To unveil the 'true nature of things', an actor must be in complete control of his feelings. To move his audience in a morally instructive way, he must masterfully manipulate his own sensibilities, that he might also manipulate theirs.[23] The situation was not so different for Rouelle, the master chemist. His role directed him to act with such artifice as would simultaneously lay nature's secrets bare and, through his example, move his students to pursue the same course that he laid out – to control their bodies so that they too might sense the true beauty and richness of nature. The choice he offered them was not between abstract reason and sensuous enthusiasm, but between reason's superficial acquaintance with nature's surface and sensible insight into nature's deepest secrets. The brilliance and effectiveness of his performance were attested to by Vicq d'Azyr, who wrote: 'Rouelle was a bold and fiery genius who set everyone's

---

21 Jussieu, *Cours de chymie*, p. 2

22 Grandjean de Fouchy, 'Eloge de Rouelle', p. 148

23 D. Diderot, *Paradoxe sur le comédien*, ed. Assézat and Tourneux, *Oeuvres complètes*, (Paris: 1875) vol. 8, pp. 339–426.

heads ablaze with his enthusiasm. He became the head of a school the memory of which will honour his century and nation.'[24]

Conclusion

Linking public science and theatre as I have tried to do here is not only a product of retrospective analysis. In his *Entretiens sur le fils naturel*, for example, Diderot called for reform in lyric poetry and drama to match the recent reforms that were grounding contemporary (natural) philosophy in experience of the 'real world'. Similarly, the critic Charles-Nicolas Cochin noted that the intervention of overly elaborate machinery (comparable to the baroque structures of philosophical systems to which Enlightenment reformers were so opposed) in the staging of operas obscured the development of natural drama; the public's focus should be directed to a artist's sensible performance rather than being distracted by mechanical accroutrements.[25] In order to understand the general thrust behind such enunciations and enactments of a link between sensible drama and public persuasion, we need to note the socio-cultural web within which public spectacles were situated in the second half of the eighteenth century.

On the one hand, early-modern France knew separate institutions and loci of cultural expression for its various orders. Royally sanctioned academies and universities held monopolies for the production of high-quality literary expression, theatre, natural philosophy and learning. These institutions were simultaneously charged with the policing of outsiders who also sought to hawk their wares in the market of cultural consumption. In some cases, especially if the state stood to gain from increased productivity, outsiders were carefully encouraged – either with or without an academy's complicity. The best examples of this can probably be found in the history of the Académie royale des sciences de Paris. But, for better or for worse, even this august institution could manifest a highly pronounced corporate jealousy, leading to the strict policing and censorship of scientific pretenders who sought to gain a hearing for themselves, their ideas and their products. Prior to the French Revolution, Jean Paul Marat made a career of pointing out just how destructively opposed the Academy's corporate vanity was to the public good in this regard.[26]

While various outlets for sociability among the middle and lower classes existed as well, with their own rights and rites, it is also the case that a number of hybrid cultural centres flourished in Paris as the eighteenth century progressed. Spectators from all walks of life visited establishments ranging from the Palais Royal to the Jardin du Roy, witnessing amalgams of cultural production that were forged out

---

24   Contant, *L'enseignement de la chimie*, p. 107.

25   D. Thomas, 'Architectural Visions of Lyric Theatre and Spectatorship in Late-Eighteenth-Century France' *Representations*, 52 (1995): 52–75.

26   R. Hahn, *The Anatomy of a Scientific Institution: the Paris Academy of Sciences, 1666–1803*, (Berkeley: University of California Press, 1971); R. Darnton , *'The High Enlightenment and Low-Life of Literature'*, *The Literary Underground of the Old Regime* (Cambridge, MA: Harvard University Press, 1982), pp. 1–40.

of a dynamic tension between high and low.[27] In keeping with their own character and history, each of these establishments managed this tension in their own way, resulting in individualized recipes for success. If we want to understand Rouelle's popularity, here is a good place to look.

Rouelle's recipe for success – whether plied consciously or not – rested in his ability to maintain good relations with the cultural bastions of both reason and sense. On the one hand, his public performances managed to enliven the otherwise dry utility and academic prose manifested even in his own contributions to the Academy of Sciences.[28] On the other hand, he appealed on stage to both the evidence and proprietors of sense, without succumbing to popular excess. That is, he sought to discipline both the senses and sensibilities of his audience at the very same time that he appealed to their central importance. The public pathos engendered by Rouelle's persona – his gestural eloquence, his natural morality, pedagogical dedication and clownish manners – combined with his disciplinary mission to advance chemistry's productivity and appeal through the carefully calibrated use of human sense to ensure him years of public popularity and an important place in the cultural history of science.

---

27 Isherwood, *Farce and Fantasy*, pp. 117–49.

28 G.F. Rouelle, 'Mémoire sur les sels neutres, dans lequel on propose une division méthodique de ses sels, qui facilite les moyens pour parvenir à la théorie de leur cristallisation', *Mémoires de l'Académie royale des sciences* (Paris, 1744), pp. 353–64 ; 'Sur le sel marin. Première partie. De la cristallisation du sel marin', *Mémoires*, 1745, pp. 57–79 ; 'Mémoire sur les sels neutres, dans lequel on fait connoître deux nouvelles classes de sels neutres, et l'on développe le phénomène singulier de l'excès d'acide dans ces sels' *Mémoires*, 1754, pp. 572–88.

Chapter 10

Honoré Fragonard, Anatomical Virtuoso

Jonathan Simon

The Enlightenment is not celebrated in either the history of science or the history of medicine as the golden age of anatomy. As is the case with astronomy, the eighteenth century stands in the long shadow of the scientific revolution. Indeed, the *De Humani Corporis Fabrica* (On the Fabric of the Human Body) of Vesalius, published in the same year (1543) as Copernicus's *De Revolutionibus Orbium Celestium* (On the Revolutions of the Celestial Spheres), is usually taken to mark the entry of anatomy into the scientific era.

The History of Anatomy in the Enlightenment

The canonical story recounts how, thanks in part to the publication of Vesalius' book, dissection and first-hand experience of anatomy came to triumph over the authority of the ancients and the medieval tradition of commenting the classical texts, thereby allowing the anatomists of the seventeenth century to map the interior of the human body free from the misconceptions disseminated by Galen and his commentators. This story of anatomy plays into the master narrative of the scientific revolution that has dominated the history of science for so long. Nevertheless, revisionist historians have both challenged this hagiographic view of Vesalius and begun to look in detail at the practice of dissection associated with the Italian Renaissance.[1]

The new historiography of Renaissance anatomy removes us a certain distance from the standard narrative outlined above, and enables us to consider alternative approaches. One question that has already been posed for the sixteenth century concerns the public dissection as performance and spectacle, allowing an examination of the interplay between the status of the Italian medical faculties and this emblematic event, as well as the role of the dissection in the lives of the medical students and their teachers.[2]

Thus, anatomy is a very appropriate subject in the context of this collection of essays that proposes to reconsider various sciences in the Enlightenment not with respect to scientific discovery and progress, but looking instead at science as spectacle and its various audiences. Here I present a case study of the virtuoso anatomist Honoré Fragonard (1732–1799) and the publics for his remarkable anatomical preparations

---

1   R. French, *Dissection and Vivisection in the European Renaissance* (Aldershot: Ashgate, 1999).

2   C. Klestinec, 'A History of Anatomy Theaters in Sixteenth-Century Padua', *Journal of the History of Medicine and Allied Sciences*, 59(3) (2004): 375–412.

from human corpses. In considering his work I aim to situate it in the context of a range of eighteenth-century anatomical practices and artefacts – dissection, injection and wax models, to name but three – that brought amateurs and professionals together around the human body and its representations. Looking at Enlightenment anatomy from the perspective of the *spectacle* of human anatomy rather than the ineluctable progress of medical science leads us to view the available evidence in a new light. Indeed, what makes Fragonard a particularly interesting figure from this point of view is the existence of challenging (non-textual) artefacts from two centuries ago that force us to reflect upon how people experienced encounters with the dissected human corpse in the eighteenth century.

Anatomy in Public Culture

It appears that, like other sciences, human anatomy was very present in the public culture of eighteenth-century Paris. A tradition of anatomical displays modelled in wax that started at the beginning of the century continued into the nineteenth and even the twentieth century, whether in the form of permanent installations or travelling shows. An explicit mission of public education often served as a justification for combining anatomical figures with the perennial spectacle of prodigious diseases and other corporeal monstrosities. Occasionally, such exhibits leave traces in official administrative records, usually because of the moral concerns that they raise. Thus, in 1712, the surgeon Guillaume Desnoües, who presented anatomical material to the general public in Paris and the surrounding area, was condemned in the following terms by the Prosecutor General of the Parliament.

> The court, upholding the conclusions of the King's Prosecutor General, has commanded and commands that the aforementioned Desnoües can no longer continue to make his Anatomical Demonstrations except in plain daylight, beginning to let people enter at nine o'clock in the morning and not letting anyone enter after 5 during the winter, and from 8 in the morning until 7 during the summer, and under the obligation to publicly exhibit only those bodies from which *the natural parts have been removed*, subject to a fine and the loss of his privilege.[3]

We can see from this example how it is the threat to public morals, combined with their evident popularity, that brings these exhibits to the attention of the authorities, constraining them to intervene. Nevertheless, the exhibitions are protected from excessive censorship by the breadth of their appeal. Desnoües is not simply catering to a general Parisian public, as only one year before this incident, in 1711, he had

---

3   Arrêt de la Cour de Parlement du 19 août 1712. 'La cour faisant droit sur les Conclusions du Procureur General du Roy, a ordonné & ordonne que ledit Desnoües ne pourra continuer de faire des Demonstrations Anatomiques, qu'en plein jour, en commençant en hyver, à laisser entrer à neuf heures du matin & ne laissant plus entrer personne aprés cinq heures, & en Eté depuis huit heures du matin jusqu'à sept heures, & qu'à la charge de demonstrer publiquemment que les Corps, *dont les parties naturelles seront supprimées*, à peine d'amende & de décheance de son privilege.'

exhibited his wax figures at the Paris Academy of Sciences.[4] Thus, while evidently appealing (perhaps too effectively) to the Parisian bourgeois, this anatomical display was interesting enough from a scientific point of view to merit the attention of France's elite savants. In other words, while Desnoües made his living as a showman, he seems to have retained a certain level of respectability, as was the case with other scientific entertainers in the Enlightenment.[5] An important factor that pleaded in favour of such exhibitions, as is the case with more recent examples, is their purported educational value. Indeed, such wax anatomical models would have a long and distinguished career within medical schools and natural history museums in the nineteenth century. The institutional scientific educational trajectory of such models was paralleled by the rise in alternative popular uses of wax figures for modelling both medical conditions and historical figures. Indeed, these kinds of waxworks continue to draw visitors to places such as Madame Tussaud's in London or the Musée Grevin in Paris today.

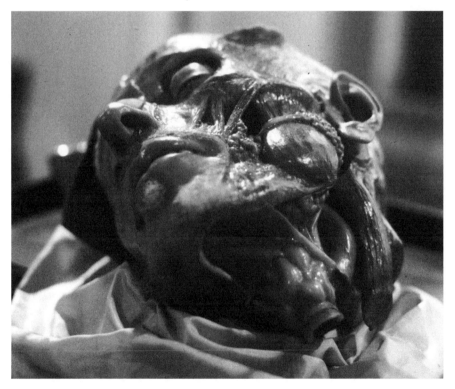

Figure 10.1   Anatomized head in wax prepared by Zumbo. Courtesy of *La Specola*, Florence.

---

4   See the entry under his name in E.J. Pyke, *A Biographical Dictionary of Wax Modellers* (Oxford: The Clarendon Press, 1973).

5   For an interesting parallel, see the discussion of the status of the itinerant electrical performer Martin Berschitz offered by Oliver Hochadel, Chapter 6 in this volume.

Anatomy in Wax, Anatomy in Texts

Guillaume Desnoües is an interesting figure in the history of the public display of anatomical models. He was a French surgeon who, while working at a hospital in Genoa at the end of the seventeenth century, formed a brief business partnership with Gaetano Zummo (or Zumbo as he became known in France). Before his meeting with Desnoües, this Italian priest sculpted tableaux in wax, many of which feature dead or decaying bodies. Under the direction of Desnoües, this extremely accomplished artisan turned his hand to creating accurate, yet lyrical anatomical figures using coloured wax (Figure 10.1).

This short-lived partnership seems to have been at the origin of the successful careers of both Zumbo and Desnoües. While the former proved a great success at the court of Louis XIV before his premature death in 1701, the latter formed a new partnership and took his anatomical collection on the road.[6] The wax anatomical figures acquired by Louis XIV through his appointment of Zumbo as a retainer were evidently of very high quality, with Diderot's *Encyclopédie* recommending a visit to the king's cabinet to see them.[7]

The production of wax anatomical figures in eighteenth-century Europe was dominated by the Italians, particularly the couple of Anna Morandi and Giovanni Manzolini in Bologna and, later, the artists brought together by Felice Fontana in Florence to prepare an unparalleled collection for the Duke of Tuscany at La Specola.[8] Nevertheless, France had its own celebrated anatomical modellers in the eighteenth century to rival the Florentines. The best known is Mademoiselle (and later *citoyenne*) Biheron (1719–1795), a pharmacist's daughter who rose to fame in Paris thanks to her dedication as an anatomist and the large collection of wax anatomical models that she prepared as part of her cabinet.[9] This collection was open to the public every Wednesday around the middle of the century. Growing old, Mademoiselle Biheron eventually sold her entire collection to Marie-Antoinette in 1786 for 6,000 *livres*. Fifteen years prior to this sale, Mademoiselle Biheron had the opportunity to present her anatomical models to the Academy of Sciences, just like Desnoües before her.[10]

Thus, while the phenomenon of wax anatomical collections spread across Europe from the centre of ceroplasty in Northern Italy, it was only natural that a fashion-conscious metropolis such as Paris should be caught up in the movement. The success

---

6   M. Lemire, *Artistes et Mortels* (Paris: Chabaud, 1990), pp. 35–6.

7   Diderot and D'Alembert (eds), *Encyclopédie ou Dictionnaire raisonné des sciences, des arts et des métiers*, 28 vols, Paris: Briasson, 1751–1772, entry for 'Anatomie'.

8   For more on this exceptional Florentine wax anatomical collection, see Anna Maerker, 'Uses and Publics of the Anatomical Model Collections of *La Specola*, Florence, and the *Josephinum*, Vienna, around 1800', in M. Beretta (ed.), *From Private to Public: Natural Collections and Museums* (USA, Science History Publications, 2005), pp. 81–96.

9   For a full biography of M.M. Biheron, see G. Boulinier, 'Une femme anatomiste au siècle des Lumières: Marie Marguerite Biheron (1719–1795)', *Histoire des Sciences Médicales*, 3(4) (2001): 411–23.

10   For a complete account of the fate of Biheron's collection, see M. Lemire, *Artistes et Mortels* (Paris: Chabaud, 1990), pp. 80–5.

of such wax anatomical models in eighteenth-century Paris is even less surprising, given the appetite for the sciences in the French capital at this time. Although the respective contributions of the demand from bourgeois enthusiasts and the supply from enterprising specialists are hard to determine, it is clear that many profited financially and socially from the movement. While anatomy does not seem to have provoked quite the same enthusiasm as electricity or even chemistry, as described in other chapters of this book, it was nevertheless one of the sciences that found an echo among the *philosophes*. In the pages of Diderot's *Encyclopédie*, the study of anatomy is explicitly promoted as an object lesson in Natural Theology:

> The human body is one of the most beautiful machines to come out of the Creator's hands. Knowledge of oneself presupposes a knowledge of one's body; and knowledge of the body presupposes a chain of causes and effects so prodigious that none other can lead more directly to the notion of omniscient, omnipotent intelligence: it is, so to speak, the foundation of Natural Theology.... Thus, anatomical knowledge is required for a philosopher.[11]

The interest in anatomy was not, however, limited to admiring or studying wax models, and there were those who encouraged even the members of polite society to dissect real human corpses themselves.[12] Thus, although this was no doubt their primary justification, dissections were not considered exclusively an element in the preparation for a medical career. Indeed, the exercise of human dissection was, according to the famous anatomist Jean-Joseph Süe (the elder), the ultimate means for an inquisitive man of letters to gain a profound understanding of nature:

> In the process of dissecting, one searches through the entrails of Nature herself, who becomes a book for us, and the impressions which stay with us are infinitely more sensible than those acquired by other studies.

> The object of anatomy is living Man.
> Its subject is the human Cadaver, or that of Brutes.

> As all who give themselves up to this science are not heading towards the same goal, one easily conceives that it is not limited to people of the art: it suits Physicists, Theologians, Jurisconsults, and almost anyone who is engaged in some liberal or mechanical profession.[13]

---

11 Diderot and D'Alembert (eds) *Encyclopédie*, entry for 'Anatomie': 'Le corps humain est une des plus belles machines qui soient sorties des mains du Créateur. La connoissance de soi-même suppose la connoissance de son corps; & la connoissance du corps suppose celle d'un enchaînement si prodigieux de causes & d'effets, qu'aucun ne mene plus directement à la notion d'une intelligence toute sage & toute-puissant : elle est, pour ainsi dire, le fondement de la Théologie naturelle. [...] Ò Donc la connoissance anatomique est requise dans un philosophe.'

12 Among the most notorious works to offer this advice were J.O. de La Mettrie, *L'Homme machine*, (Leyden, 1747) and P.L.M. de Maupertuis, *Lettre sur le progrès des sciences* (Paris, 1752).

13 J.J. Süe, *Abrégé de l'anatomie du corps de l'homme* (Paris: Simon fils, 1748), pp. 2–3.

The appeal directed at a range of liberal professionals to dissect a corpse is probably at least as rhetorical as it is sincere, and the primary interest for Süe was no doubt to sell more of his anatomy texts. Nevertheless, the alignment of dissection with philosophical empiricism by means of the idea that one gets to know oneself better by studying the detailed composition of a corpse shows more precisely how practical anatomy fitted into the world of the *philosophes*.

This discussion of texts, however important they may have been for Enlightenment culture, has, however, drawn us away from the issue of the material culture of anatomy. Nevertheless, the *Encyclopédie* and Süe provide a relevant and revealing link to the work of Fragonard that will form the subject for the rest of this chapter. In an entry on treated human skin (*PEAU, humaine passée*), we learn that this same M. Süe had donated a special pair of slippers to the king's cabinet. These slippers were made out of dried human skin, which had been prepared so skilfully that the skin had retained human hairs on the surface. From this preserved skin, it was possible to see how the individual hairs were implanted in the bulbous pores in the skin. Although it is difficult for any post-holocaust commentator not to see in this pair of slippers a precursor of grotesque Nazi dehumanization techniques, in eighteenth-century France they might well have been seen as a diverting educational gimmick. Of course, as I have already suggested, they also served to advertise Süe's skill in fabricating preparations using dried skin, a theme we will return to in the discussion of Fragonard's work.

Fragonard's speciality was not skin, but musculature and the circulatory system. His preparations from human cadavers included several full-body preparations that were (and remain) rare items in European collections (Figure 10.2). The origin of such preparations from cadavers derived from the practice of dissection as anatomical demonstration. Indeed, it is important to bear in mind that anatomical preparations ran the whole spectrum of permanence, from temporary accompaniments to particular dissections that illustrated the mechanics of the human body by, for example, injecting fluids into the arteries, to permanent preparations such as those produced by Fragonard. While it is at the level of tautology to point out that the temporary preparations prepared two centuries ago have long since disappeared, we should not let the disproportionate nature of the surviving evidence lead us to neglect the range of anatomical preparations from human corpses that were present in the eighteenth century. Nevertheless, the objects that remain today for us to study are the Fragonard-style preparations, as well as the anatomical models made from a

---

En disséquant, on fouille dans les entrailles même de la Nature qui nous devient un livre, & les impressions qui nous en restent sont infiniment plus sensibles que celles qui sont acquises par les autres études.

L'objet de l'Anatomie est l'Homme vivant.

Son sujet est le Cadavre humain, ou celui des Brutes.

Comme tous ceux qui s'adonnent à cette science, ne tendent pas tous à la même fin on conçoit aisément qu'elle ne se borne pas aux personnes de l'Art. Elle convient aux Physiciens, aux Théologiens, aux Jurisconsultes, & presqu'à tous ceux qui sont de quelque profession libérale ou mécanique.

Süe expresses a very similar position in the preface to his translation of Monro's *Osteology*, see A. Monro, *Traité d'ostéologie* (Paris: Cavelier, 1759), p. ix.

Figure 10.2 'Samson', figure of a man brandishing the jawbone of a horse, prepared by Honoré Fragonard. Courtesy of the Musée Fragonard, Ecole vétérinaire, Maisons Alfort.

variety of alternative materials, notably wax. Fragonard's preparations from dead bodies shared several advantages with their wax counterparts: first, they could serve as a permanent display of anatomy to be consulted at any time and second, they did not smell or decompose, and so could be conveniently incorporated into the private natural-history cabinets of the Parisian elite. Further, these preparations from human bodies had the advantage of being much cheaper than wax anatomical models.

These preparations from cadavers went some of the way to compensating for the lack of corpses available for dissection. Whether this shortage was due to administrative problems or to a profound popular rejection of dissection and a resistance to the trade in dead bodies, the fact had to be confronted regularly. Further, every medical educational establishment, whether public or private, needed a means to teach anatomy, and preferably one that was not bound by the vagaries of supply from willing accomplices in hospitals, or from grave robbers.[14] Thus, learning anatomy through models rather than from fresh cadavers, or an economical combination of the two, constituted an indispensable resource for the amateur anatomist and medical student alike. We know, for example, that for teaching comparative anatomy to students at the veterinary school, the professor of 1790 had at his disposal:

> [F]resh pieces of anatomy, dried pieces, injections, mouldings of natural parts, drawings, models of bandages, instruments, a botanical garden, all is collected here; the students have these objects constantly before their eyes, and they are explained to them in the different courses to which they have a bearing.[15]

Fragonard himself occupied this post of professor of anatomy at the veterinary school for six years before his dismissal in 1771, and it was here at Maisons Alfort that he produced many of his remarkable anatomical preparations.

Despite the celebrity of his work at the end of the eighteenth and beginning of the nineteenth centuries, Fragonard is essentially a figure who has been rediscovered relatively recently. There are now several publications about him available in French, although his work is less well known to the anglophone public.[16] One of the problems for biographers and commentators alike is that Fragonard published nothing during his life, and left very few written traces behind him. He did, however, leave a collection of artefacts that invite us to reflect on the question of the place of

---

14 The most thorough treatment of this issue, although it only concerns the situation in Britain, is R. Richardson, *Death, Dissection, and the Destitute* (London: Routledge & Kegan Paul, 1987).

15 From a report by Flandrin and Huzard submitted to the Assemblée Nationale in 1790, cited in A. Railliet and L. Moulé, *Histoire de l'école d'Alfort* (Paris: Asselin & Houzeau, 1908), p. 259: 'pièces fraîches d'anatomie, pièces sèches, injections, parties naturelles moulées, dessins, modèles des bandages, des instrumens, jardin botanique, tout y est rassemblé; les élèves ont ces objets constamment sous les yeux, et ils leur sont tous expliqués dans les différens cours auxquels ils ont rapport.'

16 Y. Poulle-Drieux, 'Honoré Fragonard et le cabinet d'anatomie de l'école vétérinaire d'Alfort pendant la Révolution', *Revue d'histoire des Sciences*, 15 (1962): 141–62; P.L. Verly, 'Honoré Fragonard Anatomiste, Premier directeur de l'école d'Alfort' (Diss. École Vétérinaire d'Alfort, 1963). M. Ellenberger, *L'Autre Fragonard: son oeuvre à l'École vétérinaire d'Alfort* (Paris: Jupilles, 1981).

anatomy in the public sphere, as well as the relationship that the anatomist himself had to these objects.

The Life of an Artist

A brief biographical sketch should help in situating this remarkable 'artist' (in the ambiguous sense of artisan and creative aesthete) of the body, whose career spanned almost 40 years, including the period of the French Revolution.[17] Born in Grasse, near Cannes, in 1732, he was separated in age by only three months from the painter Jean-Honoré Fragonard, his cousin, which has occasionally led to confusion.[18] Honoré Fragonard was apprenticed to a surgeon at the relatively late age of 24, and received his *brevet* in 1759, entitling him to exercise this trade, although there is no evidence he ever did, and he dedicated his life instead to the study of anatomy. Two years later, Claude Bourgelat founded a veterinary school in Lyons and appointed Fragonard as its director, a position he assumed while simultaneously occupying the chair of anatomy. It was no doubt at the time of this appointment that Fragonard started his prodigious production of anatomical preparations from dead bodies, an activity he would continue for the rest of his life.

In 1765, Bourgelat was invited to found a Royal Veterinary School in Paris on the model of that in Lyons. Unable to find a site within the city that could house the planned experimental herds of sheep and cows, Bourgelat eventually negotiated the purchase of a château at Alfort, situated several miles to the east of Paris. Here, Bourgelat founded a veterinary school that still serves as the French National Veterinary School today. Fragonard followed Bourgelat to Alfort, where he was again appointed director of the school and continued his preparations of both animals and humans that would form a large part of the school's anatomical cabinet. The reputation of this cabinet grew in parallel, attracting several foreign visitors who have left invaluable contemporary descriptions of the collection. I will return to these accounts of the cabinet later.

Fragonard spent six years teaching at Alfort before being dismissed from his position in 1771 on the grounds of insanity (ascribed by Bourgelat to kidney stones). Commentators on the affair usually put the incident down to professional rivalry. Michel Ellenberger, one of the most tendentious of Fragonard's biographers, places the renown of the anatomical cabinet at the centre of the affair, claiming that Bourgelat could not support the idea that Fragonard and his cabinet were better known than himself.[19] After his dismissal and a certain amount of negotiation, Fragonard was granted a generous pension of 1,000 *livres* a year and continued to produce his anatomical preparations in Paris. Little is known about how Fragonard occupied his time between his dismissal and his reappearance on the public scene during the French Revolution, but hints from later documents suggest that he continued to build up his collection of preparations, some of which he sold to amateurs to be placed in their natural history cabinets.

---

17 The biographical information is largely drawn from Verly, *Honoré Fragonard.*

18 The film, *Les Deux Fragonards*, presents them as brothers.

19 Ellenberger, *L'Autre Fragonard,*

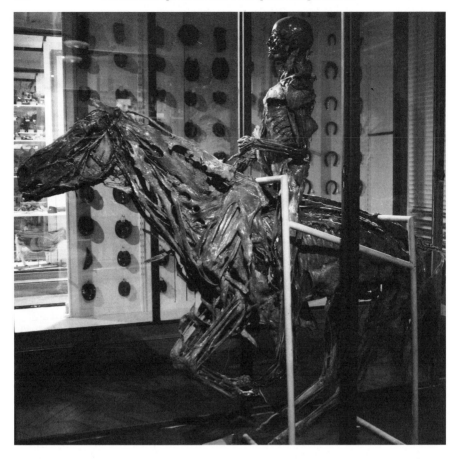

Figure 10.3   Horse and rider prepared by Fragonard. Courtesy of the Musée
Fragonard, École vétérinaire, Maisons Alfort.

Fragonard was reintroduced to the public world of anatomy in 1792, when, together with Delzeuzes and Landrieux, he proposed a project for a national anatomical cabinet for consideration by the National Assembly. The project was rejected, but Fragonard was subsequently named to both the Jury of the Arts (chaired by Jacques-Louis David and including his cousin Fragonard, the painter) and a temporary Commission of the Arts charged with the task of drawing up the inventory of anatomical cabinets across France. It was this second appointment that would take Fragonard back to the collection at Alfort, where, along with Thillaye and LeClerc from the commission, and in the company of Flandrin, his former student who now taught at the veterinary school, he drew up a list of the more than three thousand items that comprised the anatomical cabinet. In the end, the revolutionary government would revive Fragonard's career as a civil servant, recognizing his contribution to anatomy by his appointment as head of anatomy at the new Ecole de Santé in 1795. Thus, however insane Bourgelat might have considered him to be, Fragonard did not spend the last years of his life as a pariah, but was reintegrated as a respected member of the Parisian community of anatomists. He died in 1799, almost 70 years old. While we know that he underwent an autopsy, there is no evidence that his body was either put on display or permanently preserved.

Fragonard's Preparations

What is there to say about the pieces prepared by Fragonard that still exist today? The fact that a handful of these human preparations have survived over two centuries is due both to the quality of the work and to a certain amount of luck, as it was very probable that these kinds of preparations would be eaten by mites. The bulk of Fragonard's surviving work is now held at the veterinary school's own museum in Maisons Alfort, which now bears his name.[20] The outstanding piece in this collection, both for the intricacy of its construction and for the drama of its *mise-en-scène*, is Fragonard's horse and rider (Figure 10.3). This piece is often associated in commentaries with the riders of the apocalypse by Albrecht Dürer, which already suggest the force of the imagery that the anatomist managed to achieve. Judging from contemporary reports, the horse and rider had been the centrepiece of the collection since its introduction. It was accompanied by other human preparations, which were kept apart, it seems, from the general collection of comparative anatomy.

Looking at these preparations, the modern viewer cannot fail to be struck by their distinctive appearance. Their baroque aesthetic recalls a genre of religious sculpture that presents an image of death as a reminder of mortality. Nevertheless, the violence of the expressions and poses in Fragonard's work recalls the grotesque figure of Christ as portrayed by Matthias Grünewald in the Issenheim altarpiece rather than the more staid visions of saintly suffering seen in the works of the Renaissance master. The Christian funerary message concerning the brevity of life and the immanent presence of death is a figure that is ubiquitous in representations of anatomy, but, despite the overall style of Fragonard's preparations, their status as *memento mori* is not spelled out with the same literal insistence as it was by his seventeenth-century predecessors such as Zumbo working in wax, or, more particularly, Frederik Ruysch. The latter was renowned for his baroque dioramas made out of an assortment of human remains, which often featured Latin inscriptions concerning the vanity of life.[21]

The tortured appearance of Fragonard's work is in large part due to the preservation techniques used. The bodies had to be dissected and the internal organs and muscles treated with solvents before being thoroughly dried. All the time, these parts had to be carefully held in place so as not to deform the preparation. The most striking parts of these preparations were the vascular (veins and arteries) and musculo-skeletal systems, which can be seen quite clearly on the face and chest of the rider (Figure

---

20 The Fragonard Museum has an informative web page: www.vet-alfort.fr/

21 For more on Zumbo (or Zombo) (1656–1701), see M.L. Puccetti, L. Perugi and P. Scarani, 'Gaetano Giulio Zumbo: the founder of anatomic wax modeling', *Pathology Annual*, 30 (1995): 269–81. For more on Ruysch (1638–1731), see A.M. Luyendijk-Elshout, 'Death Enlightened: A Study of Frederik Ruysch', *Journal of the American Medical Association*, 212(1) (1970): 121–5.

Figure 10.4   Head and chest of the rider prepared by Fragonard. Courtesy of the
Musée Fragonard, École vétérinaire, Maisons Alfort.

10.4). The blood drains out of the veins and arteries soon after the heart stops, and the veins in particular become flaccid and shapeless. To preserve these vessels in a state approximating that of a living human, Fragonard first completely emptied them of blood and then filled them with coloured resins injected using a syringe. Each anatomist had his own secret recipe for these liquids for injection, although in general they consisted of a mixture of wax and resins, using turpentine as a solvent.[22] The idea was to inject the mixture as a liquid and let it solidify in the vessels, using a blue dye (usually azurite) for the veins and a red one (usually vermilion) for the arteries to illustrate the functioning circulatory system. Nevertheless, the injection of the resin into the blood vessels unnaturally enlarged them, giving an effect of swelling that is not found in the wax models, where the proportions observed in the freshly dissected cadaver can be accurately reproduced. Furthermore, the sheets of dried and varnished muscle stuck back onto the body in irregular panels, rather than the neatly pinned-back skin of drawings or wax models, reinforce the impression of a Christian imagery of saintly suffering.

While the technical constraints imposed by the arduous preservation techniques largely determined the appearance of the finished pieces, the anatomist still had a certain degree of liberty. Thus, a comparison between a human torso prepared by Fragonard and one prepared about half a century later by Christian Bunger in Marburg using similar techniques (Figure 10.5) suggests that the French anatomist chose to emphasize the fixed stare of the eyes and the expressive curl of the lips around the teeth. Furthermore, the dramatic *mise en scène* of the rearing horse and rider or the full-body figure brandishing the jawbone of a horse clearly illustrate Fragonard's desire to impress his audience.

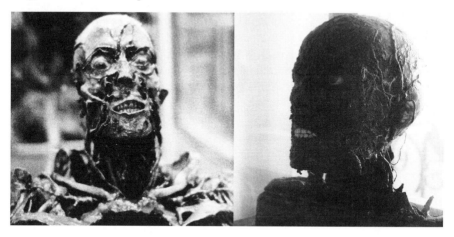

Figure 10.5   Bust prepared by Fragonard (left). Courtesy of the Musée Fragonard, Ecole vétérinaire, Maisons-Alfort. Bust prepared by Bunger (right). Courtesy of the University of Marburg anatomy collection.

---

22   Reportedly, the greatest threat to such preparations was mites and other insects. Thus, it is a credit to Fragonard's material that it has survived for over 200 years, while other collections have been eaten.

Students of Anatomy

It should not be forgotten, however, that the primary role for Fragonard's anatomical pieces was explicitly meant to be as teaching aids for the students at the veterinary school, where they formed a part of a cabinet intended for use in the teaching of comparative anatomy.

Although the anatomical detail in these preparations is impressive, it is hard to see what, exactly, a student of comparative anatomy could have learned from them, beyond the most general notions concerning the location of muscles, arteries, veins, nerves, muscles and ligaments. The bodily systems (circulatory, lymphatic, nervous) are not presented with the same analytic logic or thoroughness found in the wax models. Working in wax, the elements of the relevant system could be more easily separated out and could also be readily constructed, based on ephemeral observations made on a fresh cadaver. In Fragonard's horse and rider, for example, myology and angiology are mixed in with neurology in the same parts of the body, and when viewed from a distance, the details are quickly lost in the overall conception of the piece, an effect only exaggerated by its dramatic staging. Furthermore, the nature of these pieces meant that they did not lend themselves to student interaction; rather, as in the case of the wax models, these preparations were simply too delicate to be handled.[23]

Rumpelt, the chief veterinarian for the Elector of Saxony's Royal Stables, who visited the collection in 1779, had a somewhat different complaint about the scientific status of the preparations. For him, Fragonard's major fault was that he failed to demonstrate new discoveries in anatomy, and seemed content to display his mastery of the art of injection and preservation in ever more elaborate projects. In the end, for Rumpelt, the Anatomical Cabinet at Alfort was a triumph of artisanal virtuosity that left no place for true science. Rumpelt felt that the collection at Alfort was too geared towards providing an attractive spectacle for a public that remained ignorant of innovations in anatomy, and thus that it had gained renown at the expense of scientific interest.[24] Nevertheless, it is certain that few of the visitors to the cabinet at the veterinary school were as high-minded as Rumpelt. While we do not know who exactly visited the collection, in the 1795 report drawn up by Fragonard and his colleagues, they specifically warn against the possibility of theft in light of the large numbers of people coming to the collection. No doubt the bulk of this audience did not come from abroad but from Maisons Alfort and the Paris area. Indeed, when the veterinary school was first founded, Bourgelat had to go to great lengths to try and counter local distrust of his venture. It is reasonable, therefore, to ask what non-specialist visitors saw when they came to visit.

---

23 It was this feature that led Fontana to develop his wooden demountable figures that would allow students to take the models apart and reassemble them.

24 Cited in Verly, *Honoré Fragonard*, p. 14.

The Sentimental Side of Anatomy

Karl Rudolphi, a Swedish naturalist, who made a special journey to visit the collection during his short trip to Paris in 1802, is our source for quite a different side of Fragonard's reputation. He tells how he had read in another travelogue that the rider in the celebrated preparation of the horse and rider was Fragonard's sweetheart. The story recounts how she had died of grief after her parents' refusal to give her hand in marriage to the anatomist, who, on hearing of her demise had promptly dug her up, prepared her and put her on the horse. To add credibility to this tale, it was said that when asked about the rider, Fragonard became melancholic. Rudolphi was quick to uncover the roots of the story in local history and pointed out with a certain delight that this young woman was in fact a young man, although he had had his penis partially amputated to seat him better on the horse. Rudolphi finishes this story with a rather curious remark; that the preparation was 'tender enough' (*zart genug*) to be presented to a woman.[25]

This elaborate macabre story serves to underline the importance of the affective relationship between the public and the anatomical preparations. Indeed, the sensibility associated with anatomical displays was a central theme in the mythology of seventeenth- and eighteenth-century anatomical collections, with a key element being the lifelike nature of the preparations. As Fontenelle recounts in his life of Frederik Ruysch, Czar Peter I was moved to such a point by Ruysch's preparations that 'he tenderly kissed the body of a small child – still lovable – who seemed to smile at him'.[26] Looking at the horse and rider, it is hard to believe that the 'lifelike' appearance of these preparations could provoke a sentimental attachment like that ascribed to the Czar. Nevertheless, we can detect certain details in the commentaries of visitors that suggest the affective appeal of these figures. The blue silk reins that the rider held in his hands are remarked upon as an attractive feature. Further, there was an accompanying miniature version of the horse and rider that Fragonard describes in his inventory as the 'myology of a human foetus mounted on the fetus of a donkey, holding the reins in its hands', and that was condemned by a visiting German naturalist as an uncalled-for example of 'the frivolous spirit' of the 'French nation'. Probably the surviving preparation that is the most shocking to modern sensibilities is the figure of the dancing baby, a preparation of a foetus or young child that appears to be dancing a jig for its audience. This was not, however, a figure that visitors drew any particular attention to in their descriptions, and so we can imagine that it was intended to have a similar sentimental effect as Ruysch's earlier preparations that so affected the Czar. Nevertheless, despite these clues provided by the published reports of scientific tourists, we are largely left in the dark concerning the reactions of the bulk of the anonymous audience for this collection. Overall, I suspect that the ordinary visitor was impressed by Fragonard's virtuosity, as well as enthralled by the sentimental and/or titillating subtexts of macabre romance and sexuality.

---

25   K.A. Rudolphi, *Bemerkungen aus dem Gebiet der Naturgeschichte, Medicin und Thierarzneykunde auf eine Reise durch einen Theil von Deutschland, Holland und Frankreich* (Berlin: Realschulbuchhandlung, 1805), vol. 2, p. 45, footnote.

26   B. Le Bovier de Fontenelle, *Eloges des académiciens* (La Haye: Isaac van der Kloot, 1740).

Figure 10.6   Detail of the 'Samson' piece shown in Figure 10.2. Courtesy of the
Musée Fragonard, Ecole vétérinaire, Maisons Alfort.

Thus, the last point that I want to raise is the sexual content of Fragonard's collection. If we look at the Samson figure, where Fragonard has posed a body in an aggressive attitude wielding the jawbone of a horse, we clearly see the prepared man's genitalia (Figure 10.6). While the human reproductive organs were a legitimate theme for anatomical display, there were anatomists such as Ruysch who carefully clothed a number of his human preparations. Further, anatomical illustrations and artificial models not specifically dealing with reproduction were also often cleverly contrived to hide the external genitalia.

It seems reasonable to speculate that the sexual content of the collection at Alfort may have constituted at least a part of its appeal, just as the story about the spice-merchant's daughter had piqued the interest of the otherwise rather dry natural historian Rudolphi. Furthermore, we can recall that Desnoües was brought up almost a century earlier, presumably for the sexual content of his wax anatomical displays. Apart from the complete male figures, Fragonard's other preparations of human sexual organs were to be found among those of the other animals, as would be expected in a display designed to illustrate comparative anatomy. Nevertheless, the human genitalia were accompanied by a supplementary moral message. In the catalogue of the collection meticulously drawn up by Fragonard in 1795, we find a detailed exposition of a woman's reproductive anatomy that pays particular attention to the signs of virginity. Thus, in the fourteenth display table, there was an injected preparation of a woman's reproductive organs including the hymen, to which the note is added: 'this membrane is the indicator of virginity, it is pierced in the middle'.[27] Not only was there this mix of sexual education and sexual moralizing in the presentation of reproductive anatomy, there was also a helping of sexual exoticism. Under the glass of the display cabinet containing the human male reproductive organs there were two examples of unspecified, and hence presumably white men's, genitalia, as well as the reproductive organs of a 'Negro'. While those of other animals remain, the displays of human reproductive organs have disappeared, either transferred away from Alfort, or removed from display by subsequent curators reluctant to display such material. Nevertheless, none of these pieces was a cause for comment by the late eighteenth- and early nineteenth-century visitors to Alfort.

Conclusions

While it is impossible to generalize about Fragonard's public on the basis of the few accounts that survive, we can nevertheless hazard some observations. First, it is worth insisting on the variety of the audience for Fragonard's preparations. While the accounts of visits come from elite natural scientists, there is evidence that points to the presence of a non-scientific audience that was more diverse socially. Of course, the main public for these pieces was the students of comparative anatomy at the veterinary school, but Rudolphi's talk of the travelogue and rumours circulating around the horse and rider suggest a different public that was not looking to pass examinations, but was rather impressed by the sheer spectacle of these preparations.

---

27   Archives Nationales, Paris: F[10] 1294, '14e table vitrée.'

Further, Fragonard's business supplying private natural history cabinets suggests that the peculiar aesthetics of his preparations were appreciated in the refined circles of Parisian amateurs of natural history.

Turning the question around, I want to close by asking what the preparations might have meant for Fragonard in relation to his public. It is clear that they were meant to contribute to anatomical education, although their value compared to other forms of anatomical models was questionable. Nevertheless, they were also intended to exhibit Fragonard's virtuosity in this difficult art of preparing cadavers, and to impress in doing so. Thus, we can surmise that the dramatic *mises-en-scène* and the macabre and sometimes moralizing tone of Fragonard's work were part of the anatomical model as spectacle. While it is tempting to see Fragonard as the antithesis of the classic Enlightenment scientific attitude of detached objectivity, taking the theme of science as spectacle allows us to situate him more comfortably and probably more accurately in this period.

Acknowledgements

I would like to thank Dr Christophe Degueurce for granting me permission to photograph Fragonard's work. The Fragonard Museum has recently benefited from state funding that will allow it to keep more regular opening hours. For those who can, I strongly recommend visiting the collection.

Index